FREE ENTERPRISE—THE AMERICAN ECONOMIC SYSTEM

Robert F. Smith
Professor, Department of Economics
Louisiana State University
Baton Rouge, Louisiana

Michael W. Watts
Assistant Professor of Economics
Indiana University-Purdue University
at Indianapolis
Indianapolis, Indiana

Vivian D. Hogan
Teacher
Milford Mill Senior High School
Baltimore, Maryland

LAIDLAW BROTHERS • PUBLISHERS
A Division of Doubleday & Company, Inc.
RIVER FOREST, ILLINOIS

Irvine, California Chamblee, Georgia Dallas, Texas Toronto, Canada

Editorial Staff
Project Director K.A. Kruse
Staff Editors Veronica Micklin-Pajonk, Michael P. Plumpton
Associate Editor Darrell J. Kozlowski
Production Director LaVergne G. Niequist
Production Supervisor Kathleen Kasper
Production Associate Lisa Palmisano
Photo Researcher William A. Cassin
Indexer Joan M. Shotola
Art Director Gloria J. Muczynski
Assistant to the Art Director Dennis Horan

Illustrators
John D. Firestone & Associates, Inc., Paul Hazelrigg

ISBN 0-8445-6870-8

1984 Edition

PRINTED IN THE UNITED STATES OF AMERICA 56789 10 11 12 13 14 15 098765

Contents

Chart, Graph, Map, and Table List

To the Student

This book will help you to understand our country's free enterprise economic system—a subject that is very important in your life. Take some time to think about the many ways in which your life is affected by economic matters. In the free enterprise system, the prices you pay for records, for jeans, for concert tickets, or for gasoline; the pay you earn for the work you do; and the choices you make in planning a career are all affected by economic factors. The economy affects what courses are offered in your school and the number of students in your classes. The availability of part-time jobs in your area is also shaped by economic matters.

Every day you are confronted with information on economic issues. You read or hear about subjects ranging from energy and tax problems to government spending and the causes of unemployment. And each day you must make a range of economic decisions. The decisions that you make affect the overall economy. This book will enable you to better understand the economic information that you receive and will help you to make wise economic decisions.

The free enterprise system in America is a distinct system in which the citizens, rather than a central authority, are largely responsible for making economic decisions. We live in a free country where citizens, acting in their own self-interest, direct how resources should be used. Our economy is based on the private ownership of property and on freedom of enterprise. Americans have the right to choose their own jobs. They are also free to save, to invest, or to spend their incomes in the ways that they choose. To become a full participant in the economy—as a producer and as a consumer—you must have an understanding of the organization and operation of the economy. The material in this book will provide you with the knowledge and insight needed to develop this understanding.

As you use this book, you should think about the ways in which the American economy suits the political beliefs and the goals of the American people. From the founding of our country, political and economic freedoms have been two of the major goals of Americans. The free enterprise economy allows us the opportunity to fulfill these goals. True, our economy today is far more complex than that of years ago. Nevertheless, the underlying characteristics of economic freedom and private enterprise remain the same. In this book you will learn how the free enterprise system allows Americans to meet their economic goals.

This book is divided into four units. Unit I begins with the study of economics. It also gives an overview of the American economy. Unit II looks at how the economy works. It presents detailed examinations of the activities of producers and consumers in the free market system. Unit III explains the major organizations and institutions that make up the economy. In Unit III you will learn about business, labor, and government. Unit IV studies the United States as a part of the world economy. It also looks into our country's future to discuss the challenges that face our economy.

This book presents several highly readable and interesting features. These features focus on practical, up-to-date subjects. Consumer guidelines and career information are among the subjects presented. Some of the features provide an opportunity for you to develop your social-studies skills and decision-making abilities.

Our country faces many economic problems. Inflation, unemployment, and competition from foreign businesses are among the subjects that concern Americans today. There are no easy answers to these problems. However, the free enterprise system does provide ways for Americans to meet these challenges. The free enterprise system works best when citizens understand how it works. This book will help you to analyze economic problems. It will also help you to make wise economic decisions as a producer, as a consumer, and as a citizen.

Camerique

Unit 1 The Study of Economics

H. Armstrong Roberts

Chapter 1 The Nature of Economics

In the United States we have an abundance of natural resources. The quality and quantity of these natural resources have allowed our country to become a leading industrial power in the world today. And most Americans are now able to enjoy a standard of living unmatched in any other country. Even so, when compared to our many needs and wants, our supply of natural resources is limited. Economics is concerned with the decisions we make in allocating our limited natural resources to best satisfy our unlimited needs and wants.

Section 1
What Is Economics?

Economics is about everyday life. That is, it is concerned with the many ways in which people make a living. It is also about how people make important choices between the many things that they want and the small number of things that are available. How and why people try to buy more and better things than they did in the past is another subject covered in economics.

Simply stated, economics is about how people and countries try to answer three basic questions: *(1) What should be produced? (2) How should products be produced? (3) For whom should these products be produced?* As you read this section, ask yourself the following questions: *Why do we study economics? What are needs? What are wants? Why has the American standard of living improved over the past 200 years? What are the basic economic questions?*

Why Study Economics? For many people economics is viewed as a rather dull subject. In the past it was known as the dismal science, because some *economists*—people who study economics—predicted a dismal future for society. So, why should economics be of any interest to the average person today? One answer is that economics constantly enters into everyday life. For example, when you go to the store to buy groceries, or to the theater to see a movie, or to work to earn wages, you are making important economic decisions.

Finding a job, earning a good wage, and spending or saving that wage are problems that everybody faces. Economics can help people to better understand and cope with such problems. But economics is far more than just the study of how people make a living. It is also the study of the connection between the unlimited number of things that people want and the limited amount of materials available to make these things.

Needs and Wants. We all want many things. Some things—such as food, clothing, and shelter—are necessary for survival. These things are *needs,* because they are essential to life. Desirable things and luxuries—such as cars, color televisions, and dishwashers—are called *wants.* These are not essential to life, but they make life more comfortable. People's needs and wants are never satisfied, because as one need or want is fulfilled, another comes along to take its place.

People's wants are constantly changing. As people grow older, or as they become better educated, or as they move from one part of the country to another, their wants change. All this creates a problem, as the materials, or *resources,* that are available to make the things that will satisfy these wants are in limited supply. Another problem is that people have a limited amount of money with which to buy all the things that will satisfy their unlimited wants.

Camerique

Economists call the problem of having limited resources to satisfy unlimited wants a problem of *scarcity*. That is, resources are scarce—in limited supply—while wants are unlimited. Thus, individuals and countries must always make *economic choices* of how to use their limited resources to satisfy their unlimited wants.

Economics is the study of how and why these choices are made. Throughout this book you will look at many economic concepts that are involved in making these choices. And you will study closely the way the American economy makes economic decisions.

A High Standard of Living. Over the last 200 years the way in which Americans live has changed. This is due, in great part, to the growth of the American economy. Overall, our economy has been one of increasing production and efficiency. *Mass production*—producing things in large quantities; *automation*—using machines instead of human labor; and new ideas about how to use land, labor, and machinery have made this possible.

Everett C. Johnson/De Wys, Inc.

Economics plays a part in everyday life. The ways in which we satisfy unlimited needs and wants with the limited resources that are available are the concern of economics.

Today, average workers can produce twice as much as they could produce only 20 years ago. The United States has only about 6 percent of the world's population and only about 7 percent of the world's land area. Nevertheless, our country produces about 33 percent of the world's total goods and services.

This high level of production means American workers can earn higher wages. In addition, mass production and automation have reduced working hours and given American workers more vacation and leisure time than ever before.

(Text continues on page 14.)

Using Social Studies Skills

Interpreting graphs

The bar graph at the right shows the United States *per capita disposable personal income* in dollars for the years 1950 through 1980. A country's *personal income* is the annual income received by all the country's people from all sources. These sources include such things as wages, interest from savings accounts, and dividends from business corporations. The *disposable personal income* of a country is what remains of the personal income after income taxes, property taxes, and so on, have been paid. The disposable personal income of each person in the country is found by dividing the disposable personal income by the total population. This gives the *per capita* disposable personal income of the country.

Study the bar graph at the right; then answer the questions that follow.

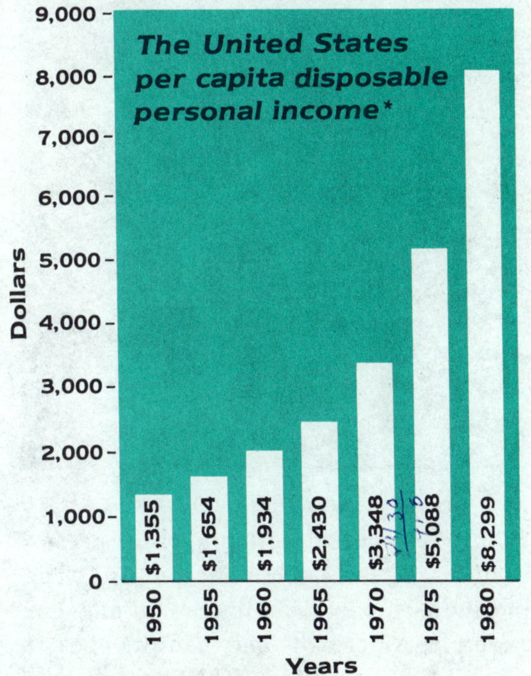

*Figures prior to 1960 do not include Alaska and Hawaii.

Source: U.S. Bureau of Economic Analysis.

1. What was the per capita disposable personal income for the year 1960?
2. By how many dollars did per capita disposable personal income increase between the years 1965 and 1970?
3. In what five-year period was the smallest dollar increase in per capita disposable personal income?
4. Why do you think the standard of living within a country *may* improve when the per capita disposable personal income increases?
5. The actual increase in per capita disposable personal income for the five-year period 1975 to 1980 was large. Do you think there will be a similar improvement in the standard of living? Why or why not?

Harold M. Lambert

In a market economy, consumers are free to choose the goods and services that best satisfy their needs and wants. Young Americans between the ages of 13 and 19 spend billions of dollars each year making such economic decisions.

But what part does the average person play in the total economic picture? The individual's part is an important one. For example, Americans between the ages of 13 and 19 spend 10 to 15 billion dollars a year. Most of this money is spent on such things as clothes, record albums, movies, and music concerts. The producers of these and other goods and services pay close attention to the tastes of the *consumers*—people who buy and use the goods and services—who are spending this large amount of money. By spending this money, consumers are playing a part in the American economy, because they are making economic choices. In this way they help to provide an answer to one of our society's basic economic questions, the question of what should be produced.

The Basic Economic Problem. As you have learned, economics is a study of making choices. More specifically, it is a study of how we use the scarce resources available to satisfy unlimited wants. This is the basic economic problem that all countries face. If an individual or a country is to make the best possible economic choices, then three basic questions must be answered carefully.

The first basic economic question is *What should be produced?* The way a country decides what it will produce is based on several things. For example, the resources that are available are important. A country cannot produce gasoline if no crude oil is available. By the same token, the skill of the people is important. A country with an untrained labor force cannot produce automobiles.

An important part of deciding what will be produced is deciding what people want or will be willing to buy. In a free society, like the United States, the people tell producers what they want produced by what they buy. Today, few, if any, manufacturers make covered wagons. There is a much more efficient form of transportation available in the automobile. Very few people would buy covered wagons, so producing them would not be a wise economic choice.

The second basic economic question is *How should products be produced?* This involves the way the available resources are best used. It is the process of making sure that products are produced in the correct quantity, in the least time, and at the lowest cost. There are no easy answers to this question. For example, when growing wheat, the United States would answer this question differently than would India. In India the skills of the labor force generally are not highly developed, and there are many workers for each acre of land. Therefore, using machines might not be a good economic choice, as training the laborers to use the machines would be costly in time and in money. The cheapest way to grow the wheat might be to use more human labor and fewer machines, since human labor is cheap and plentiful in India. However, this is not the case in the United States. In our country human labor is scarce and expensive. But the level of skill of our labor force is high. So it is better to use machines and a small labor force to grow wheat in the United States.

How much of any one product is produced affects the resources available for other goods. If, for example, Americans want to buy 8 million automobiles this year, steel, glass, plastic, rubber, and so on, must be used. These resources are scarce and expensive, and when they are used to make automobiles, they are not available to make other products. Thus, when American consumers indicate what they want produced, they also decide how scarce resources are to be used and how much will be produced.

The third basic economic question is *For whom should these products be produced?* We know that even the richest country can never hope to produce enough to satisfy all the wants of all the people. Some way to share what is produced must be established. In the United States, workers are usually paid according to the contribution they make in producing desired goods and services. For example, a new salesclerk will usually not receive as much money as a skilled store manager. However, nearly

In industrialized countries, such as the United States, agriculture is highly mechanized. This allows fewer farmers to produce more farm products.

Leonard Lee Rue III/Photri

all workers are able to earn enough money to meet their needs and satisfy some of their wants.

In summary, we see that the way a country answers the questions *what, how,* and *for whom* depends on a number of things. In our country all individuals play a major part in answering these questions. The United States has a *free economic system.* A country's economic system is really just the way in which people go about producing and distributing the goods and services that satisfy their needs and wants. Other kinds of economic systems are discussed in the last section of this chapter.

Section Checkups

1. *What is economics about?*
2. *What are needs and wants?*
3. *List the three basic economic questions.*

Section 2
Economics and Society

All countries—large or small, rich or poor—face many difficult economic problems. The task of satisfying unlimited wants with limited resources must be faced. Answers to the basic economic questions—*what to produce, how to produce, for whom to produce*—must also be found. Each country must find ways to provide for the needs and wants of its people. To do this, each country develops an *economic system* that answers the basic economic questions.

As you read this section, ask yourself the following questions: *What are free goods? What are economic wants? What are the four factors of production? How do we economize? Why do we need economic systems?*

Economic Wants. You have already learned that people's wants are unlimited and that each person wants a large number of different things. But economics is not interested in all the wants and needs of every individual. For example, most people have emotional needs and wants that must be satisfied. They desire the love and affection of their families, the respect and admiration of their friends, and recognition and success at work or school. These are all important wants, but they are not necessarily important to economists. Since emotional wants are not thought of in terms of scarce resources, they are not important to the study of economics. Some needs also have no economic importance. For example, all people need to breathe the

Camerique

Both the sun and oil are sources of heat. We do not have to give up anything of value to enjoy the warmth of the sun's rays. Therefore, the sun is considered to be a free good. However, to enjoy the heat produced by oil, we have to pay. Oil, therefore, is an economic good.

Standard Oil Company

air to live, but they do not have to give up anything of value to do so. Therefore, we say that air is free. Things that can satisfy people's needs and wants but have no economic value are called *free goods*.

The wants that economists are interested in are *economic wants*. These can be satisfied only by *economic goods and services*. An economic good is any material thing that satisfies people's wants and needs and is scarce enough that people are willing to pay for it. A stereo system is an economic good. It satisfies the want of listening to music. However, it is not free; it is scarce and it costs money. Therefore it is an economic good. In much the same way, an economic service is a personal service that satisfies a want or a need and can be valued in terms of money. The health services a doctor offers are economic services because we must pay for them.

The economic wants of individuals, and of countries, are unlimited. It is impossible to satisfy all of them because *resources*—the things needed to produce goods and services—are in limited supply.

Scarce Resources. Economists define *resources* as those things that can be used to produce goods and services. Resources are normally divided into four groups. These are *land*, or *natural resources*; *labor*; *capital*; and *entrepreneurship*. These are sometimes called *productive resources*, or *factors of production*. The importance of these factors of production will be looked at in much greater detail in Chapter 4. However, a brief discussion of these factors will be helpful here.

Land, or *natural resources*, is all the things in nature that can be used to produce goods and services. Soil, rivers,

H. Armstrong Roberts

Coal is one natural resource that the United States has in abundance. As the supply of foreign oil becomes more uncertain, our coal supplies will become increasingly important as a source of energy.

forests, coal, oil, and so on, are all natural resources. *Land* is sometimes used as the general name for all these natural resources.

Labor is all the human physical and mental activity that goes into the production of goods and services. The physical work that goes into the assembly of an automobile is an example of labor. So, too, is the thought that the engineers put into the design of that automobile.

Capital is often used to refer to money. But in economics it is a term used to refer to all the tools, machinery, and buildings used in producing goods and services. The assembly line, welding tools, spray-paint guns, and buildings where they are used are all examples of capital used in the automobile industry. Tools, machinery, and buildings are sometimes called *capital goods*. These capital goods are used in the production of goods and services; they are not used directly to satisfy people's wants.

In simple terms, *entrepreneurship* is the bringing together of the first three resources. It gathers together all the natural resources, capital goods, and labor needed to produce goods and services. But entrepreneurship involves something else. It is the taking of risks to ensure efficient and successful production of goods and services.

These resources needed for production are scarce when compared to our never-ending wants. Natural resources, for example, may not be available, except at very high prices. In the same way, there is a limit to the number of workers available. Capital goods may be expensive and in limited supply. As a result, choices must be made about how to use our scarce resources. The practice of making economic choices is known as *economizing*.

The Need to Economize. All countries are faced with the problem of economizing. This problem involves sharing the scarce resources among a large number of possible uses. But this must be carried out in an

(Text continues on page 20.)

Looking at Careers
The food-store manager

What does a food-store manager do? The food-store manager is responsible for the efficient and profitable operation of a food store. The manager has to order stock for the store and hire staff. In addition, the manager has to plan staff work schedules. The manager also has to make sure that the store is protected against robberies and shoplifting. Sales and advertising campaigns are other responsibilities of the manager. And the manager has to maintain good relations between the store, its staff, and its customers.

What qualifications does a food-store manager need? Most food-store firms have training programs for their managers. Generally, several years of work in a food store are needed before a person is made a manager. Educational requirements may differ. Some firms like their managers to attend college or training school. Others like their managers to get on-the-job training.

Brent Jones

What about pay and working conditions? New managers may earn a starting wage of more than $10,000. Experienced managers often earn much more. But managers frequently work long hours. They have to stay after regular store hours to check work schedules, plan sales campaigns, take stock, and do the paperwork.

How does a knowledge of economics help? If a store is to run smoothly, the manager must find answers to the three basic economic questions. By talking to customers and knowing their tastes and what they will be willing to buy, the manager is answering the problem of what and how much to sell. By planning work schedules and generally organizing all the store operations, the manager is deciding how the goods will be sold. This involves using the available resources—namely labor—in the best possible way to make sure that sales are high. The manager decides to whom to sell by running advertising campaigns and choosing the types of goods to be offered at sale prices. The kind of advertising used and the level of prices will determine who buys what. For more information on careers in the food-store industry, write to **National Association of Retail Grocers, P.O. Box 17412, Washington, DC 20041.**

orderly fashion. A country's economic system allows this to be done. Through its economic system, a country will make orderly decisions about the sharing, or *allocation*, of its scarce resources.

Throughout history people have established a variety of economic systems to meet their needs and wants. Whatever economic system is developed, it will reflect the cultural and social values of the people. For example, over the years, we in the United States have developed a democratic system of government. In a democracy values such as personal freedom and individual rights are important. These values are reflected in our free enterprise system, where the individual answers the questions *what*, *how*, and *for whom*.

The leading economic problem—how to meet unlimited wants with limited resources—has always been the same. The ways of dealing with it, however, have differed widely. The next section and Chapter 2 will discuss several types of economic systems. The rest of the book will be concerned with the American economic system. It will explain how we in America go about answering our basic economic questions.

Section Checkups

1. *How are economic wants satisfied?*
2. *What are the four resources needed to produce goods and services?*
3. *What is the function of an economic system?*

Section 3
Types of Economic Systems

Although all countries face economic problems, they do not handle them in the same way. You have already learned that a country's economic system will provide the answers to the many economic problems that country will face. To help people understand how economic systems work, economists, as a rule, divide these systems into three types. These are *traditional*, *controlled*, and *market* (or *free*) economic systems. Today, few, if any, economic systems are fully traditional, fully controlled, or fully free. Most are a mixture of two or more types.

As you read this section, ask yourself the following questions: *What are the main features of each of the three basic economic systems? How do the three basic*

Lomen Family Collection in the Archives, University of Alaska, Fairbanks

In traditional societies like that of the Eskimo, economic problems, such as food production, are solved by methods passed down from generation to generation.

types of economic systems differ in the way they answer the basic economic questions?

Traditional Economic Systems. In a traditional economic system, the three basic economic questions are answered, "As we have always done." In other words, nearly all economic decisions are based on age-old traditions, customs, and beliefs. A look at the traditional way of life of the Eskimo will make this clearer.

Until recently, the Eskimo of North America lived a traditional life. Almost all problems were solved in the same way as they had been solved in the past. Following age-old customs, the Eskimo survived in a very cold, harsh environment. They saw no reason to change their way of life.

The first people who came to North America, many thousands of years ago, settled in the far north. This area was cold and icy. These people soon learned that seals were a good source of food and skins. The seals' fat, or blubber, was the answer to survival during the cold northern winters. As well as being a source of food, blubber was burned to give heat and light. Each generation of Eskimo since that time has answered the question of what to produce in the same way. For example, they hunted seals, just as their ancestors had done.

Age-old methods, passed from one generation to the next, showed the Eskimo the best ways to produce the food that was needed. They learned where to find the best holes in the ice where seals come to the surface for air. They learned how to crawl, facedown, on the ice, in order to quietly approach the seals. These methods had been used successfully for thousands of years. No one questioned the old ways because they were effective.

The distribution of food also followed long-established traditions. Seal meat was shared among all the families so that all might have enough food to survive. Not following this tradition was a grave matter, and punishment was severe. The offender who refused to share might have all the meat taken. Also, the offender was often avoided by the other Eskimo. Life alone in the harsh northern environment was hard and severe.

Today, pure traditional societies are rare. However, tradition still plays a part in decision making in some modern societies. In certain Arab countries, for example, women are allowed to do only household work. It is rare for an Arab woman to go to school and have a career in these countries. Thus we still can find in some countries an economic system that is influenced by age-old traditions.

Soviet consumers have access to large department stores, such as Moscow's GUM. However, consumer decisions may have little direct effect on the Soviet economy.

Daniel Simon/Gamma—Liaison

Controlled Economic Systems. In a controlled economic system the average person has little influence on how the basic economic questions are answered. The questions of *what to produce, how to produce,* and *for whom to produce* are basically answered by a group of government planners. A brief look at the economy of the Soviet Union will help to illustrate this.

In the early 1980's, the Soviet Union produced about a million automobiles per year. Soviet consumers had very little to do with the making of this economic decision. The question of what to produce was answered by the Soviet economic planners. They decided if many different kinds of consumer goods or large amounts of capital goods were to be produced. In the late 1970's, they drew up the list of what was to be produced. The automobile was one consumer good that was chosen.

The planners also decided how to produce the cars. When considering how best to use the limited resources available, they decided there were enough resources to make 1.2 million automobiles. They also decided which factories throughout the country would be used to produce these automobiles.

How to distribute these automobiles was another decision of the planners. They decided how many automobiles would be exported and also how many would be sold in the Soviet Union. The planners then set the price of each automobile. In this way they decided who would receive what was produced. The high price set for the cars meant that only the better paid—mainly top government and Communist-party officials—could afford to buy an automobile.

Chevrolet Public Relations

Automation and mass-production methods have enabled American automobile companies to produce millions of automobiles per year. However, the large numbers of automobiles were produced in response to the demands of American consumers.

As you can see, in a controlled economy the average person has little influence on the way economic decisions are made. Most major economic questions are answered by government planners. The individual has little choice but to follow the planners' decisions.

Market Economic Systems. In a *market*—or free—economy the average person has much to say in the making of economic decisions. By buying or not buying goods and services, consumers are helping to provide answers to the basic economic questions. A look at the market economy of the United States will help make this clearer.

The United States in the early 1980's produced about 7 million automobiles per year. The consumers played an important part in the making of this economic decision. When trying to decide *what to produce,* American producers noted the willingness of consumers to buy automobiles. Producing automobiles to meet this demand seemed to be a wise economic choice.

The answer to the problem of *how to produce* also was influenced by consumers. Because of the great demand, the producers moved more of their resources to the production of automobiles. The consumers' demand for automobiles helped the producers to decide how many automobiles to produce. Competition between producers kept prices down and production methods efficient.

Consumers also helped to determine the distribution of these automobiles. The amount of money consumers were willing and able to spend on such goods as automobiles influenced the prices that producers charged. The level of prices, in turn, helped decide who would be able to afford to buy an automobile. Therefore, we can say that in our free market economy, consumers, and producers reacting to consumers' choices, provide most answers to the basic economic questions.

However, we must understand that our government also plays a role in the marketplace. Government usually plays a limited part in our market economy. At all levels government collects taxes and pays for certain public goods and services, such as roads, schools, and so on. In a sense, our government is a consumer as well. In addition, government at all levels regulates businesses, protects consumers, and does other things to keep our economy strong. (See Chapter 12.) Still, our government's influence on the American economy is limited. In the final analysis, private consumers and producers play the major roles in answering the basic economic questions by buying and selling products in the marketplace.

The three kinds of economic systems—traditional, controlled, and market (or free) systems—are just models—the ideal types. Few, if any, economic systems are fully traditional, fully controlled, or fully free. Most are a mixture of two or more kinds. And even economic systems of the same kind may differ in some ways. But, even though economic systems differ, the basic economic problem they all face is the same. The following chapter will discuss the ways in which three modern economic systems have developed answers to meet the economic problem of scarcity.

Section Checkups

1. *What are the three basic types of economic systems?*
2. *How does each of the three basic types of economic systems answer the basic economic questions?*
3. *Why do you think that an economic system reflects the values of the society?*

Chapter Summary

In many ways, economics is the study of everyday life. It is concerned with how people make choices to satisfy their unlimited wants with limited resources. Put in simple terms, economics is the study of how people and countries answer the three following questions: *What should be produced? How should products be produced? For whom should these products be produced?*

Economists are interested in people's economic wants. These are unlimited. But the resources available to fill them are in limited supply. Important choices have to be made concerning the use of these scarce resources. This is called economizing.

Decisions on economizing are made through a country's economic system. Economists generally divide economic systems into three kinds—traditional, controlled, and market economic systems. Although economic systems differ, the basic problem they face is the same.

Reviewing the Chapter

Identifying Terms

Explain or identify the following:

Economics	Consumers
Needs	Capital goods
Wants	Economic system
Scarcity	Allocation
Automation	Controlled economy
Economic goods	Market economy

Analyzing Information

1. Economics is the study of what?

2. What is the basic economic problem facing all people?

3. What is the difference between free goods and economic goods?

4. What are the factors of production?

5. Why do we have economic systems?

6. How do traditional economic systems, controlled economic systems, and market economic systems differ in the ways they answer the basic economic questions?

Analyzing Visual Material

1. Study closely the pictures on page 12. Which picture shows something that is a need? What qualities make the subject of the picture a need? Which picture represents something that is a want? What qualities does the subject of the picture possess that make it a want?

2. Carefully examine the picture on page 21. What activity is shown in the picture? What tools and equipment are shown in the picture? In what ways might the tools and equipment be used? How does the way in which we obtain food differ from what is shown in the picture?

Research and Projects

1. Imagine that you have been given $50 to spend. Make a list of the things you would like to buy with your $50. Be sure to list the approximate price of each item. When you have completed your list, add up the prices to see if you have spent more than your $50. If you have, remove those items you want least from your list until you have spent $50 or less. Divide the class into groups of five. In your group discuss the choices you made, and why you made them. Compare your list with those of other students. Which items were chosen most often by the class? Make a list of the most popular items.

2. George Bernard Shaw, the famous writer, once said that if you laid all the economists end to end they would not reach a conclusion. Collect as many definitions of *economics* as you can from dictionaries, encyclopedias, textbooks, and other sources. Compare your definitions with those of the rest of the class. Choose a definition you think best describes economics and explain why.

Chapter 2 Modern Economic Systems

H. Armstrong Roberts

We in America enjoy the benefits of a free enterprise economic system. In our economic system, the individual is the major economic decision maker. It is consumer demand that determines what will be produced. And private individuals and businesses, rather than the government, control most production. Today many other nations of the world have economic systems that place less emphasis on private enterprise and greater emphasis on government control. And in communist nations, all major economic decisions are made by government agencies. In contrast, Americans enjoy the freedom of choosing their jobs and, through their consumer demand, Americans determine the production of most goods and services.

Section 1
Capitalism

Even though most Americans can describe the benefits of our free enterprise system, not all of us understand the ideas behind our economy. Basically, free enterprise is a capitalistic economic system. The major forces at work in capitalism are competition and self-interest. This section explains how capitalism developed. As you read this section, ask yourself the following questions: *Why did some people want to end mercantilism when the Industrial Revolution began? In what ways does capitalism allow individuals to serve their self-interests? How is modern capitalism different from laissez-faire capitalism?*

The Rise of Capitalism. As you remember from American history, many colonists came to the New World from Europe for economic reasons. At that time, the major countries of the Old World favored colonization. They saw colonies as a source of wealth for the home country. During the 1600's and 1700's, England, France, Spain, and other European countries competed for overseas lands first for gold and later for other raw materials. These countries had economic systems based on *mercantilism*. Mercantilism was a controlled economic system. In it the government regulated trade and business in an attempt to bring greater wealth, stability, and power to the country.

The need for colonies became greater as the Industrial Revolution came to the countries of Europe. Cotton, for example, was needed for the expanding textile mills. But as industries developed, business owners often found that the regulations set by the government limited their growth. A feeling began to grow that mercantilism should be changed. At the same time, many colonists in America also came to dislike the economic controls that were imposed on them by the British government. Thus by the mid-1700's, many different groups were saying that there was a need for more freedom from government control.

One major writer who called for more economic freedom was Adam Smith. In 1776, Smith published *An Inquiry Into the Nature and Causes of the Wealth of Nations*. In this very influential book, Smith criticized the British government for interfering with the economy. He said that more progress would be made if people and businesses could operate freely. Overall, Smith wanted the government to keep its hands off business and allow a free-market economy.

Adam Smith believed that each country should allow its citizens to follow their own self-interests in business. Smith said that the desire to make money would lead business owners to make those things that the people wanted to buy. Businesses would succeed if they supplied the goods that people wanted at the prices that people were willing to pay. On the other hand, businesses that offered unwanted goods or overpriced items would not stay in business. According to Smith, everyone would benefit from this type of economic system in which the main forces were self-interest and competition. The economic system outlined by Adam Smith became known as *free enterprise,* or *capitalism.*

Capitalism in America. Adam Smith's ideas on economics were popular among the colonists who wanted independence from Great Britain. Individual freedoms—religious, political, and economic—were highly valued by the American colonists. After winning independence, these Americans—led by Thomas Jefferson, John Adams, James Madison, Alexander Hamilton, and others—wanted to make certain that the rights of citizens would be protected. As you know, the Bill of Rights was added to the United States Constitution to protect certain personal freedoms. The Constitution also reflected Adam Smith's ideas about economic freedoms. The framers of the Constitution believed that free enterprise would be the basis of the American economy.

The Growth of Capitalism. Capitalism took the place of mercantilism in England and other countries. Many people came to believe that government regulations were really harmful for business growth and the good of the nation. In the early days of capitalism, it was widely believed that the government should only undertake a few activities. These included defending the nation, providing a stable currency, and keeping law and order. This was called *laissez-faire* capitalism. *Laissez-faire* is a French term that means "let the people make or do." Those who favored this kind of capitalism believed that government interference in the free flow of competition would damage the overall economy.

Over the years, however, many countries have taken steps to modify capitalism to fit their needs. For example, in the United States, we have laws that restrict child labor. Our government has also taken steps to protect consumers. In later chapters, you will read more about the different ways in which the American government has become more involved in our economy.

Even with these changes, the American economy is a capitalist system. In the United States, the factories and resources used to make goods are in private hands. *Demand*—what people are willing to buy—determines what is produced. In the American free enterprise system, individuals are free to decide how to use their wealth and skills.

The Bettmann Archive

America's seaports, such as New York, were important centers of trade in the early years of our nation. Trade was an important part of our country's developing economy.

(Text continues on page 30.)

Being a Wise Consumer
Social security and you

If you have a job, you know that certain deductions are taken from each paycheck that you receive. One of these deductions pays a *social-security tax*. About nine out of ten workers in the United States have this deduction taken from their paychecks. Each worker's social-security deduction, along with an equal sum contributed by the employer, is sent to the Department of the Treasury. This money is used to fund the various social-security programs of the federal government.

Many people think of social security as only a type of old-age insurance. This is because the social-security programs provide benefits for retired workers who have worked under the system long enough to qualify. However, more than a million high-school students also receive social-security checks each month. These young people are eligible for benefits because of the death, the disability, or the retirement of a parent.

Take the case of Clara M., a 17-year-old high-school student in Chicago. Clara lives with her mother, a retired librarian. Both Clara and her mother receive monthly checks from social security. Clara will receive benefits until she is 18. However, if Clara decides to go to college, and if she is enrolled in college by May 1982, she can qualify for monthly social-security checks until April 1985.

Today, monthly benefit amounts are based, in part, on an insured worker's average earnings. The table below shows some average benefits paid in 1981.

Range of monthly social-security payments

	Average *	Maximum*
Worker retired at age 65	$400.00	$540.00
Disabled worker	427.00	540.00
Disabled worker with dependents	542.00	810.00[1]
Surviving spouse and/or children	520.00	946.00[2]

*Based on maximum average indexed monthly earnings in 1981
[1]Maximum paid to families with three or more qualifying dependents
[2]Maximum paid to families with three or more qualifying survivors

Source: Social Security Administration.

* By June 1984, average payments ran $542.80, $441.00, $841.00, and $912.00, respectively.

R. Harrington/Miller Services

This flea market in Ontario, Canada, illustrates free enterprise in operation. In this type of market, buyers and sellers freely meet to make exchanges.

Other countries in the world also have capitalist economies. West Germany, Japan, Canada, and France all have a large degree of free enterprise. In these countries, the three basic economic questions that face all countries are answered, for the most part, by private individuals and organizations. Many other countries allow some free enterprise, while depending more heavily on the government for decision making.

Section Checkups

1. *What economic ideas did Adam Smith put forth in* An Inquiry Into the Nature and Causes of the Wealth of Nations?
2. *What are the main forces in a capitalist economy?*
3. *In what two ways have some capitalist countries modified capitalism to fit their needs?*

Section 2 Socialism

If you were traveling in England, you would probably notice that the British government owns and operates the nation's largest broadcasting system. If you needed medical aid, you would learn that most British doctors work for the National Health Service. In England, the government owns many types of businesses that are privately owned in the United States. England has replaced some features of capitalism with socialism. This section explains how socialism developed. As you read this section, ask yourself the following questions: *How does socialism differ from capitalism? Why do socialist countries nationalize certain industries? How do socialist nations attempt to narrow the gap between the rich and the poor?*

The Rise of Socialism. Many social problems developed in Europe during the early days of the Industrial Revolution. As machines replaced farm workers, more and more people crowded into cities to find jobs. Working conditions in factories were often poor, and wages were frequently very low. In many cases, entire families, including young children, had to work long hours in the factories in order to meet the needs of the family.

Reformers in several European countries called for government action to improve the conditions of the working class.

During the early years of the Industrial Revolution in Europe, many socialists claimed that poor working conditions were the result of capitalism. They called for more government control of the economy.

Culver Pictures, Inc.

Some of these reformers believed that laws to protect wage earners would not be enough to solve the problems that had developed under capitalism. They claimed that capitalism allowed wealthy individuals too much power over the lives of others. They also argued that capitalism allowed a small group of people to control a country's resources. They warned that private control made it possible for these important resources to be used for the good of certain people rather than the well-being of all the people.

To change this situation, these reformers proposed public, or government, control over the country's major industries. In this way, they planned to replace the *market economy* with a partially *controlled economy.* The type of economic system called for by these reformers became known as *socialism.*

The Goals of Socialists. One of the major goals of the socialists was to end the great inequalities of wealth that had come about under capitalism. They said that the government should end poverty. The socialists also wanted the government to prevent individuals from using their wealth to control others. Most socialists felt that the people, through their government, should control the basic resources of the country. The socialists wanted the government to make economic decisions. They believed that the economic security that would come with government direction was more important than economic freedom.

Throughout history, however, socialists have not agreed with one another on many points. Karl Marx, for example, outlined a kind of socialism that would end all private ownership of property. This kind of socialism became known as communism, which will be discussed in the next section. Many other socialists, however, did not think that the extreme measures suggested by Marx were necessary or desirable. They wanted to maintain some private ownership. Socialists also differed because they were looking for solutions to the particular problems of their own countries. Thus, today, while a number of countries have developed *socialist* economies, there is a wide range of differences among them. There are, however, some basic features shared by these countries.

The Nature of Socialism Today. In most socialist countries, the government owns and operates all basic industries. This usually includes those industries that affect the whole population and are important to the country's welfare. In most cases, transportation and communication services are *nationalized*—owned by the government. For example, railroads, airlines, radio stations, and telephone services are owned by the government in Great Britain, Sweden, and other socialist countries. Public utilities and energy industries—coal, gas, and oil—are also under public ownership. Socialists believe that government ownership of these industries best serves the interests of the country. For the same reason, the steel and iron industries are usually nationalized.

One of the major charges that socialists made against capitalism was that under capitalism, working-class families often lived without the basic necessities and comforts of life. There was a wide gap between the living conditions of the rich and those of the poor. Because of this, most socialist countries today control income levels to reduce extremes in poverty and wealth. Social welfare programs also serve to narrow the gap between the upper and lower classes. Education, health care, and public housing are often provided by the government in socialist countries.

These Concorde supersonic airliners at Great Britain's Heathrow Airport are part of British Airways, a government-owned airline. The development of the Concorde was a joint venture of the British and French governments.

British Airways

In Sweden, comfortable housing is considered a social right. The Swedish government supplies this type of housing by planning and financing its construction.

Steven A. Seidman

Even though the major industries in modern socialist countries are owned by the government, some private ownership of business is allowed. However, private ownership is permitted only in nonessential businesses. This means that individuals do have the freedom to own and operate some kinds of businesses. Nevertheless, the government shapes the activities of these privately owned businesses through regulation and taxation. In this way, the country's resources are used to meet national needs and goals. Therefore, it can be said that socialism, unlike capitalism, is based on government planning. The control the people have over this planning varies. To understand this point, it is important to remember that the term *socialism* describes a country's *economic* system. In some cases, socialist countries today have *democratic* governments. Thus, decisions made by the government represent the desires of the majority of the voters. But in countries that do not have democratic governments, the people usually have little or no power over the planning.

In recent years, many developing countries have adopted socialist economies to take the place of their traditional economic systems. Often, these countries have limited natural resources. Many of them have a low standard of living. Through socialism, the leaders in these countries are trying to form overall economic plans to speed up their country's economic growth. Whether or not these plans will be successful remains to be seen.

Section Checkups

1. *What common criticisms have socialists made of capitalism?*
2. *Why do socialists want certain industries to be nationalized?*
3. *In what ways does socialism differ from capitalism?*

Section 3
Communism

About one third of the people in the world live in communist countries. The economic systems of these countries are based on ideas developed by Karl Marx over 100 years ago. Marx believed that capitalism would destroy itself. He predicted that after capitalism fell, the working class would build an ideal society—communism. There is, however, a wide gap between the communism that Marx described and the systems that are practiced in communist countries today. As you read this section, ask yourself the following questions: *What criticisms did Karl Marx make of capitalism? How did Marx describe communism? What are the major features of communism as it is practiced today?*

The Roots of Modern Communism. The major ideas behind modern communism were put forth by Karl Marx—a German philosopher who lived from 1818 to 1883. In 1848 Marx, along with Friedrich Engels, offered a powerful attack on capitalism in the *Communist Manifesto.* This pamphlet also contained an explanation of *communism*—the controlled economic system that Marx believed would take the place of capitalism.

The *Communist Manifesto* claimed that throughout history, economics had been the most important factor in shaping people's lives. Marx claimed that wealthy people had always been able to control those in the lower classes. Marx also said that politics and religion were tools that wealthy people used to strengthen their power.

Karl Marx charged that in capitalism, owners held complete power over the working class. Marx said that factory owners took advantage of workers by not paying the workers the full value of their labor. Marx claimed that labor was the only truly productive resource. Marx also predicted that as capitalism developed, the already poor conditions of workers would become worse. This would happen as wealth became concentrated in the hands of a few individuals. The *Communist Manifesto* said that workers, not factory owners, should benefit from the wealth created by their labors. For this to happen, Marx said it would be necessary for the workers to control the factories, stores, and other businesses.

The Call for Revolution. In the *Communist Manifesto* and also in his later work *Das Kapital,* Karl Marx explained that capitalist factory owners would not volunteer to turn their wealth and power over to the workers. Therefore, according to Marx, workers would have to take control of their countries, either through political means or by actual revolutions. Marx said that after these revolutions, the workers would set up a communist state. In this system, all forms of private property would end. Farmland and industry, for example, would no longer belong to private individuals. *Common ownership*—ownership by all the people—would replace

(Text continues on page 36.)

Using Social Studies Skills

Interpreting tables and graphs

Karl Marx had predicted that as capitalism developed, workers would be given a continuously smaller share of the nation's income. The table and the line graph below contain useful information for evaluating Marx's prediction. *Total national income* includes the money made each year from the production of goods and services. *Total workers' income* shows how much of the national income went to workers. Study the table and the graph carefully; then answer the questions that follow.

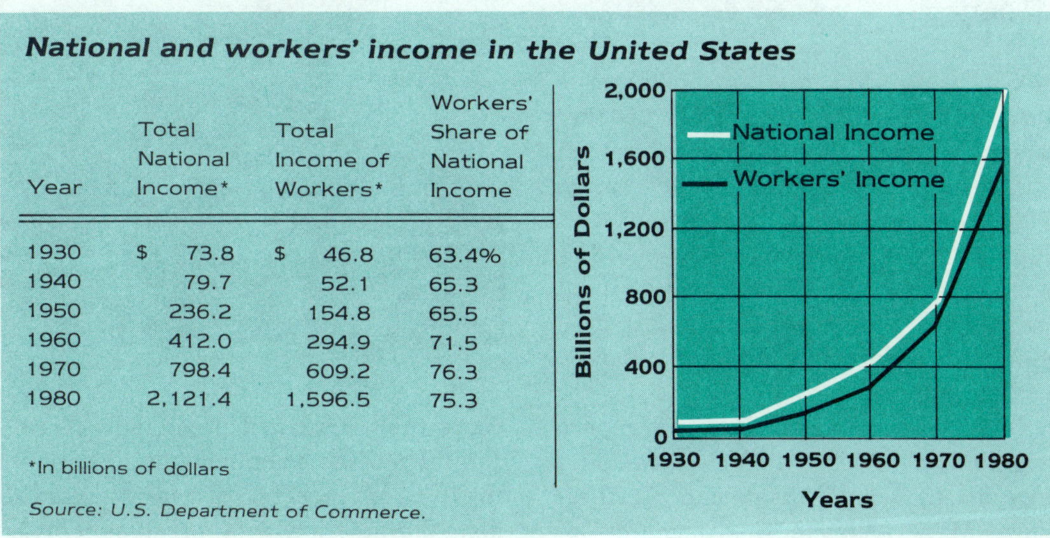

National and workers' income in the United States

Year	Total National Income*	Total Income of Workers*	Workers' Share of National Income
1930	$ 73.8	$ 46.8	63.4%
1940	79.7	52.1	65.3
1950	236.2	154.8	65.5
1960	412.0	294.9	71.5
1970	798.4	609.2	76.3
1980	2,121.4	1,596.5	75.3

*In billions of dollars

Source: U.S. Department of Commerce.

1. What was the national income of the United States in 1930?
2. What share of the national income in 1930 was paid to workers?
3. During what ten-year period did the national income of the country increase by the greatest amount?
4. By what dollar amount has the national income of the United States increased between 1930 and 1980?
5. What percent of the national income in 1980 was paid to workers?
6. Drawing information from the table and the graph, what conclusions can you make about the workers' share of national income and workers' rewards under capitalism in the United States?

Karl Marx (left) argued for the overthrow of capitalism. He believed that the working class would eventually unite and revolt against capitalism. V. I. Lenin (below) led the communist seizure of power in Russia in 1917.

Culver Pictures, Inc.

private ownership. Just as capitalism is based on competition, Marx predicted that communism would be based on cooperation.

In communism, the needs of the nation would come before individual wants. Karl Marx also said that communism would be a *classless* system. This meant that all people would be rewarded and treated equally regardless of their family history or their occupation.

Karl Marx believed that under pure communism the need for police and government would disappear. Furthermore, Marx believed that communism would spread to all nations as workers in other lands revolted against capitalism. In the end, according to Marx, communism would achieve world peace, since countries would no longer be in competition with one another.

During Marx's lifetime, England, Germany, and France were the leading capitalist countries. Because of this, Marx expected a workers' revolution to happen in one of these countries. However, this did not occur. The workers in these countries did not react to capitalism in the ways that Marx had predicted. Overall, capitalism was bringing improvements to the lives of workers. As a result, communism did not gain widespread support.

Communism in Russia. In 1917, a group of communist revolutionaries took control of the Russian government. They were led by Vladimir Ilyich Ulyanov—also known as Lenin. This group claimed to represent all the workers of Russia. Their goal was to establish communism in Russia. The Communists established political and economic controls over the Russian people.

At that time, however, Russia was not an industrialized country. It was an agricultural country with a traditional-type economic system. Despite this situation,

Lenin believed that Marx's ideas could be altered to fit Russia. However, it would be necessary to industrialize the country. To accomplish this, the citizens would have to be willing to make many sacrifices. Furthermore, many Russians, as well as leaders from other countries, were against Lenin's plans for setting up communism in Russia. Faced with widespread opposition, the Communists used force against those who would not go along with the programs of the Communist party. This force was often met with more resistance from Russians who were unwilling to give up their personal freedoms.

The Communists claimed that their dictatorship would only be a temporary step. They promised that Russia—later called the Soviet Union—would gradually move closer to communism. Yet, even today, the Soviet Union is far from the system that Karl Marx had outlined. The Soviet Union has *fully controlled* political and economic systems. The government answers the three basic economic questions. Since the Soviet Union is not a democracy, the average citizen has no say in these government decisions.

Communism in Other Countries. The People's Republic of China, Czechoslovakia, Poland, Cuba, and East Germany are among those countries ruled by Communist parties. There are differences between the economic practices of these countries. These differences are partly due to the special circumstances of each country. There are, however, some major similarities among all communist countries.

In all communist countries, for example, the government is the major decision maker in economic matters. Consumers in these countries do not direct production with their purchases. Instead, government planners decide what is produced and how it should be distributed. Thus, consumer demand is not a major force in communism. In the same way, workers do not enjoy the freedoms that are common to workers in noncommunist countries. Communist backers, however, believe that national goals should come before the wants of individuals. Industrial progress and military growth, for example, are often given great attention. On the other hand, consumer goods, such as blue jeans and automobiles, are not as important.

Semyon Maisterman/Tass from Sovfoto

This photograph shows a Soviet supermarket. Although Soviet consumers have some supermarkets to shop in, they often face shortages of food and other basic products. The Soviet government determines what goods are to be available to consumers.

As with capitalism and socialism, communism has been adapted to fit the special needs of different countries. There is a wide range in the amount of private property allowed in communist nations. Some free enterprise is carried on in many communist countries. For example, while all Soviet farmers work for the government, some of these farmers spend their extra time working on private plots. The food produced on this land can be sold by the farmer. In Yugoslavia, another communist country, people are even allowed to own small businesses.

Section Checkups

1. *Why did Karl Marx believe that workers should control a country's businesses and industries?*
2. *In what ways does the role of the consumer in a communist economy differ from the role of the consumer in a capitalist economy?*
3. *What are the main features shared in common by communist countries in the world today?*

Chapter Summary

There are three major types of economic systems in the world today—capitalism, socialism, and communism. We can compare these systems by looking at the process of economic decision making in each system. Capitalism is based on the rights of individuals to make economic decisions. The government has a very small role in economic matters in capitalist countries. For the most part, consumer choice determines what is produced.

In a socialist system, the government directs the national economy. It makes a wide range of economic decisions. In socialism, the government owns or controls the country's major resources and industries. There are many different kinds of socialism. In some democratic-socialist countries, the government owns only certain basic industries. Other privately owned businesses are allowed. Consumer decisions play some part in shaping production.

Communism is an extreme form of socialism. In a communist country, the government is in nearly full control of the economy. Communists believe that the interests of the country are more important than the economic rights of citizens. Because of this, government planners closely control production and total consumption. Consumer demand does not shape production activities in most communist countries.

Reviewing the Chapter

Identifying Terms

Explain or identify the following:

Capitalism	Controlled economy
Mercantilism	Nationalized
Adam Smith	Karl Marx
Laissez-faire	*Communist Manifesto*
Demand	Lenin
Socialism	Communism

Analyzing Information

1. Why did free enterprise appeal to the American colonists?

2. In what type of economic system is the role of the consumer more important? Explain your answer.

3. How do socialists determine which industries should be nationalized?

4. How has capitalism changed since the days of Adam Smith?

5. What are the major differences between socialism and communism?

6. In what ways did the actual development of capitalism differ from the predictions made by Karl Marx?

7. How did Karl Marx describe the relationship between factory owners and workers under capitalism?

Analyzing Visual Material

1. Look at the picture of the pier that is shown on page 28. List the different types of economic activity that are shown in the scene. What present American cities were important ports during the colonial era? What cities are important ports today?

2. Examine the engraving of the English knife grinders that appears on page 31. In what different ways were the health and safety of these workers endangered? In what other industries during the early days of the Industrial Revolution were workers endangered in their jobs? How are American workers protected from dangers on their jobs today?

Research and Projects

1. You can learn more about the economic systems of other countries by examining the ways in which they solve their economic problems. Select one country to study. For one week, collect newspaper and magazine articles about economic news from that country. Then, summarize this news in an oral report to your class. If possible, present illustrations, such as photographs and maps, with your report.

2. Interview five people to learn their views of capitalism, socialism, and communism. Discuss your findings with your class.

3. Throughout modern history, several nations developed fascist governments and economic systems. Investigate these economies. In a class report, explain fascism and compare it to other types of economic systems.

Francene Keery/De Wys, Inc.

Chapter 3 Characteristics of the American Economy

SECTIONS 1 Basic Principles
2 The Growth of the American Economy

As we move toward the end of the twentieth century, the United States stands as one of the world's industrial giants. And a majority of Americans enjoy a high standard of living. But how was our country able to achieve these things? The United States does have abundant natural resources and a large, healthy, and well-educated labor force. This, however, is not the complete picture. Other countries have had advantages similar to those of the United States but have not matched our economic advance. The very nature of our economic system—free enterprise—has made rapid industrial growth and a high standard of living possible.

Section 1
Basic Principles

The economy of the United States is basically a free enterprise economy. A free enterprise economy has no controlled central plan. Rather, it is based on economic freedom. The characteristics of the American economy allow for the making of free economic choices. These characteristics are such things as private property, freedom of choice, competition, and profits.

However, the American economy is not completely free. It is, in part, regulated by government. But the part government plays is limited. As you read this section, ask yourself the following questions: *What are the basic characteristics of the American economy? What is the driving force of the American economy? What part does government play in the American economy?*

Private Property. The right to own *private property* is a cornerstone of the American economy. This right of ownership includes productive resources as well as personal property. The abilities and talents a person may have are also a part of that person's private property. In general, people who own private property are free to use it without interference from others. In other words, they can use what they own as they see fit.

As important as the ownership of private property is the way people feel about that ownership. People often gain a sense of pride in maintaining and improving something they own. Also, ownership of private property often leads people to be more efficient. If their income depends on how they use their private property, peo-

H. Armstrong Roberts

Homeowners often gain personal satisfaction from taking care of and improving their homes. They can also increase the value of their homes through home-improvement projects. In today's market, most homes increase in value each year.

AT&T Photo Center

In the United States, workers are free to enter the line of work of their choice. In recent years women have been entering jobs, such as that of telephone engineer, that were once traditionally held only by men.

ple will try to be more efficient. By doing this, they can increase their income.

Property rights are limited sometimes, just as some laws limit individual behavior. None of us are completely free. The taxes that federal, state, and local governments collect limit our private property rights. Zoning laws may prevent us from building a factory on residential land we own. Our government also may forbid us to produce certain goods, such as narcotics, with the resources we own. However, these limitations are safeguards built into the economy to protect the American people. In many ways, these safeguards have been designed to maintain the institution of private property.

Freedom of Choice. Another important feature of the American economy is *freedom of choice.* This means that people have the right to organize and take part in any *lawful* business they choose. They are free to own productive resources. They are also free to use these resources to make whatever products they choose. Likewise, they are free to sell these products in the markets they choose. As you can see, freedom of choice is a natural outcome of owning private property.

Freedom of choice also means that workers are free to enter any line of work they choose. However, they must be physically and mentally equipped for that line of work. Consumers also have freedom of choice. Within the limits of their income, consumers can decide to buy those goods and services that most closely satisfy their needs and wants. By buying or not buying, American consumers directly influence what is produced. The owners of productive resources must make their free choices within the limits set by consumers.

As with private-property rights, there are some limits to freedom of choice. For example, public utilities, such as natural gas and electricity, cannot be operated without government permission. And certain licenses have to be obtained before entering certain businesses or professions, such as law or medicine. Even so, people do have a great deal of freedom of choice in the American economic system.

The Market System. To be successful, private-property rights and freedom of choice must work within an economic system. In the United States our economic system is based on the *market system.*

(Text continues on page 44.)

Innovation and Opportunity
The Wham-O Mfg. Co.

Did you ever play with a Hula Hoop or a Super Ball? More than likely, you have tossed a Frisbee disk around. These toys have one thing in common. They were developed and marketed by the Wham-O Mfg. Co. of San Gabriel, California. Wham-O's owners, Dick Knerr and Arthur Melin, have developed many similar toys.

The name of the company comes from the first product that Knerr and Melin made, the Wham-O slingshot. The slingshot was originally made for their own use, but friends began to ask for copies. To meet demand, Knerr and Melin set up a workshop to produce the slingshots. As business grew, they began to make other products. In time, they opened the Wham-O plant in San Gabriel.

Few of Wham-O's ideas come directly from Knerr and Melin. For the most part, they work with other people's ideas. But they may have to go through a thousand ideas before they find one worth the risk of investment. One of Wham-O's biggest successes, the Hula Hoop was adapted from a piece of exercise equipment used in Australia. The Super Ball was the idea of Norman Stingley, a research chemist for a rubber company. By and large, Knerr and Melin happened on the Frisbee disk by accident.

P. Vannucci/De Wys, Inc.

Knerr and Melin had frequently noticed people playing on the beach with plastic "flying saucers." The partners discovered that the saucers were made by an inventor named Fred Morrison. In 1955, they came to a business agreement with Morrison. By 1957, Wham-O was producing the plastic saucers. To help sales, Wham-O representatives went on promotion tours across the country. On one of these tours, Knerr learned from students that they played a similar game using Frisbie Pie Company tins. Knerr borrowed the name, but spelled it *Frisbee*. Frisbee® is a brand name and a registered trademark of Wham-O Mfg. Co.

Since that time, Wham-O has produced more than 100 million Frisbee disks in 16 different models. Today, Frisbee disks are almost a national pastime. There are even international Frisbee disk championships. The success of the Frisbee disk has assured Knerr and Melin of a comfortable income for life.

Through it the free economic choices of millions of individuals are put into effect. The American economy depends on the market system to perform its major economic functions. Put in simple terms, the market system answers the basic economic questions *what, how,* and *for whom.* The way in which the market system works will be discussed further in Chapter 5.

A market system relies on certain characteristics, such as *competition, profits,* and *self-interest.* These characteristics separate the market system from all other economic systems. Taking each of these characteristics in order, we can see how the American market system serves our free economy.

This dam is part of the Southern California Edison Company's Big Creek-San Joaquin River hydroelectric development. Public utilities—such as electric companies—are natural monopolies and not competitive businesses.

Southern California Edison Company

Competition. The right to compete is one of the major characteristics of the American economy. *Competition* refers to the many things that businesses will do to attract customers. These things include lower prices, better quality goods and services, new and different goods and services, advertising, and so on. With competition no one business has total command of the supply of certain goods or services. This forces businesses to keep prices low and to produce what consumers want to buy. Competition ensures that consumers will have a choice in the kinds of goods and services they can buy. For example, in the United States a number of automobile manufacturers sell cars. They compete with one another, and with foreign automobile manufacturers, to sell cars to American consumers. This competition means that American consumers have a wide choice of models when buying a car. Competition also leads to greater efficiency. This leads to lower production costs, which allows producers to charge more competitive prices.

Not all businesses are competitive. Public utilities—such as natural gas, electricity, water, and telephone services—are legal *monopolies.* A monopoly exists where one business has command of the production and supply of a certain good or service. With public utilities, organization and supply are more efficient if handled by one company. For example, if five telephone companies provided service in your community, to be certain that you would be able to telephone all your friends you would need five telephones and five telephone books. There would also be five telephone bills to pay! So, such things as telephone services for a given area are normally provided by one company. However, public commissions oversee these "natural" monopolies to make sure that fair rates are charged.

Profits and Self-interest. Another characteristic of the market system is the search for profits. In simple terms, profits are what is left from a company's receipts after all expenses have been paid. But profits are also viewed as the return for taking risks in business. In short, profits are the payment for organizing a business and taking the chance that the business may or may not be successful. The search for profits is probably the key driving force of the American economy. It helps explain many of the economic decisions made in the American economy.

The search for profits tends to benefit the economy as a whole. Highest profits go to businesses that produce products consumers want at prices they can afford. Greater profits lead to greater income for producers, and this should result in higher levels of economic growth. Greater profits also mean that more money is available to invest in and to improve businesses.

In trying to increase profits, businesses will try to improve efficiency. This lowers production costs, so overall business costs should be lower. Businesses also try to increase profits by improving the quality of their goods or services and selling them at a fair price. Consumers are more likely to buy fairly priced, high-quality goods. So, the efforts of businesses to increase profits often work in favor of consumers.

The drive to increase profits is only one kind of economic self-interest. All economic units, whether businesses or individuals, try to do what is best for themselves. Businesses seek to increase their profits. Consumers try to buy the best goods and services at the lowest price. But there are some limits on the ways we can fulfill our economic self-interest.

The Role of Government. Perhaps only a person living alone on an island is completely free. Everyone else must always limit his or her actions when dealing with others. He or she must respect the rights of others. In much the same way, the American economy is not a completely free market economy. It is influenced by government laws and rules. However, in a free society the government is controlled by the people. At election time, voters in the United States select leaders. These leaders make the laws that must be followed. We in the United States are free to change our leaders through the system of free elections. Though we are bound by laws, we are free to choose our leaders and, therefore, to determine what those laws will be.

In influencing the economy, our government tries to protect the economic freedom of both businesses and consumers. In the American economy, government rules and the market system are mixed together. Because of this some people say that the American economy is a *mixed economy*.

Our government's influence on the American economy is usually of two kinds. First, our government provides a number of necessary public services. These services are the basis of our political system. They include the defense of our country, help for the poor, the administration of justice, and so on. To pay for these public services, government collects taxes from businesses and individuals. There is no legal choice in the matter of paying taxes. There may be a choice in producing or buying certain goods or services, but as far as taxes are concerned there is no choice, taxes *must* be paid.

Second, federal, state, and local governments pass laws that regulate the ways in which businesses operate. Such laws prevent illegal business practices, like *price-fixing*—competing businesses joining together to decide on set prices for their goods or services. Businesses and consumers alike have little choice but to work within the limits set by these laws.

It should be noted that, in comparison to other economic systems, the part played by government in the American economy is limited. Over the last few decades government influence has been growing. But there is a great difference in the way our government influences the economy and the way government controls the economy in communist countries such as the Soviet Union. The role of government in the American economy will be discussed further in Chapter 12.

Section Checkups

1. *What are some of the things that are usually considered to be private property?*
2. *Which characteristics make the market system distinct from other economic systems?*
3. *Why is competition so important to the American economic system?*

Section 2
The Growth of the American Economy

The rapid growth of its economy has made the United States one of the world's leading industrial nations. Because of this, the American people enjoy a high standard of living. But how was this economic growth possible? Some people have said that it was possible because the United States has many natural resources. Other people have also stated that technological changes caused the American economy to grow. Still others have said that economic growth was possible because America's growing population provided a labor force of skilled and healthy workers. All these explanations have some truth. But the driving force behind the growth of the American economy is the American economic system—free enterprise. As you

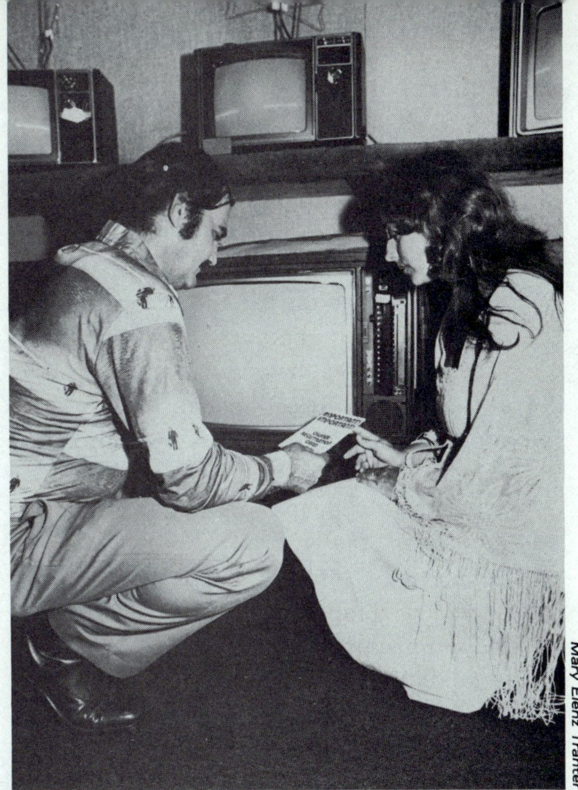

Mary Elenz Tranter

Many Americans own laborsaving and luxury appliances. By the early 1980's, almost every household in the United States had at least one televison set.

read this section, ask yourself the following questions: *In what way has the standard of living changed in the United States in recent years? How have technological advances affected productivity? What are the advantages and the disadvantages of rapid economic growth?*

A Rising Standard of Living. Today, we often hear that Americans have one of the highest standards of living in the world. But what is meant by this statement? A country's *standard of living* can be measured by the amounts and kinds of goods and services the people enjoy. In simple terms, standard of living is the measure of how people live.

As Americans, we consume very large amounts of a great variety of goods and services. For example, by the early 1980's nearly every household in the United States had a radio, a black-and-white television, and a refrigerator. Nearly 85 percent of American households had a color television. More than 95 percent had a toaster, a coffee maker, and a vacuum cleaner. And more than 75 percent of American households had a washing machine.

Other things can be used to measure the rising standard of living. Over the last 100 years or so, the per capita income of the population of the United States has risen by about 6 times. The quality of life in the United States has also improved. American workers enjoy much more leisure time than they did in the past. In 1920, for example, the average American worker could expect to spend about 48 hours a week at work. By the 1980's, this figure had been cut to 36 hours a week. And during this period, the length of time the average American could usually expect to live also increased. In 1920, life expectancy was 54 years. By the early 1980's, it was more than 75 years.

The American people are able to enjoy this standard of living because of the rapid growth of the American economy. Many reasons have been given to explain this growth. They include such things as the large American work force, technological developments, and a vast store of natural resources.

Abundant Natural Resources. The United States is rich in natural resources. This has been true throughout our country's history. The earliest European settlers in America found abundant woodland, fertile soil, and a favorable climate.

All these things encouraged the growth of American agriculture. As the frontier moved west, more fertile land was opened for agricultural use. When hardy European strains of wheat were introduced on the western plains during the second half of the nineteenth century, food production soared. The western plains became known as America's breadbasket. Today, our
1 country provides about 14 percent of the world's wheat production. And American wheat feeds people in many countries throughout the world.

America's mineral deposits were not widely developed until the second half of the nineteenth century. During this time, large deposits of iron ore and coal helped the growth of the steel industry. In 1876, less than 600,000 tons [about 550 000 metric tons] were produced in the United States. One hundred years later, about 128 million tons [about 116 million metric tons] were produced, about 17 percent of the world's production. Oil was first discovered in the United States in 1859. At first, oil was used for kerosene and for lubricating machinery. But with the coming of the internal-combustion engine and the automobile, gasoline was refined from crude oil. Today, the United States is one of the world's leading oil producers. In 1980, our country produced about 3 bil-

* In 1983, the United States produced 83.4 million tons of steel and about 3.2 billion barrels of oil.

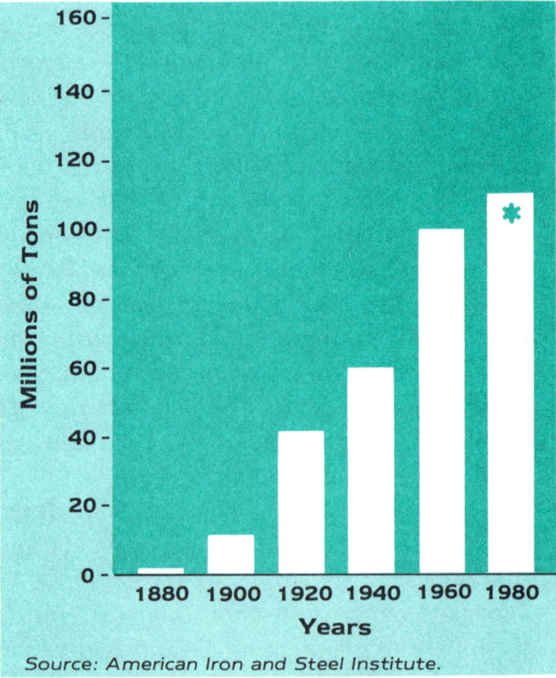

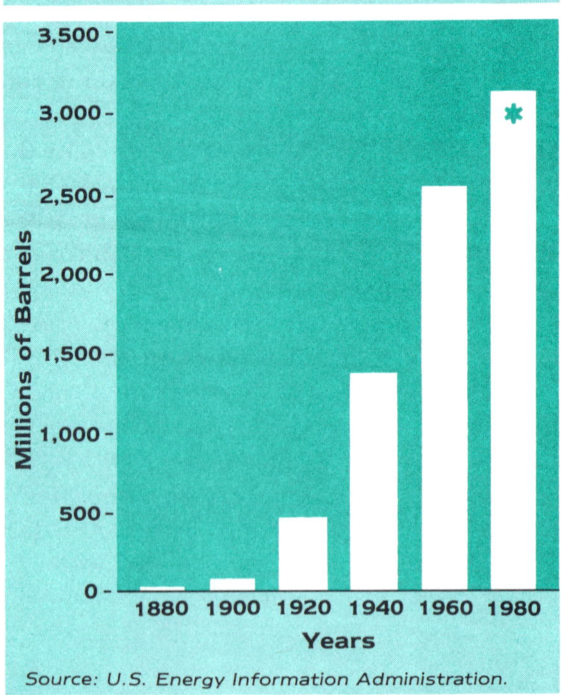

Over the last 100 years, the United States has become one of the world's leading industrial nations. By the 1980's the United States was producing about one seventh of the world's total steel production and about one seventh of the world's oil production.

1. By 1983, our country provided about 17 percent of the world's wheat production.

lion barrels of oil, 14 percent of the world's total production. Even so, this is not enough to meet our needs, and we must buy oil from other countries.

A good supply of natural resources is important to economic growth. But some countries that are rich in natural resources have yet to show any real growth. Technical knowledge on how to develop and then use these resources is also needed.

Technological Change. Ever since the birth of our nation, American businesses have tried to develop new technology. This new knowledge has then been applied to increase productivity. New machinery and new ways to use machinery have cut down costs and saved time. Generally, this saving has led to an increase in overall output. And this, in turn, has led to a higher standard of living.

Throughout our country's history, many technological changes have helped the economy to grow. But the second half of the nineteenth century was a time of rapid technological change. For example, before 1865, only 62,000 *patents*—papers giving people exclusive rights to make and sell inventions—were issued to American inventors. But between the years 1865 and 1900, more than 500,000 new patents were issued. The technological advances resulting from these patents helped to change the United States from an agricultural country to one of the world's leading industrial nations. In recent years we have experienced a similar period of rapid technological change with the development of the computer.

Economic growth would be impossible without technology. But other things, such

The introduction of computer technology has opened up many new jobs that require new skills.

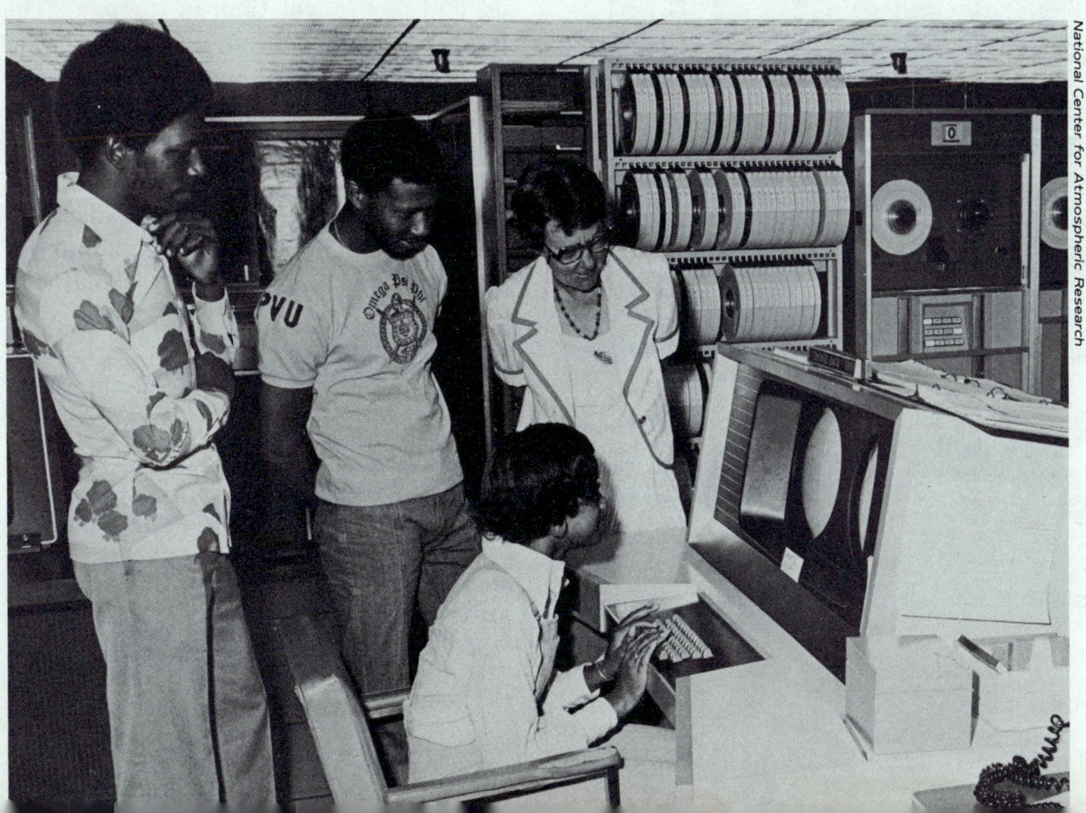

National Center for Atmospheric Research

as a growing population to provide a work force, are needed if a country's economy is to grow.

Population Growth. Since its birth, the United States has had a growing population. In the late 1700's, there were only about 4 million people in the United States. These people lived in a few cities and on farms along the Atlantic coast. By 1880, the population had grown to about 50 million. About a quarter of the 1880 population lived in urban areas—towns and cities of more than 2,500 persons. By 1980, the population was more than 226 million. Nearly three quarters of this figure lived in urban areas. This rapidly growing population swelled the ranks of the American work force.

There are a number of reasons why our country's population grew. First, there was a rise in the birthrate and a decline in the death rate. This was a result of such things as better living conditions, better nutrition, and improved medical practices. The second reason for population growth was large-scale immigration. Between the years 1820 and 1980 more than 48 million people came to the United States. Immigration was at its highest in the last years of the 1800's and the early years of the 1900's. Immigration was so high during this time that in 1920 nearly 15 percent of the population was foreign-born.

The quality, as well as the quantity, of a population must improve if economic growth is to take place. You have already seen that the American people are healthier and live longer than in the past. The American people also are generally better educated than in the past. In 1980, more than 89 percent of Americans between the ages of 5 and 19 were enrolled in school. And by 1980, nearly 70 percent of Americans who were 18 years or over had graduated from high school. A high quality population is important for growth. A

Total immigration to U.S., 1885-1915

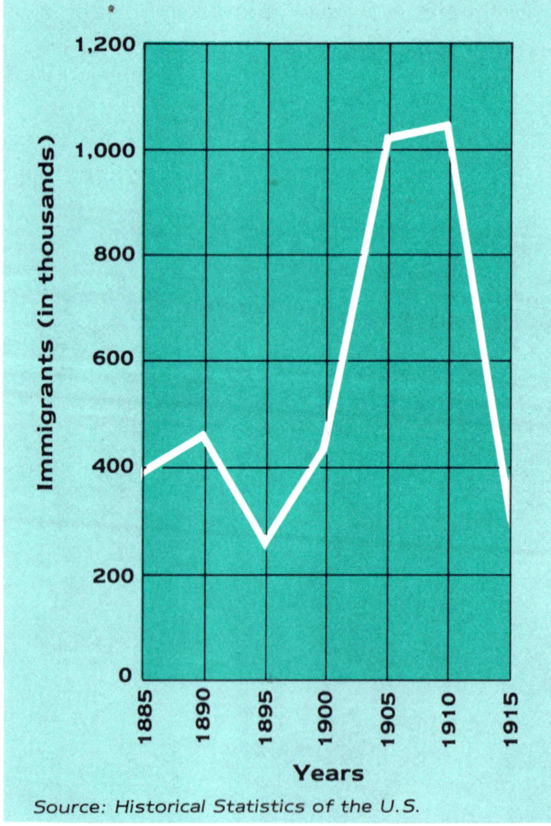

High rates of immigration were a major cause of the rapid increase in the American population. Immigration was at its highest point in the early years of the twentieth century. During this time, millions of immigrants entered the United States.

(Text continues on page 52.)

Using Social Studies Skills
Interpreting graphs

The bar and circle graphs below contain information on the growth of the United States labor force in the twentieth century. The bar graph gives information on the total labor force for the years 1900 to 1980. The circle graphs show the percentage distribution of the labor force in various industries for the years 1900, 1940, and 1980. Study the graphs carefully; then answer the questions that follow.

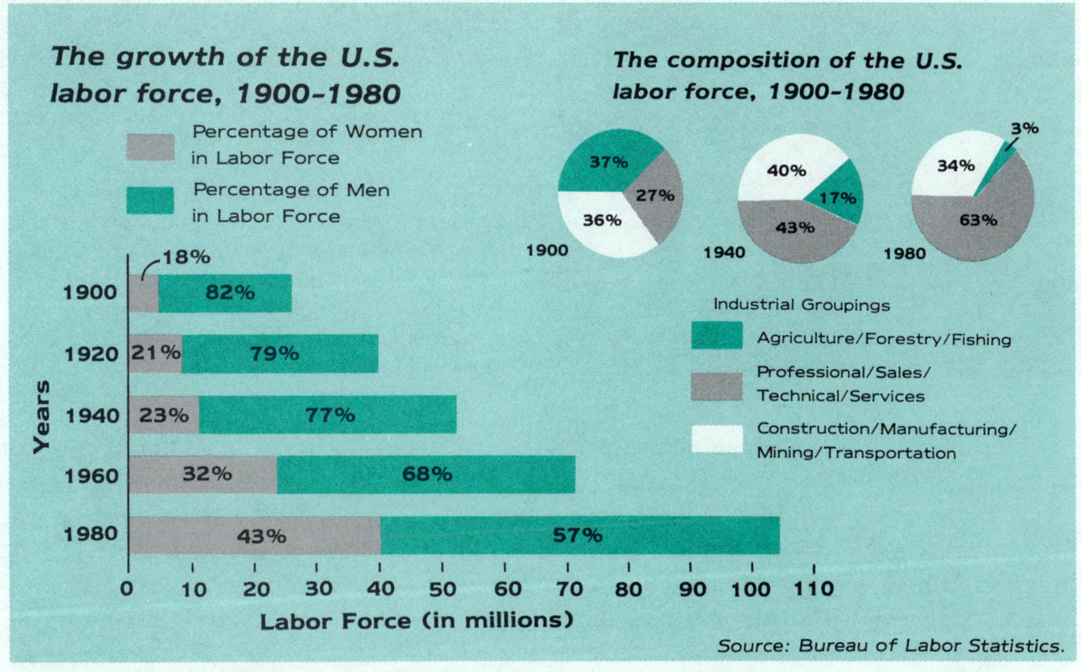

1. In which industrial grouping were most workers in 1900?
2. Which industrial grouping grew most between 1900 and 1940?
3. Between which years did the total labor force show the greatest growth?
4. Which incident during the 1940's might have accounted for the increase in the percentage of women in the labor force?
5. Since 1940, the percentage of women in the labor force has nearly doubled. In your opinion, which industrial grouping has absorbed this increase? Give reasons for your answer.

Dave Healey/Liaison

USDA

Two major problems facing the United States today are industrial pollution and the need for new energy sources. Improved pollution control is becoming an important goal for most industries. And solar energy is just one alternative source being developed to meet our energy needs.

work force of healthy, educated people is likely to be more efficient and productive.

This, however, is not the complete picture of growth. Natural resources, technological change, and a growing population are all important. But other things have influenced the growth of the American economy.

The Free Enterprise System. A rich supply of natural resources, technological developments, and a growing population have all played a part in the growth of our economy. But other countries have had similar advantages, yet they have not matched the economic growth of the United States. What has made the growth of the American economy special is our economic system—free enterprise.

Through its basic characteristics—private property, freedom of choice, competition, profits, and self-interest—free enterprise has encouraged growth. The right to own private property and the freedom to enter any lawful business and compete for profits have been the real driving force of the American economy. In this way free enterprise has given people the incentive to search out and use natural resources. It has also encouraged people to develop and apply inventions and new technology to the economy. And it has given encouragement to workers and business leaders who are willing to work harder, longer, and faster than others.

The Problems of Economic Growth. Rapid economic growth has given the

American people many good things. But it has also brought problems. In the last few years, questions have been raised about the cost of a high rate of growth. The United States does not have limitless natural resources. To go on at our present rate of growth means that some of our resources will soon be exhausted. And growth has brought with it such problems as pollution of the water and the air. These things have made it clear that greater attention must be paid to the *quality* of growth.

The United States is well aware of these problems. We are continually searching for ways to conserve our scarce resources. Many companies are looking for new deposits of oil and coal. Other forms of energy, such as solar energy, are being developed. All sectors of the economy are trying to avoid causing such problems as pollution. These things are important if our economy is to continue growing and if we are to enjoy a rising standard of living.

Section Checkups

1. *How has the standard of living changed in the United States in recent years?*
2. *What is the real driving force of the American economy?*
3. *How are we in the United States attempting to solve the problems caused by rapid economic growth?*

Chapter Summary

In the United States we have a free enterprise economy. This kind of economy is based on individual economic freedom. The characteristics of the American economy—such as freedom of choice, competition, and profits—encourage free economic choices. But our economy is not completely free. Government regulation plays a limited part. Because free enterprise and government rules are mixed together, our economy is often referred to as a mixed economy.

The American people enjoy a high standard of living. This is possible because our economy has grown rapidly. Many reasons have been given for this growth, such as abundant natural resources, technological advances, and America's large labor force. But a major reason for this rapid economic growth is our economic system—free enterprise. In recent years, however, people have noted that a rapid rate of growth often brings problems. Efforts are being made to solve these problems so that we in America can continue to enjoy a high standard of living.

Reviewing the Chapter

Identifying Terms

Explain or identify the following:

Private property	Profits
Freedom of choice	Self-interest
Market system	Mixed economy
Competition	Standard of living
Public utility	Patent
Monopoly	Urban area

Analyzing Information

1. What is the importance of the way people feel about the ownership of private property?

2. What part does competition play in the American economy?

3. How does government influence the American economy?

4. How has the quality of life in the United States improved?

5. Why is a high-quality population important to economic growth?

6. In what ways do the basic characteristics of the American free enterprise system aid economic growth?

7. What problems arise from rapid economic growth? What is being done in the United States to solve these problems?

Analyzing Visual Material

1. Look at the graphs on page 48. Between which years was there the greatest increase in steel production? Between which years was there the greatest increase in crude-oil production? What differing trends do the two graphs show?

2. Study the pictures on page 52. What source of energy is being used in the dairy-farm picture? What problems might be associated with the use of this energy source? What kind of fuel might be used by the factory in the other picture? What problems might arise from the use of this kind of fuel?

Research and Projects

1. New industries and shifting population patterns have caused many places in the United States to become well-known, if only for a short time. Select four places from the list below; then find out how and when these places were affected by industrial, technological, or population changes. With this information prepare a report to be presented to the class.

Abilene, Kansas
Detroit, Michigan
Hollywood, California
Kitty Hawk, North Carolina
New Orleans, Louisiana
Promontory Point, Utah
Spindletop, Texas

2. From newspapers and magazines, collect articles and advertisements that show the standard of living we enjoy in the United States. With these items make a collage for posting on the bulletin board.

Unit 1

Reviewing the Unit

Understanding the Unit

1. Why do we study economics?

2. What function does an economic system perform?

3. Explain the main forces in a capitalist economy.

4. Which economic activities handled by government in a socialist system would be handled by private industry in a capitalist system?

5. How does modern communism differ from the theory of communism developed by Karl Marx?

6. When does a monopoly exist? In which industries are natural monopolies found?

7. Why is the American economy often called a mixed economy?

8. What has made the growth of the American economy different from economic growth in other countries?

Questions for Discussion

1. Make a comparison of capitalist and communist economies. What are the advantages and disadvantages of each system?

2. Should the private-property rights and freedom of choice of both individuals and businesses in the American free enterprise system be unlimited?

3. Are there any limits placed on the economic freedom of American individuals and businesses that should be removed? Are there any new restrictions that should be imposed?

Recommended Reading

Galbraith, John Kenneth, and Nicole Salinger. *Almost Everyone's Guide to Economics.* Boston: Houghton Mifflin Company, 1978. An entertaining look at economics by one of today's leading economists.

Grossman, Gregory. *Economic Systems,* 2nd ed. Englewood Cliffs, N.J.: Prentice-Hall, 1974. A study of capitalist, communist, and socialist economic systems.

Hacker, Louis M. *The Course of American Economic Growth and Development.* New York: John Wiley and Sons, 1970. A review of the forces responsible for economic growth.

Haveman, Robert H., and Kenyon A. Knopf. *The Market System,* 3rd ed. New York: John Wiley and Sons, 1978. A detailed study of how the market system works.

Heilbroner, Robert L. *The Worldly Philosophers,* rev. ed. New York: Simon and Schuster, 1972. An introduction to the lives and ideas of some great economists.

Silk, Leonard. *Economics in Plain English.* New York: Simon and Schuster, 1978. Economic concepts in everyday use explained in everyday language.

Economics at Work

Making economic choices: Planning the junior-senior prom

Through a number of fund-raising projects over the last few years, your class has raised a total of $5,086.43. Your years of hard work and sacrifice can now be rewarded with the junior-senior prom. You *cannot* spend more than $5,086.43 on the prom. And there has been discussion on giving the school a gift. This will require some money.

You have decided that there are three things on which to spend the money for the prom: (1) hiring a band; (2) renting a place to hold the prom; and (3) providing for refreshments, decorations, and so on. Investigation into the costs of these things has provided the following information:

Bands Available

$ 200 Local band, plain but cheap
$ 500 Very loud rock 'n' roll band
$1200 Good, pleasant-sounding country band
$2500 Better, solid rock 'n' roll band
$3500 Good, but not big-name, band from England
$4500 Nationally known, versatile rock 'n' roll band

Places Available

$ 100 School gym
$ 250 American Legion hall
$ 750 Banquet hall at a large downtown restaurant
$1000 Ballroom at a large downtown hotel
$1500 Wallow Springs Country Club

Refreshments and Decorations

$ 250 Home economics classes fix sandwiches and decorations
$ 750 Catered—simple snacks and decorations
$1200 Catered—fancy snacks and decorations

Using this information, arrive at a decision concerning the prom. You must decide which band to hire, where to hold the prom, and what refreshments to have. You should also decide what things will be covered by the senior-class gift.

In what ways are the problems faced by the class similar to those faced by you and your family? What steps must an individual or a group take in solving budget problems?

C. E. Pefley

Unit 2 The American Economy in Action

CHAPTERS

4 The Role of Production
5 The Role of the Market
6 Profits and Competition
7 Income and the Market System
8 The Role of the Consumer

Chapter 4 **The Role of Production**

SECTIONS **1 The Factors of Production**
2 Demand Leads to Production
3 The Principles of Production

Camerique

Land, labor, capital, and entrepreneurship are the four categories of resources that go into the production of goods and services. In our free enterprise system, consumer demand is a major force in determining production. Through our purchase decisions, we direct production and, therefore, determine how our nation's factors of production will be used. Businesses work to meet our demand by producing goods and services in the most efficient way possible. Two ways businesses increase their efficiency are through specialization in certain areas of production and through careful management of resources.

Section 1
The Factors of Production

Take a few minutes to think about the clothes you are wearing. What was needed to produce each item? What raw materials were used? What tools were used in the production? What human skills and activities were needed?

You can see that a wide range of materials, goods, and human activities were used in the production of your clothes. This section takes a close look at the resources that are needed in all production. These factors of production, which were introduced in Chapter 1, are grouped into four categories. This section takes a close look at each of these categories. As you read this section, ask yourself the following questions: *What are the four factors of production? In what ways is the United States dependent on foreign sources for factors of production? What two factors of production involve human resources?*

Land or Natural Resources. Oil, diamonds, salt, and farm fields all fall into the category that we call *land* or *natural resources.* We use the term *land* to describe all natural resources, including the very surface of the earth. Land is used in many different ways to produce the things that we need and want.

Much of human history has been shaped by the need for natural resources. In part, this is because there is a wide difference

The United States is rich in natural resources. Lakes, such as this one in California, can be used in many ways to produce the things we need and want.

Camerique

between the natural resources found in different parts of the world. Some countries are rich in only one main resource, while others are rich in a variety of resources. The United States, for example, has rich mineral deposits, fertile land, good water supplies, and other needed resources. Land has been important to our history and economic growth. However, over the years, the United States has grown more dependent on the natural resources of other countries. Oil is one of the important resources that we must import. Furthermore, we depend on other countries for diamonds, bauxite, natural rubber, and several other materials. This means that in many cases Americans must go to a foreign source for one factor of production.

It is important to remember that natural resources are limited. However, these resources could be used to make many things. One parcel of land, for example, might be used for recreation, for housing, or for industry. The problem is that the land cannot be used for all of these things.

Some natural resources, such as forests, are renewable. Others, such as oil and minerals, are not. The conservation of natural resources is a key task for our country as well as the whole world. At the same time, we must find replacements for resources that are in short supply.

Labor. As you know, people are needed in the production of all goods and services. The factor of production that refers to human resources—people and their skills—is *labor*. Through labor, land is changed into a useful good. Also, as is the case with land, the nature of available labor is not the same in all countries. The size of a country's population and the job skills of its people shape production within a country.

In the United States, labor is very productive. Most American workers have high levels of education and job training. Eating regular meals and receiving good medical care also improves productivity. And, most Americans have strong incentives to work harder and better. In a market economy very productive workers earn more income than less-productive workers. The chance to earn higher wages and salaries encourages workers to improve their job skills.

The American labor force includes many workers in occupations that require a great deal of education. Pharmacists, for example, must complete a program of specialized training beyond their college education.

Mario Petitti

Photri

Capital goods, such as this dock and loading equipment, are essential to industry.

It is easy to see that over the years labor needs have been constantly changing. In the 1800's, most Americans worked on farms. Today, fewer workers are needed in agriculture. Many other changes have taken place as the result of technological development. Fifty years ago there were about as many unskilled workers in the United States as skilled workers. Today, American industry demands fewer unskilled workers. For the most part, machines can do the work that was once done by unskilled workers. Now less than 1 in 20 workers is classified as unskilled. In the same way, the labor needed for production in 50 years will be different from what it is today. Higher levels of job skills and education will be needed. For these reasons, workers will have to be flexible if they are to meet the challenges of the future.

Capital. Throughout history, people have developed many aids to use in the production of goods and services. Tools, machines, docks, and factories are among the aids that we call *capital* or *capital goods*. Capital also includes many resources used to distribute goods to consumers, such as highways and trucks. The term *capital* is sometimes used to describe the money available to a business. Used as an economic term, however, *capital* refers to actual goods.

It takes land and labor to make capital goods. Because of this need, the production of capital requires resources that could otherwise be used to make consumer goods.

©Walt Disney Productions

Walt Disney was one of America's best-known entrepreneurs. Disney, who began his career as a free-lance artist, became a major innovator in the animated-cartoon and motion-picture industry.

In the long run, however, the production of capital goods aids the production of consumer goods. To understand this relationship, imagine that you must make 100 posters to announce a school event. You could make the posters with no capital investment by printing each poster individually. Or, you could first make a capital investment in the form of a stencil. Although making a stencil might take as much time as it would take you to make several posters, the time would be well invested. Your overall production time—the time it takes to make the stencil and then to make 100 posters—would be shorter than it would be to print each poster individually.

The United States has a large supply of capital. Sophisticated farm machinery and computers are among the long list of goods that have increased our output of goods and services. Much of this has been made possible because individual Americans were willing to put their resources into the production of capital goods. Yet, even though the United States has so many capital goods, the possible uses for these goods are even greater. Due to this scarcity, there is the ongoing need for decision making to determine how capital will be used.

Entrepreneurship. Behind every business venture, there is a person or group of persons who are willing to take risks. Persons who undertake business risks are called *entrepreneurs*. Entrepreneurs take the initiative in putting together the other productive resources—land, labor, and capital. For this contribution, risk takers earn profits from successful business ventures. On the other hand, these risk takers must bear some of the losses of business failures.

In a small business, the owner-manager is normally the entrepreneur. In large corporations, most risks are assumed by the owners. In some cases, however, the managers of corporations share directly in the business's profits and losses. When this happens, managers can be called entrepreneurs.

Entrepreneurship is as important as the other factors of production. Businesses are started only when a key person sees a need for the enterprise. This person must put together all of the resources—land, labor, and capital—needed to open the business. In many ways, entrepreneurship is the spark that drives our American free enterprise system.

Section Checkups

1. *What are five resources that come under the classification of land?*
2. *What are four reasons that explain why American labor is very productive?*
3. *How do capital goods aid in production?*

Section 2
Demand Leads to Production

Have you ever thought of starting your own business? If so, how would you determine which goods or services that you would provide? What would you need to carry out this production? This section examines some forces that have shaped production in the United States. As you read this section, ask yourself the following questions: *What is the difference between consumer wants and consumer demand? Is consumer demand always the same? In what ways does production in modern America differ from production during earlier periods of our history?*

The Role of the Consumer. In the first section, you learned about the entrepreneurs' part in production. They take risks in starting new businesses. Entrepreneurs and managers also make the decisions for ongoing businesses. How do managers decide which business ventures will probably be successful and profitable? These decisions are based on information about consumer demand and production costs. In the United States, consumers play a key role in determining what gets produced.

Most consumers have unlimited wants. All have limited amounts of money. A large number of students in your school, for example, might want to own a sports car. Most of these students, however, do not have enough money to buy a sports car. Some of the students who have enough money might not be willing to spend it on a car.

If you were interested in opening a business, you would need to know about more than the wants of consumers. You would also want information on the consumers' *ability* and *willingness* to buy. The amount of a product that people are willing to buy at all prices is called *demand.*

(Text continues on page 65.)

Looking at Careers
The market researcher

What do market researchers do? Market researchers provide businesses with information on demand. They investigate the demand for consumer goods as well as the demand for goods used by businesses. Market researchers collect, analyze, and interpret data on the sale and promotion of products. They collect facts from a variety of sources, ranging from business records to telephone surveys.

What qualifications do market researchers need? A bachelor's degree is generally needed for a career in marketing research. Majors in economics, business administration, or psychology are best suited for the field. In most cases, graduate degrees are needed for the top jobs in the field. Courses in statistics, data processing, sociology, and journalism are important preparation for market research. The job requires careful attention to facts and figures. The work is best suited to individuals who enjoy problem solving and have the ability to work under the pressure of deadlines.

What about pay and working conditions? Salaries differ, depending on the educational background and the experience of the market researcher. College graduates who entered the field as trainees in 1980 earned more than $12,000 a year. Persons with master's degrees and experience in the field earned more. The field offers many opportunities for advancement. Most market researchers work in offices located in major cities. Some market researchers must travel in their work.

American Marketing Association

How does a knowledge of economics help? Market researchers are at the forefront of business decision-making and investment decisions. Market researchers must be able to determine what customers are willing and able to buy. Businesses rely on market researchers when planning their production and sales operations. In order to make sound recommendations, researchers must understand production, advertising, and marketing. For more information on careers in market research, write to **American Marketing Association, 222 South Riverside Plaza, Chicago, Illinois 60606.**

Entrepreneurs pay close attention to the demands of consumers. Businesses will produce a good or service when they believe that people are willing to buy it at a price that is higher than the cost of production. Imagine that you could make candles at the cost of $1.00 each. If your neighbors were willing to buy these candles for $1.50 each, you might be willing to make some candles for sale. However, if no one was willing to pay more than $1.00 for a candle, you would not make any for sale. Remember, demand measures consumers' willingness and ability to buy at different prices.

All businesses in our country are concerned with demand. To be successful, businesses must determine consumer demand. With this information and information on production costs, production can be properly planned.

The Production of Goods and Services. Factors of production must be used in making all goods and services. This is true for small-scale production as well as for large enterprises. It is true whether the production is carried out at home or in a factory.

During the early years of our history, Americans produced a large part of the things that they needed and wanted at home. Farm families were often quite *self-sufficient*—able to provide for themselves. They raised crops and animals, constructed buildings, and gathered fuels for heating, cooking, and lighting. Families made their food, their clothes, and their furnishings. Limited transportation, education, and even medical care were often carried out within the family. A great deal of work went into these activities.

Production is certainly very different now in late-twentieth-century America.

The Bettmann Archive

Early American families had to make most of their household items, as is shown in the picture above. Today, however, specialization enables us to buy many of the goods we use.

Photri

Developments in production have given us a very high standard of living. Production still requires a combination of the factors of production. But, today we are much more efficient in our use of these resources. For example, the population of the United States today is about two and one-half times larger than it was in 1900. Despite this great increase, far less labor is needed to meet our agricultural needs. In fact, the number of Americans working in agriculture today is less than one third the number for 1900. Furthermore, this small number of workers also provides many agricultural goods for export.

The more efficient use of labor benefits all Americans. In the past, children were part of the work force. Adults and children worked long hours, six days a week. Today, child labor is outlawed, and the workweek for adults has been cut. Many goods and services that were once produced at home are now made by businesses through specialized production. The buying power of Americans has risen greatly. This, in turn, has increased consumer demand, leading to even more production.

Section Checkups

1. *What is consumer demand?*
2. *How does consumer demand affect production?*
3. *In what two ways has production in the United States changed during our history?*

Section 3
The Principles of Production

Businesses must first examine consumer demand to make production decisions. However, demand is not the only force that shapes production. For example, there is a demand for automobiles in Oklahoma. But, it is not likely that an automobile factory will be built on a rich oil field. This land can be used more efficiently. This section explains how producers look for the best use of resources. As you read this section, ask yourself the following questions: *Why do businesses specialize? How is productivity increased? Why is investment important to production?*

Specialization. One major practice that makes the production of goods and services efficient is called *specialization.* To specialize is to focus efforts on a certain task. Specialization can be used at all levels of production.

People specialize in the jobs that they do best. Cooks, farmers, and butchers all do different tasks in food production. It is easy to see how the specialization of labor increases efficiency. Try to imagine a world without this specialization. Each person would have to master many trades just to satisfy the basic needs of food, clothing, and shelter. Life would certainly be very different if you had to do all of these things for yourself.

Businesses specialize for the same reasons as individuals. By specializing in a particular type of good or service, they can become more *efficient*—make better use of scarce resources. Like individuals, a business should undertake the activities best suited to its resources. This allows a business to invest in capital goods that will produce the greatest return.

Regions and countries also specialize. As in all other cases, this specialization occurs because producers want to use their resources efficiently. In the United States, Texas, Louisiana, and California lead all other states in oil production. New York is the country's top state for the manufacture of clothing. Kansas leads all other states in wheat production. Among the countries of the world, Japan and the Soviet Union lead in fishing.

When specializing, an individual, a state, or a country is making economic decisions. It is deciding to use its re-

Specialization in the food industry is illustrated by the equipment and the operation of this modern dairy.

William L. Means

sources for the greatest possible efficiency. Throughout our history, individual Americans, as well as the nation, have moved from a high level of self-sufficiency to a high level of specialization.

Improving Productivity. Productivity is the measure of goods and services made with a set amount of resources. Producers are always interested in increasing their productivity. They want to find better ways to use their resources in order to increase their output.

The history of American industry shows a tremendous increase in productivity. Because of this, Americans today enjoy more goods and leisure time than ever before. A number of factors have combined to make this possible.

These scientists are part of a research team that is experimenting with soybean plants to learn how sludge can be used as a safe and effective soil conditioner and fertilizer.

Robert C. Bjork/USDA

Over the years, the productivity of American labor has risen greatly. In fact, American workers are among the most efficient in the world. This means that American workers produce more goods and services than workers in other countries make in the same amount of time. Education and job training has made American workers highly skilled. Training has also improved management decisions regarding the use of labor.

Americans have also become more efficient in the use of land. Farmers have learned more about soil, crops, and weather. Education has also improved the use of energy resources.

The increase and improvement in capital, such as machines and tools, have been the chief reasons for increased productivity. Thousands of inventions serve to make production faster and easier. Think about the changes that have been made possible by computers. Telephones, lasers, jet engines, and copying machines are among the other goods that have changed our productivity.

All of these advances in *technology*—methods of production—have brought about more products and free time for Americans. Improvements in technology also cause higher wages, salaries, and profits. For these reasons, Americans are willing to use some resources to develop better technology. Using resources in this way is one form of investment.

Investment. The word *investment* describes the activities undertaken to increase or improve future production. The technology that we have today was made possible through past investment. In the same way, investments must continue so that new technology can be developed.

(Text continues on page 70.)

Using Social Studies Skills
Interpreting pictographs

The high standard of living enjoyed in the United States is closely related to our high level of productivity. American productivity has increased greatly during the twentieth century. The highest increase has occurred in agriculture. Improved technology has made American farms the most productive in the world.

One way of measuring productivity is in terms of output per labor hour—the amount of goods or services a worker can produce in an hour. These two pictographs use this method to illustrate the increase in farm productivity. Study the pictographs carefully; then answer the questions that follow.

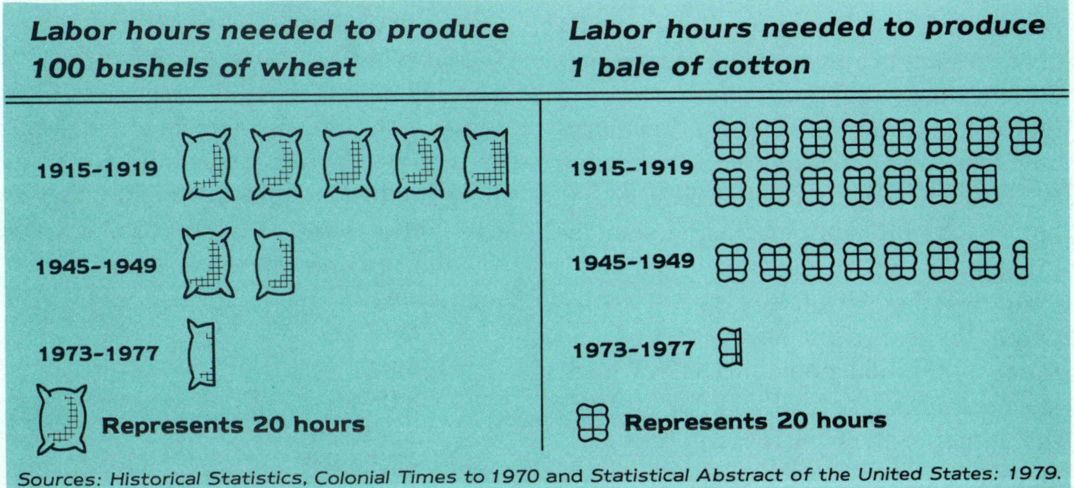

Sources: Historical Statistics, Colonial Times to 1970 and Statistical Abstract of the United States: 1979.

1. What does each symbol represent in the pictograph for wheat production? In the pictograph for cotton production?
2. How many labor hours did it take to produce 100 bushels of wheat between 1915 and 1919? Between 1973 and 1977?
3. What was the decrease in labor hours required to produce 100 bushels of wheat between 1919 and 1973?
4. How many labor hours did it take to produce a bale of cotton between 1915 and 1919? Between 1973 and 1977?
5. What was the decrease in labor hours required to produce a bale of cotton between 1919 and 1973?
6. How do you think the changes in agricultural productivity have affected the size of the country's farm population?

Furthermore, some investment is always needed to replace or expand capital.

When investing, a person or business is making an important economic decision. Resources that are invested cannot be used for current consumption. The money used to build a new printing press, for example, cannot be used to buy ink or paper. The new press, however, will serve in later production.

Part of the money invested by businesses is used for capital goods. Tools, machines, buildings, and power generators are some of these goods. Businesses must also make investments for communications and transportation. Investments are also made in human resources. Managers and other workers are given training to improve their abilities. In the same way, you invest in yourself by going to school. While in school, you are not earning money, but you are probably increasing your future earning power.

Increasing Efficiency and Output. One of the goals of management is to keep the costs of production down. Often, management must also find ways to increase the output of their businesses. There are several ways to increase the amount of goods or services made by a business.

First, managers can use higher quality factors of production to increase output. Highly skilled workers and dependable machinery will usually result in greater output than untrained workers and poor machinery. Second, managers can work out better ways to use the factors of production. This might involve changing the position of machines within a plant. Or, managers might improve productivity by using workers' time more efficiently.

The third way to increase output is to increase the input of the factors of production. In order to make more chairs, for example, a furniture company might have its carpenters work extra hours. Or, more carpenters might be hired. In all cases, however, management must see that the factors of production are used efficiently.

Diminishing Returns. When adding more inputs to the production process, businesses want to know how much extra output will result from each addition. Adding more and more of one factor of production will not always increase productivity. This is explained by the *law of diminishing returns.*

An example of diminishing returns

Number of Workers	Cars Washed Each Hour
4	10
5	14
6	19
7	25
8	32
9	36
10	39
11	40

As more workers are hired at the car wash, the number of cars washed each hour increases. However, at a certain point, the addition of each extra worker results in a smaller increase in the total output.

It is easiest to understand this idea through an example. There is a busy car wash that employed 4 workers. These workers had to complete 8 different steps to wash a car. The manager of the car wash decided that another worker should be hired. Look at the table on page 70 to see how the extra worker changed production. After obtaining such good results with this fifth worker, the manager hired even more workers.

The table shows how production changed as the work force expanded to 11. You can see that the total output increased as each worker was added. However, the manager should have paid close attention to the extra output that was occurring with the addition of each new worker. The eighth worker added 7 cars to the total, whereas the ninth worker added only 4. The law of diminishing returns had set in when the ninth worker was hired.

The law of diminishing returns applies to all factors of production when they are added to fixed amounts of other inputs. Because of it, managers must always search for the best combination of land, labor, and capital for efficient production.

Section Checkups

1. *What are the reasons for specialization in production?*
2. *What is the relationship between productivity, capital goods, and technology?*
3. *How is technology improved?*

Chapter Summary

The production of goods and services requires a combination of the four factors of production. The factors are land, labor, capital, and entrepreneurship. *Land* describes all natural resources. *Labor* includes the human skills needed in production. *Capital* refers to the aids that are used in production. *Entrepreneurship* describes the activities undertaken by those who make business decisions that involve economic risks.

Managers depend on information about consumer demand to make their business decisions. They also want to use the factors of production in the best possible way. This ongoing drive for efficiency has brought about many changes in industry. Better technology has also shaped these changes.

The expansion and development of technology requires investment. The resources used in the development of capital cannot be used for other goods. Investments, however, are necessary for businesses to maintain or improve their productivity.

Reviewing the Chapter

Identifying Terms

Explain or identify the following:

Land	Demand
Labor	Specialization
Capital	Productivity
Entrepreneurship	Technology
Efficiency	Investment

Analyzing Information

1. What factors make the American labor force highly efficient?

2. How do capital goods aid in the production of goods and services?

3. Why is the entrepreneur also called the risk taker?

4. How do consumer wants differ from consumer demand?

5. In what ways does production today differ from production 100 years ago?

6. Why is investment necessary for future production?

7. What are ways in which managers can attempt to increase the output of a business?

8. Why must managers understand the law of diminishing returns when they attempt to increase production?

Analyzing Visual Material

1. Examine the two pictures that are shown on page 65. What activities are shown in these pictures? How do these pictures suggest changes in life-styles that have occurred as the result of changes in the production of goods and services? What other activities might a family have done for itself 150 years ago that are now completed by specialists working away from the home?

2. Look at the picture of the Department of Agriculture scientists that is shown on page 68. How does this picture illustrate that advanced technology allows us to make better use of our natural resources? What other agricultural projects make similar use of technology to improve production?

Research and Projects

1. To learn more about the relationship between technology and productivity, interview a business owner. Ask questions to learn how the owner's company has used technology to increase its production over the past years.

2. Explore the changes that have taken place in the makeup of the American labor force since the beginning of the century. Prepare oral reports and charts to share this information with the class.

3. Divide into small groups to prepare reports on the natural resources of different nations. Each group should focus on one nation. The reports should include information on types of resources and how the nation uses those resources.

New York Convention & Visitors Bureau

Chapter 5 The Role of the Market

Our economy is a market system in which consumers try to buy products for as low a price as possible while producers try to sell their products for as high a price as possible. The price at which a sale will take place is determined through the market forces of supply and demand. Generally, the price of a product depends on the amount of that product that is available for sale and on people's ability and willingness to buy that product. Businesses use prices as guides in determining the types and quantities of goods and services to produce.

Section 1
The Law of Supply

How many students in your class earn money by offering their services for gardening, house painting, or baby-sitting? What is the average hourly wage in these jobs? Imagine that the people wanting these services doubled the wages that they offer. How would this change affect the number of students who would make their services available? According to the law of supply, more students would offer their services at the higher rate of pay. This section examines the law of supply. As you read this section, ask yourself the following questions: *What is supply? How does price affect the amount of a product offered for sale by producers? What causes changes in supply?*

Charles J. Quinlan

In many areas, the amount of land supplied for parking spaces depends on the rate that drivers are willing to pay for parking. Parking lots at airports, sports stadiums, and downtown business districts often charge parking fees.

The Nature of Supply. *Supply* refers to the amounts of goods and services that producers are willing to offer for sale at all possible prices. It is important to remember that *supply* does not refer to one fixed amount of goods or services. Rather, it refers to a range of amounts. The *law of supply*, stated most simply, says that producers will offer more goods and services for sale in markets if the prices they receive for their products are relatively high.

Consider, for example, an airport where there were two parking lots. Each lot charged 25 cents an hour for each car. As the local population grew, more air travelers began to drive to the airport. The two parking lots were usually filled up by 11:00 A.M. The two parking-lot owners then expanded their lots. They also raised the parking rates.

Yet, even with more available space and higher rates, travelers continued to fill the lots. Owners of other property in the area began to offer their land for parking spaces. Thus, more parking spaces were made available as the price of parking went up. In this example, as in most cases, the amount of a product or service offered for sale depended upon the price offered in the market. The *quantity supplied* increased as the price offered for the good or service was increased. For the same reason, more students from your class would be willing to baby-sit if the wage paid for this service was doubled. It is likely that even more students would baby-sit if the pay was raised even higher.

Using Economic Models. As we study the law of supply and other economic principles, keep in mind that we are presenting economic models. Models are generalizations. They offer a way of simplifying one part of the economy. Models describe overall patterns, not what happens in each case. There are exceptions for every model.

To explain some economic models, we will use hypothetical examples throughout this book. The parking-lot case is one of these examples. Each example will help you to understand the model that is being presented.

Models and examples are designed to provide focus. They will help you to find the relationship between two factors of the economy. In the parking-lot example, we looked at the relationship between price increases and quantity supplied. As we isolated these factors (price and supply), we assumed that other things, such as the wages for parking-lot attendants, remained the same. Throughout this book we will use this "all things equal" assumption in order to isolate the effect of one specific factor on another.

The Supply Schedule. Economists use a *supply schedule* to indicate how different amounts of a product would be made available at different prices. On this page there is a supply schedule for the parking-lot example. The supply schedule lists the number of parking spaces offered at different prices.

You can see that when shoppers were paying 25 cents an hour for parking, producers (lot owners) were able to offer 40 parking spaces. At 50 cents an hour, they could build and rent 60 spaces. As the parking rate climbed higher, more spaces were made available.

Supply schedule

Parking Rate per Hour	Parking Spaces Supplied
$1.00	100
.75	80
.50	60
.25	40

This supply schedule lists the quantities of parking spaces that would be supplied at each possible parking rate. As this schedule indicates, more spaces would be made available with each parking-rate increase.

The Supply Curve. The information from the supply schedule on page 75 can also be presented in a graph. Graphs are important tools in economics. They offer a way to show changes and to show the relationships between two sets of information. The graph on this page shows the relationship between price and the quantity supplied.

On this graph, price is shown on the vertical axis. Quantity is shown on the horizontal axis. The information from the supply schedule has been plotted on the graph by first finding the correct points on each axis. Perpendicular lines were then drawn from the correct points. The broken lines on this graph indicate how this was done. A point is placed at the intersection of each pair of lines. One point, for example, shows that 100 parking spaces would be supplied at a rate of $1.00. The upward-sloping line that connects the 4 points is called the *supply curve*. The supply curve shows how the quantity supplied goes up with increases in price.

This supply curve presents the information from the supply schedule on page 75. Prices are shown on the vertical axis and quantities are shown on the horizontal axis. The upward-sloping curve shows that the producers would offer more parking spaces as the parking rate is increased.

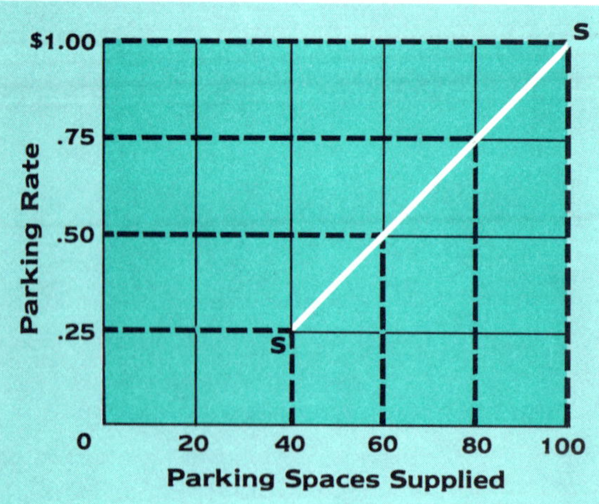

Changes in Supply. Changes in the cost of production are the major reasons for changes in supply. Producers must pay for the scarce goods and services that they use. If the prices that producers pay for land, labor, and capital go up, they may supply fewer goods and services.

Anything that lowers producers' costs will tend to bring about greater production. For example, technological advances sometimes have the effect of lowering the costs of production. When cost is reduced in this way, supply will most likely be increased. The supply of pocket calculators, for example, went up as new technology was developed and the cost of production went down.

It is important to remember that *changes in supply* refer to changes in the amounts offered at each different price level. Imagine that the cost of land near that airport went up greatly as more businesses moved into the area. The parking-lot owners might find that their land could bring higher profits if it was used for building sites. A restaurant or a gift shop might be built on the land. If this happened—if one lot was no longer available for car parking—fewer spaces would be available to travelers. There would be a decrease in the supply of parking spaces. This change in supply can be seen on the graph on page 77. As you can see, a decrease in supply caused the supply curve (S^2) to move to the left on the graph. On the other hand, an

Changes in supply

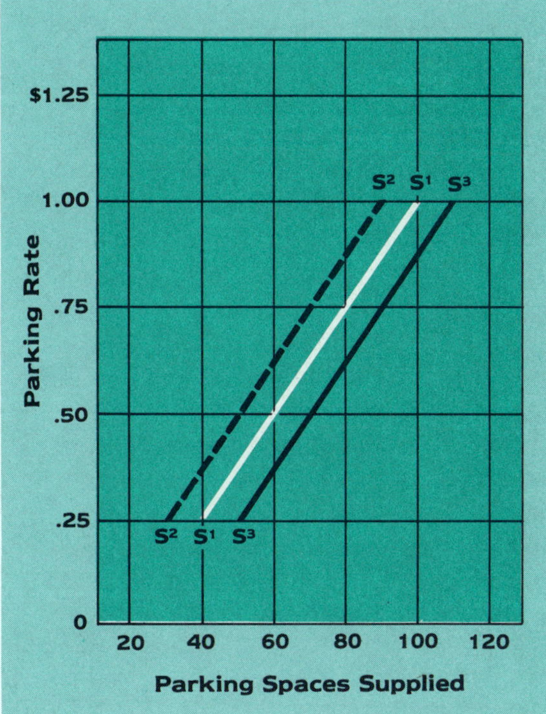

This graph shows how an increase in supply (S^3) and a decrease in supply (S^2) would change the position of the supply curve.

increase in supply would cause the curve (S^3) to move to the right on the graph. Changes in supply, such as those illustrated on this graph, are usually the result of changes in the costs of production.

Section Checkups

1. *What is the law of supply?*
2. *What information is provided in a supply schedule?*
3. *What is the relationship between producers' costs and supply?*

Section 2 The Law of Demand

The law of supply explains only one side of the market. The other side—the activities of buyers—is explained by the forces of demand. This section explores demand and the factors that shape it. As you read this section, ask yourself the following questions: *What is the relationship between price and demand? What does it mean to say that demand is elastic? What are the main causes of changes in demand?*

The Nature of Demand. As you recall, *demand* refers to the amount of a good or a service that buyers will purchase at various prices at a given time. In Chapter 4 you learned that in economic terms demand depends on the consumer's willingness and ability to buy. Therefore, to understand the nature of demand, we must look at the factors that determine what consumers buy.

Price is one of the major factors that shape demand. Generally, people will buy more of a good at a low price than they will at a high price. This is the *law of demand.* This law merely states that there is an *inverse*—opposite—relationship between price and quantity demanded.

The Demand Schedule. Think back to the airport parking problem that we discussed in the first section of this chapter. The law of demand would also be present in that situation. More people, for example, would want parking spaces at a low parking rate than at a higher parking rate. The *demand schedule* on this page shows how many parking spaces would be demanded at different rates.

You can see that the highest number of parking spaces would be demanded at a rate of 25 cents an hour. At 50 cents an hour, 100 drivers would want to rent spaces. The schedule also shows that as the price goes higher, fewer travelers would be willing and able to pay the rates.

The information from the demand schedule is also shown on the graph. Price is shown on the vertical axis. Quantity is shown on the horizontal axis. Points that represent the information from the demand schedule have been plotted. The line that connects these points is called the *demand curve.* The demand curve indicates the relationship between price and demand.

This demand schedule lists the quantities of parking spaces that travelers would demand at each possible rate. The information from the schedule is also shown on the graph.

Demand schedule

Parking Rate per Hour	Parking Spaces Demanded
$1.00	60
.75	80
.50	100
.25	120

Demand curve

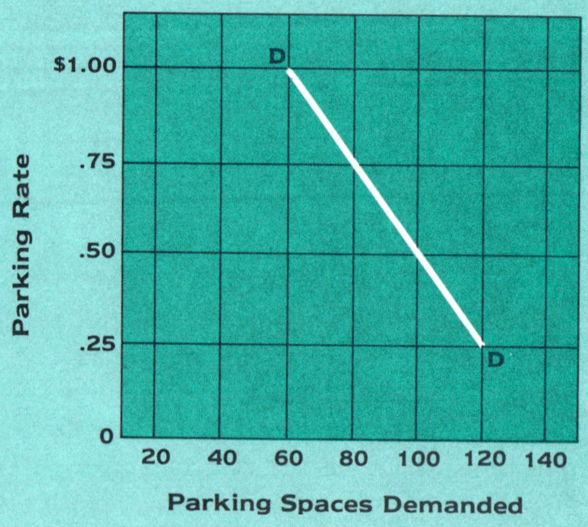

(Text continues on page 80.)

Being a Wise Consumer
Unit pricing

You know that the price of a product is one of the main factors that you must consider when you buy something. For you to get the best possible buy, it is often necessary to do comparison shopping. This involves comparing the prices of different brands and also comparing the prices of different-sized packages. How can you determine which package offers you the most for your money? Is the largest package always the best buy? These questions can be answered through *unit pricing*.

Unit pricing is the way of determining the price of a product per comparable units of measure. The units of measure might be ounces, pounds, pints, liters, or another measure. The following example illustrates how unit pricing works:

One store offers four different-sized packages of notebook paper. The chart lists the package size, package price, and unit price for each product.

Size of Package (# of sheets)	Package Price	Unit Price
50	$0.79	$0.0158
75	0.99	0.0132
100	1.19	0.0119
200	2.76	0.0138

Which of the packages offers the best buy?
Which package involves the highest price per sheet of paper?

The unit price is figured by dividing the price of the package by the number of sheets (units) contained in the package. Some stores, particularly food stores, provide unit-price information for each product on their shelves. Some cities require food stores to provide this information for consumers. In many cases, this information is listed on the shelf near the product. However, where it is not provided, the unit price can be determined easily. It will serve you as a valuable tool for comparison shopping.

De Wys, Inc.

Clothing and entertainment are two areas in which consumer preferences frequently change.

Changes in Demand. A change in demand refers to an increase or a decrease in the amount of a product that people will buy at all possible prices. There are several factors that might cause a change in demand.

Changes in consumers' preferences or tastes are one reason for changes in demand. The demand for many goods and services is subject to these changes. Clothing styles, forms of entertainment, and even eating habits are continuously changing. As these and other changes occur, there are changes in the demand for goods and services.

Demand also changes with the income levels of consumers. When their incomes rise, consumers have more money to spend on all goods and services. The sale of *normal goods* increases when buyers have more money to spend. *Normal goods* is the term used by economists to describe all the products for which the demand is greater when the income of consumers rises. Many products fall into this group. Steak is a good example of a normal good.

Other Relationships There are, however, some goods for which demand decreases as the income of consumers increases. Economists refer to these products as *inferior goods*. Cheap cuts of meat are examples of these products. Middle-income families are likely to buy less hamburger as their incomes increase. To those families hamburger would be an example of an inferior good.

The demand for a product also changes when there is a price change in a related product. Many products have close substitutes. A consumer has to consider the price of several products in deciding how much of any one product to buy. In general, an

A change in demand means an increase or a decrease in the quantity of a product that could be sold at all possible prices. This graph shows how a decrease in demand (D²) causes the demand curve to shift to the left.

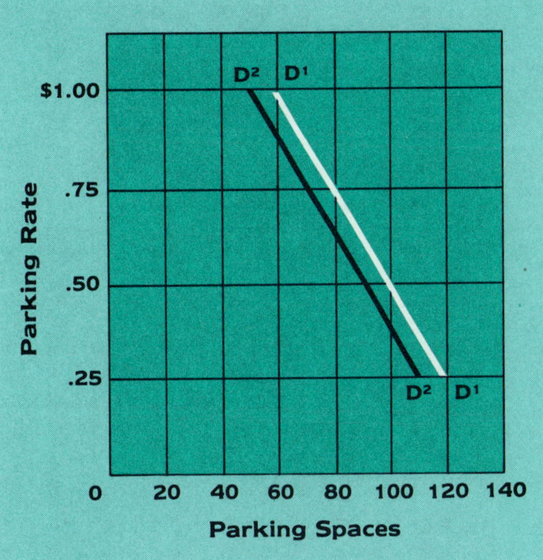

increase in the price of a product will cause an increase in the demand for close substitutes for that product. For example, if the price of butter goes up, many people will buy more margarine.

On the other hand, some products are used together. Goods related in this way are referred to as *complementary goods.* Tires and automobiles are complementary goods. Automobile buyers must also purchase tires. If the prices of automobiles go up, consumers will demand fewer tires. If the prices of automobiles go down, consumers will demand more tires. Cameras and rolls of film are also complementary goods. If the price of cameras falls, people will use more film.

Let us return to the airport parking problem in order to illustrate a change in demand. Imagine that a bus service has been opened in the area. This service would allow travelers to ride a bus to the airport from several points in the area. At the same time, the price of gasoline has gone up. These two factors have resulted in a decrease in the number of parking spaces that will be rented at each possible price. The graph on this page contains the original demand curve (D^1) and the new curve (D^2) that reflects this decrease in demand. You can see that a decrease in demand shifts the demand curve to the left on the graph. An increase in demand would move the curve to the right on the graph. Note that a change in demand means that either more or less will be purchased at all possible prices.

The Elasticity of Demand. With many goods and services, the amount purchased varies greatly with the price. When the amount demanded varies greatly with price changes, the demand is said to be *elastic.* The demand is called *inelastic* if a change in price does not result in a large change in the quantity demanded.

The demand for new automobiles, for example, is elastic. Buyers will increase their purchases more than proportionately if the price of cars drops. If, on the other hand, the price goes up, buyers will reduce their purchases.

The demand for table salt is considered inelastic. Variations in price do not bring about large changes in the amount purchased. Your family would not greatly

Inelastic demand curve

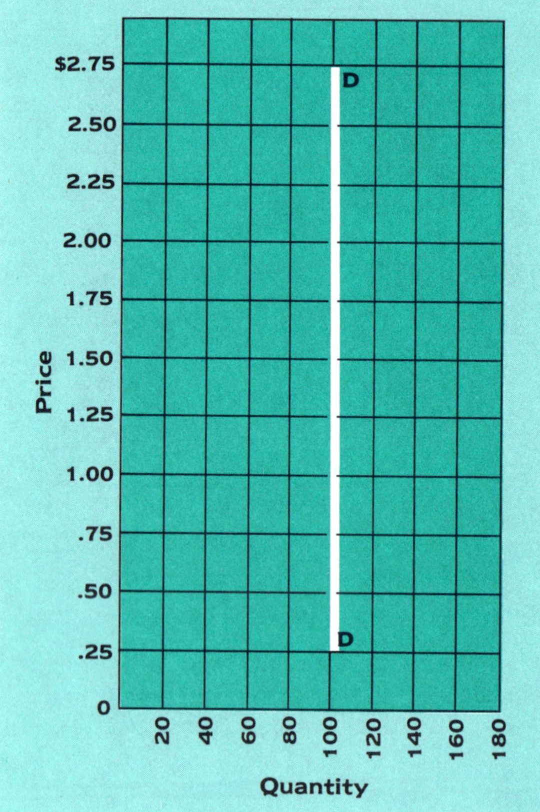

This graph shows a demand curve for a situation in which the demand for a product is perfectly inelastic. In this situation, a change in price would result in no change in the quantity demanded.

change its buying habits of salt if the price was doubled or if it was cut in half.

The graph on this page shows a demand curve (D) for a *perfectly inelastic* demand. The curve shows that changes in price would not change the quantity demanded. It is not likely that the demand for any product would be so inelastic over any appreciable length of time. The demand for most goods and services is neither totally elastic nor totally inelastic. Rather, there is a range in the degree of elasticity that a good or service might have. There are several conditions that determine the elasticity of demand for a given good or service.

Determinants of Elasticity. What makes the demand for new automobiles elastic? Why is the quantity demanded so responsive to price changes? Why is the demand for new cars different from the demand for salt? There are some close substitutes available for new automobiles. If new car prices soared, people would buy fewer new cars. Instead, they might buy used cars or use more public transportation to satisfy their transportation needs.

Another factor that enters the picture is the amount of the buyer's income spent on the product. Generally, if the amount spent on a product is small in relation to the buyer's income, that person's demand for the good will be inelastic. The demand for new cars, therefore, will be more elastic than the demand for salt. Your decision to purchase a new car would be much more sensitive to a 5 percent price change than would be your decision to buy a box of salt.

Time is also an important determinant of elasticity. The more time consumers have to adjust their purchases in light of price changes, the more elastic their demand will be. For example, it took several years for a large number of people to buy smaller cars and to better insulate their homes when energy prices rose very rapidly. But, over a number of years, Americans have cut their energy consumption per person quite dramatically.

From the above three points, you can see why the demand for salt is inelastic. Salt is needed in our diets. There are few close substitutes for salt. Furthermore, the cost of salt takes only a small part of most persons' incomes.

Elasticity describes the changes in quantities demanded that occur with price changes. Other factors, independent of price, change overall demand.

Section Checkups

1. *What generally happens to the quantity demanded when price is increased?*
2. *How can you determine the elasticity of demand for a given product?*
3. *Why might the price of one good affect the demand for a related good?*

Section 3
Price Determination

All consumers have a limited amount of money to use to buy goods and services. They want to get the most for their money. Producers, on the other hand, want to get the highest possible price for the products that they sell. How, then, do producers and consumers agree on price? This section examines how the forces of supply and demand interact to set prices. As you read this section, ask yourself the following questions: *How are prices determined? Why are prices related to shortages and surpluses of products? In what ways do prices determine production?*

The Market. In a free enterprise system, prices are set in markets. The term *market* is used to describe any place where buyers and sellers make exchanges. In any given market, goods and services that are similar tend to have similar prices.

It is not necessary for buyers and sellers to physically meet together in one place in order to form a market. Long-distance transportation and communication draw people together into the same market even though they are separated by large distances. Some products have a worldwide market. Whether a market is local or worldwide, prices in a free market are determined by the same forces.

The Determination of Prices. It is through the actions of consumers and producers that market prices are established. Consumers enter a market seeking the lowest price possible. Producers enter the market seeking the highest price possible. Market prices are determined by this interaction of demand and supply.

We can illustrate this interaction by combining the information from a supply

Barry Edmonds/Corn's Photo Service

At an auction, the market price for a particular item is determined through competitive bidding.

schedule and a demand schedule. The price schedule on page 85 combines this information from the airport parking problem that was presented earlier in this chapter. The schedule lists four possible prices. It also lists the amount of parking spaces that would be demanded and supplied at each of those possible prices. From this information, we can determine what would be the market price for parking.

The Market Price. The market price is the price at which the amount of a product that producers want to sell is equal to the amount that consumers want to buy. Therefore, there is an *equilibrium,* or balance. Economists refer to the market price as the equilibrium price. At any price higher than the market price, producers want to sell more than consumers want to buy. There will be a *surplus* of unsold products. At a parking rate of $1.00 an hour, for example, there would be a surplus of 40 parking spaces.

When a surplus exists, there is a strong pressure for the price to go down. A price decrease will then increase the amount of the product that consumers will buy. It will also reduce the amount that producers are willing to sell. The downward pressure will continue until the market price is reached.

At any price lower than the market price, consumers will want to buy more products than the producers are supplying. There will be a *shortage.* The schedule on page 85 shows that shortages would develop at hourly parking rates of 25 cents and 50 cents.

When a shortage exists, consumers will begin to bid against one another to get the products that are offered at this "too low" price. This will result in an upward pressure on the price. This pressure will continue until the market price is reached.

The market price in this case is 75 cents. At this price there is balance between

Price schedule

Parking Rate per Hour	Parking Spaces Supplied	Parking Spaces Demanded
$1.00	100	60
.75	80	80
.50	60	100
.25	40	120

The price schedule above combines the information from a supply schedule and a demand schedule. Market price is determined through the interaction of supply and demand.

Equilibrium price and quantity

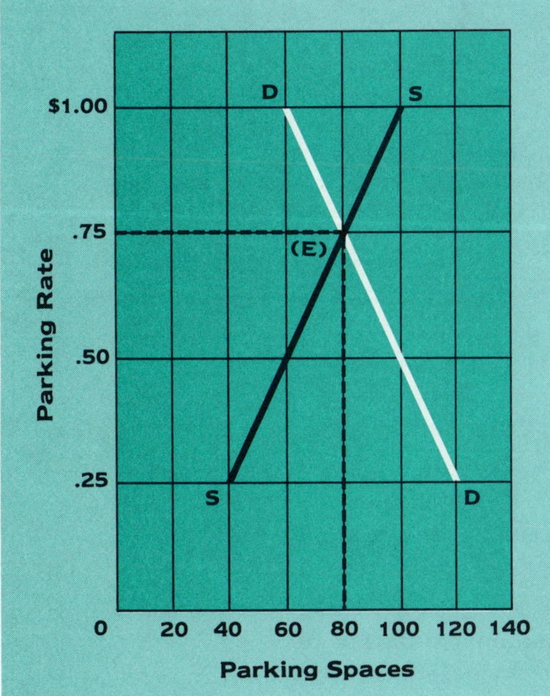

supply and demand. There would be no shortage or surplus at this price. Only at this price will everything that the producers supply be purchased.

From the graph on this page you can see how the market price is arrived at by the forces of supply and demand. The supply curve and demand curve have been plotted on this graph. The two curves intersect at the point (E) at which supply is equal to demand. The quantity represented at this point is the ideal level of production for this market. There would be no shortage or surplus.

Once a market price is reached, that price will not be changed if the market conditions remain the same. These conditions can change, however, for any one of several reasons. Changes can occur in the supply or demand side of the market.

Price and Competition. Under the free market system, we rely on competition among suppliers to keep prices at market levels. With competition, no one producer can control the price of a product. For the same reason, no one producer will charge very high prices for a good that is being sold by other suppliers at a lower price. Consumers will buy products from the sellers who offer their products at lower prices.

Pricing Factors of Production. The prices of the factors of production are also

The graph on the left shows a supply curve and a demand curve. The market price is established at the point where the quantity demanded at a certain price equals the quantity supplied at the same price.

(Text continues on page 87.)

Using Social Studies Skills

Interpreting graphs

The graph below contains information on the supply and demand for one style of printed T-shirts. From this graph, you should be able to determine the market price, the quantity that will be sold at this price, and other information. Study the graph; then answer the questions that follow.

Interaction of supply and demand

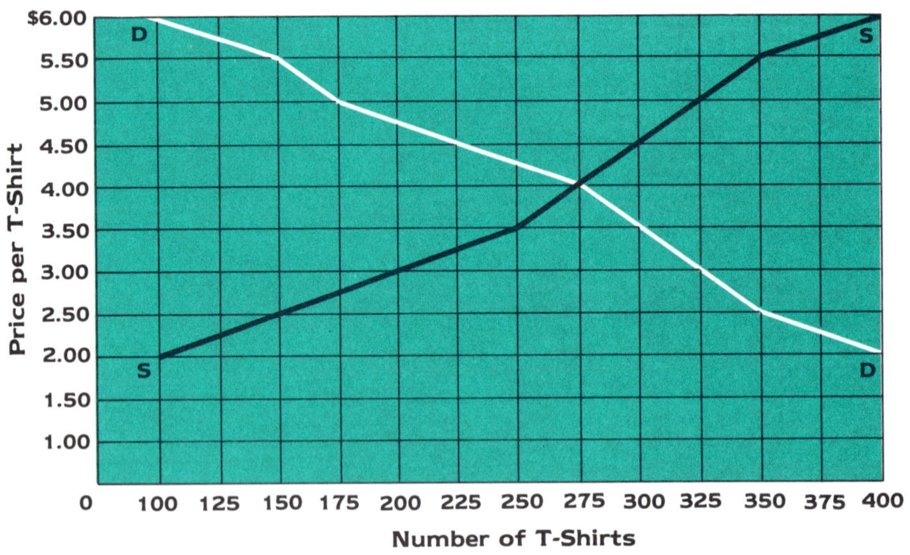

1. How many T-shirts would be supplied at a price of $2.00 each? How many T-shirts would be demanded?
2. Would there be a surplus or a shortage of T-shirts at a price of $3.00 each?
3. At which price would there be a surplus of 75 T-shirts?
4. What is the market price for these T-shirts under these supply and demand conditions?
5. What quantity of T-shirts would be sold at the market price?
6. What changes could occur that would cause an increase in demand for this type of product? How would an increase in demand change the demand curve on this graph?

determined primarily by the market forces of supply and demand. The prices of these factors of production have special names. The price of land is called *rent*. The price of labor is called *wages*. The price of capital is known as *interest*. The price of entrepreneurship is referred to as *profit*.

Factors that are relatively scarce and that are very productive tend to receive higher prices. Thus, a property lot in the heart of a business district will attract a higher rent than that same size lot in many other parts of the city.

Supply and demand forces also determine wages. An increase in the demand for workers with special technical skills would tend to increase the salaries of engineers. But higher pay for engineers would soon encourage more people to become engineers. An increased supply would tend to bring these salaries back down. In this way the price system serves as a basic coordinating device in two kinds of markets—in setting prices of goods and in setting people's incomes.

The Function of Prices. Prices can be seen as signals in our market economy. Prices serve as a guide to resource owners, producers, and consumers. Each of these groups learns about the choices and activities of the other groups through prices.

Prices work as signals between producers and consumers. Producers must learn about prices when they make decisions concerning the use of resources. Producers must know about the price of each input (factor of production) used in the production process. This information must be considered along with the information on market price. In this way producers can

Rent is determined by the forces of supply and demand. This vacant lot will be sold at a price set by these forces.

Jack Rudman

tell what goods or services can be produced profitably. Nevertheless, risks are involved because market conditions can change during the time between planning the production and actually offering the product for sale.

If consumers show an increased preference for a certain good or service, the price can be expected to rise. But a rise in the price of a good or service is a signal that profits may be rising for those who are producing this good or service. Resource owners will respond by shifting their resources from lower-profit opportunities to higher-profit opportunities. Through this signaling, consumers decide what goods will be produced. In that way they really decide how resources will be used.

Once prices are set, businesses know how much to produce. No government planning is required to decide how our scarce resources should be used. The market system will provide answers to those questions in accordance with the actions of consumers and producers. But market forces are not always allowed to operate freely. In later chapters you will learn about other factors that shape price levels.

Section Checkups

1. *What is a market price?*
2. *In what ways does price lead businesses to produce certain goods and not make other goods?*
3. *How does the price system give consumers control over what is produced?*

Chapter Summary

In a free market system, most economic decisions are made by private individuals and businesses. The cumulative decisions of all consumers and producers lie behind the main forces of the economy. These forces are known as supply and demand.

Demand refers to the quantities of any good or service that buyers would be willing to buy at each possible price. *Supply* describes the amounts of goods and services that producers would offer at each possible price. Both supply and demand may change for a number of different reasons.

Market prices are determined by the interaction of supply and demand. Prices guide resource owners, entrepreneurs, and consumers in making free choices that further their own self-interests. Because prices are determined in this way, it is the consumer who ultimately decides what will be produced. This means that consumers direct how resources are used.

Reviewing the Chapter

Identifying Terms

Explain or identify the following:

Supply	Shortage
Demand	Surplus
Elastic demand	Wages
Normal goods	Rent
Market	Interest
Market price	Profits

Analyzing Information

1. Why does a supply curve slope upward? What happens to a supply curve when supply is increased?

2. Why might the demand for a product be elastic over one range of prices but inelastic over another range?

3. List five pairs of complementary goods. What would happen if the price of one item from each pair was increased?

4. Why do sellers reduce prices for clearance sales?

5. Why do many professional athletes, singers, or film stars earn higher salaries than most teachers?

6. What price conditions might result in a shortage of a line of products? What conditions would result in a surplus?

Analyzing Visual Material

1. Examine the graph on page 77, which shows how a supply curve changes with changes in supply. How many parking spaces would be supplied in the original situation at a parking rate of 50 cents? How many spaces would be supplied at 50 cents after the supply is decreased? How many spaces would be supplied at 50 cents after the supply is increased?

2. The photograph on page 84 shows an auction. How do supply and demand determine prices in an auction?

3. Look at the picture of vacant property that is shown on page 87. Name some possible uses for this lot. What do you think would be the best use for this lot? Why would property in this area be higher priced than property in other parts of the same city? Do you know of any areas where property values are very high?

Research and Projects

1. Work in small groups to make a list of items for which prices have gone down during the past few years. Why have these prices declined? Make another list of items for which prices have gone up. Why did these prices increase? Did people change their spending patterns in response to the price changes? Why or why not?

2. Imagine that you and a friend decide to make some extra cash by producing and selling silk-screened T-shirts. How would you determine the designs for your products? How would you try to sell your products? How would you determine the prices for these products?

Chapter 6 **Profits and Competition**

SECTIONS
1 The Nature of Profit
2 What Profit Does
3 The Role of Competition

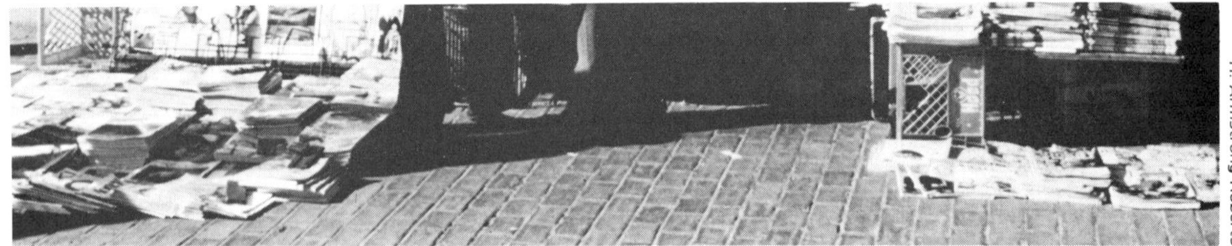

H. Armstrong Roberts

In our free enterprise economy, entrepreneurs are willing to take risks because they have the opportunity to earn profits. The competition between businesses for profits is an important force in our free enterprise system. Price competition, product innovation and improvement, and advertising are among the forms of competition undertaken by businesses in their search for profits. Competition between producers provides us, as consumers, with high-quality products at low prices. Competition between producers also makes it possible for us to exercise our freedom to choose between different products.

Section 1
The Nature of Profit

What is the objective of entrepreneurs? In other words, why do people go into business? Why are they willing to undertake the risks involved in business? For both of these questions, the answer is *profit*. Profits provide the basic motivation for businesses in a free enterprise economy. This section deals with profits. As you read this section, ask yourself the following questions: *Why are profits uncertain? How is profit a return to entrepreneurship? What are economic profits?*

Profits. In common usage, profit is said to be the money that's left for a business after costs have been paid from revenue. There is, however, a common mistake tied to this description of profit. This mistake arises when only the costs of land, labor, and capital are thought of as the costs of production. Businesses also need entrepreneurship. Profit, in economic terms, is a return for entrepreneurship—a factor of production.

Profit describes the income earned by entrepreneurs for their role in organizing businesses and taking the risks of these ventures. Stated most simply, profit is a reward for taking risks. It is the most unpredictable of the returns to the factors of production. The uncertainty of profit is tied to the uncertainties that are part of all businesses in a free enterprise economy. Let's look at the risks that entrepreneurs have to face.

Risks. Entrepreneurs cannot be certain which businesses will succeed and which ones will fail. Our free enterprise economy is *dynamic*—always changing. Entrepreneurs cannot control many of the forces that affect their businesses.

Consumer demand, for example, is largely beyond the control of producers. Furthermore, demand is difficult to predict. One part of demand, individual preference for a good or a service, can be changed by many factors. Many products are popular for only a short period of time. The sales of roller skates or home video recorders, for example, will depend on their popularity among consumers.

The ability of consumers to buy goods and services also changes. Unemployment and inflation are two conditions that change the buying power of consumers and therefore add to the risks of entrepreneurship. Changing conditions might also interfere with the entrepreneur's efforts to assemble the land, labor, and capital needed for production. A change in our government's foreign relations, for example, might bring about changes in trade patterns.

Think about the risks undertaken by the owner of a record store. The owner must decide what styles of music and what recording artists will be good sellers. Furthermore, the number of albums sold may be influenced by forces that are beyond the

Harold M. Lambert

Predicting consumer demand is a major risk facing many entrepreneurs in today's changing society.

control of the record-store owner. The selection of music played by local radio stations is one factor that enters the situation. Or, the appearance of a band at a local concert might bring about a sudden demand for that group's albums.

Looking further in the recording industry, we can see how risks are involved at all levels. Record companies, for example, accept many risks. These businesses produce and distribute record albums. A top-selling record may bring high profits to the entrepreneurs. However, not all record albums become "hits." In many cases, low sales result in losses for entrepreneurs. Even well-known recording artists may make new albums that do not sell well. The entrepreneurs must accept the risks if they want a chance to earn profits.

Profits and Innovation. In a free enterprise system, the chance for profit encourages innovation. Entrepreneurs are willing to use their capital and their skills to develop new products because they hope to make profits. Profits are incentives. The opportunity to make profits leads entrepreneurs to develop new production methods and discover more-efficient uses of resources. In this way, they may cut their costs and thus increase their profits.

Innovation also involves risk taking. In creating new products or trying new production methods, entrepreneurs are taking risks. Think, for example, of the many innovations that have been made in the automobile industry. Cruise control and electronic ignitions are among these innovations. For each of these successful innovations, there were other new products—such as the Edsel automobile—that did not succeed.

The risks of innovating and of producing new products are easily seen in the record industry. A record-company entrepreneur is taking a chance by introducing a new performer. The entrepreneur is willing to do so only because there is the possibility of making a profit. There is no guarantee that the entrepreneur will make a profit. However, a minimum profit will be necessary to keep an entrepreneur in the recording business or in any other business activity.

Normal Profit. Economists use the term *normal profit* to describe the minimum return that is needed to keep an entrepreneur in a certain business. Economists consider normal profit as a cost of doing business, just as is the rent paid on a building, or wages paid to employees. A

Normal profits are essential for a successful business, and the failure to receive these profits may force a business to close.

business cannot continue if a normal profit is not earned.

As you know, entrepreneurs contribute many services to their firms. For example, entrepreneurs may make capital investments, or they may contribute their labor to the business. These entrepreneurs direct their efforts and investments in the hope of receiving a profit. If no profits are received, these individuals will no longer provide the entrepreneurship needed by these businesses. They will seek other businesses where they can earn profits for their efforts and investments.

Consider the example of Michael and Mary, who own and operate a bicycle-repair shop. They perform many services for the business. They have invested money in tools and parts. They also own the building that houses the business.

These owners expect to earn income for their labor services. They also expect to earn rent for the building and interest on the money they have invested. But, in addition, they must receive a normal profit for organizing and operating the business. The profit they earn must be enough to keep them in this business. If their profit falls below this level, Michael and Mary might consider changing their line of business. They could also choose to give up entrepreneurship and work for someone else. They could then rent or sell their property to another business.

It is not possible to say what dollar amount a normal profit should be. There are too many differences in entrepreneurship. Normal profits also vary with market conditions. In general, however, we can say that normal profits will be about equal to what entrepreneurs could earn in other activities with equal risks. Each entrepreneur decides what will be the lowest acceptable payment for contributing this factor of production.

Economic Profit. Business income that exceeds costs is called *economic profit*. Remember that the costs of production include rent, wages, interest, and normal profit. *Economic profit* describes money that is left to the entrepreneur after all of these costs have been paid.

Economic profit is also called *excess profit*. Under competitive market conditions, a business that makes an economic profit may be able to do so for only a short time. These profits may be short-lived because they may draw other firms into the industry. In time, competition can cause economic or excess profits to disappear. We will take a closer look at this function of profit in the following section.

However, economic profit may be maintained if a firm is a monopoly. As you know, a monopoly has control over the supply of a certain good or service. The monopolist may set prices to keep other companies out of the market. Power over prices may allow the monopolist to maintain economic profits.

Reporting Profits. Profits are usually reported in two ways. The first way is called a company's *profit margin*. In this method, profit is reported as a percentage of the firm's net sales. The second method is called *rate of profit*. In this method, profit is reported as a percentage of the total amount of money that is invested in the business. Rate of profit is also called the return on stockholders' equity because it is based on the amount of money that the owners—the stockholders—are risking in the business.

Economists prefer to use rate of profit when evaluating the profitability of a business. This method provides the most-accurate means of comparing firms from different industries. It looks at profit as a return for taking risks. Profit margins are often misleading when used to compare firms from different industries.

Some measures of profit, 1981 *

Name of Business	Return on Stockholders' Equity
Monsanto	10.8%
Beatrice Foods	17.5
Gulf Oil	12.8
General Motors	1.7
Levi Strauss	22.3
Winn-Dixie	19.7
Lockheed	17.7
Holiday Inns	16.8
Polaroid	6.3
McDonald's	22.2
Maytag	20.9
Walt Disney	11.2

Source: Forbes 34th Annual Report on American Industry.

* For 1983, the rate of profit for these companies remained much the same. However, the rate for General Motors rose to 14.2 percent and the rate for Lockheed rose to 50.6 percent.

This table shows how businesses varied in their rate of profit for 1981. Rate of profit (return on stockholders' equity) is the dollar amount of a firm's profits, shown as a percentage of the amount of money invested in the company.

(Text continues on page 96.)

Using Social Studies Skills
Interpreting graphs

The way in which profits are reported is important to the individual business owner, to the stockholders, to the government, and to economists. Information on earned profits helps us to determine how well resources are being utilized. This information also helps us to evaluate the overall health of the economy. The bar graph below shows two measures of profits for certain industries in 1981. Study the graph carefully; then answer the questions that follow.

Average profits for selected industries, 1981

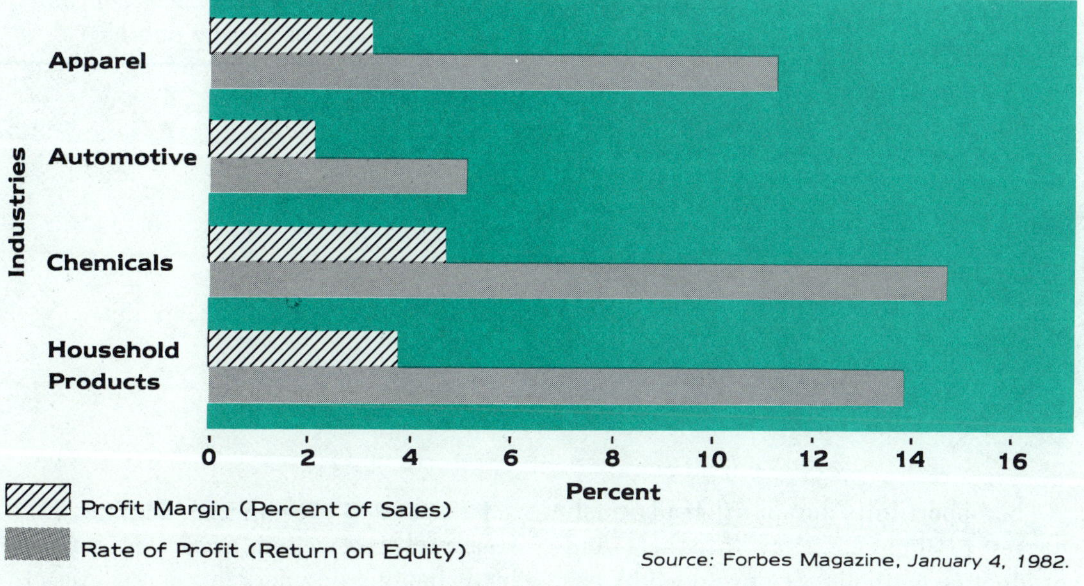

Source: Forbes Magazine, *January 4, 1982.*

1. Which of the two measures of profits is larger for each of the four industries?
2. Which of these industries had the largest rate of profit?
3. Which two industries reported similar profit margins but had a sizable difference in their rate of profit?
4. Which of these industries had the lowest rate of profit?
5. How could the information from this graph be used to aid business investors in making investment decisions?

For example, recently one company, a leader in the chemical industry, earned a profit of more than $349,700,000. This amount of profit represented a rate of profit of 40 percent. For the same year, however, its profit margin, based on sales, was only 1.9 percent. During that year, another company, a grocery chain, had a similar profit margin. The grocery chain had a profit margin of 1.6 percent of sales. Its dollar amount of profit, however, was $93,300,000. That amount was a 20.2 percent rate of profit. You can see that both firms reported similar profit margins, yet there was a wide difference in the dollar amount of profit. Furthermore, there was a great difference in the rate of profit for these firms. Profit margins are valuable for comparing firms in the same industry, but they are not accurate for comparing firms from different industries.

Section Checkups

1. *Why is a normal profit necessary for the continuation of a business?*
2. *How does the opportunity to earn a profit encourage innovation?*
3. *Why might the normal profit expected by one entrepreneur be higher than that which is expected by another?*

Section 2
What Profit Does

The opportunity for profit leads businesses to innovate. New products and production methods are developed by entrepreneurs in their search for profit. Profit leads businesses to make the products most demanded by the public. This section examines how profits serve as signals between consumers and producers. As you read this section, ask yourself the following questions: *How is profit related to the allocation of resources? Why is profit necessary for investments? How does profit affect the national economy?*

Profit and Consumer Choice. In a free enterprise system, the desire for profit leads business owners to use resources in ways that are favored by buyers. This means that the public has a say in what should be made and how it should be produced. It can be said that consumers "vote" with their dollars for the products they want. We can use a hypothetical example to show how profit works in this way.

Chuck had been working in a grocery store when he decided that he wanted to open his own business. He had given the matter much thought over the past year. He believed that his town could use a fast-food restaurant near the shopping center. Chuck thought that he had the food experience and management skills needed to enter this line of business. He would use money from his savings and a bank loan to finance the business. Chuck named his restaurant The Chili House to highlight his specialty.

Within the first month of operation, The Chili House had become very popular. The largest number of customers appeared between 11:00 A.M. and 2:00 P.M. Chuck expanded his part-time service staff when it became obvious that more workers would be needed during the lunch-hour shift. A small staff of five workers was quickly enlarged to ten.

Orders for supplies were almost double the amount that Chuck had originally planned. In particular, ground-beef orders tripled within the first month. Much of this meat was used to make chili—Chuck's fast-selling specialty. Chuck also had to triple the supply orders for cups, napkins, and plastic utensils.

This story shows how an entrepreneur organizes a business and accepts the risk that the business may or may not be successful. The early successes of The Chili House showed Chuck that he had selected a business that was demanded by consumers. The continuing opportunity for profit led Chuck to bring added resources—such as labor—to the business. The search for profit led Chuck to produce what would satisfy consumer demand.

Chuck invested in The Chili House because he believed that the demand for its products would result in a profit.

In response to consumer demand, Chuck increased his capital investment and expanded The Chili House.

Earning a Profit. Let us take this example further. After the first year of business, Chuck had earned a profit. The overall sales record proved that there was a large demand for the restaurant's products. The number of workers had been increased to meet these needs. Furthermore, Chuck had expanded the restaurant by renting an adjacent building. This added room allowed more space for tables and counters. More kitchen equipment was also bought.

After five years in business, Chuck was so successful that he was able to open a second restaurant. Further capital investment was a response to consumer demand. The Chili House II served the same menu as the original restaurant. Chuck has plans for even further growth. He also plans to begin marketing his famous chili in grocery stores.

The Allocation of Resources. From this story, you can see how profit is tied to the decisions that businesses make about the uses of resources. Chuck was able to make a profit because consumers demanded the products that he offered for sale. As sales grew, The Chili House used larger portions of the factors of production. More labor, for example, was needed to prepare and to serve the food. Further capital investments were made as The Chili House grew. If sales had been poor, the business would have been forced to change or, possibly, to close.

Business owners and managers search for ways to profit. In doing this, they use the country's labor and raw materials in production projects that will satisfy consumers' demands. Profit provides the incentive that leads business owners to be concerned with the tastes and preferences of the public.

Profits as Signals. Unusually high profits in an industry will attract new resources. In many cases, high profits will lead new firms to enter an industry. When this happens, competition will cause excess profits to disappear.

Lower-than-average profits will cause resources to be taken out of an industry. These resources will be directed to more-profitable ventures. Profits are the signals that the market system sends out to the owners of scarce resources. The history of the American coal industry shows how this works.

American coal production expanded until the mid-1900's. At that time, the use of other fuels—mainly petroleum and natural gas—expanded greatly. This caused a drop in the demand for coal. Profits fell. As this happened, factors of production—such as land—were taken out of the coal industry.

However, this trend was later reversed. The growing scarcity of other fuels led to a great increase in the demand for coal. As a result, the coal industry expanded once again. High profit served as a signal to bring more productive resources—such as capital goods—to the coal industry.

Profit and Investments. The opportunity to earn profits encourages businesses to invest in capital. Furthermore, profits provide the funds for these investments. This is an important function of profits. The investments made by private industry are a key to the prosperity and economic growth of our country.

The hypothetical example of The Chili House shows how this works on small scale. Chuck, the owner, was willing to expand the restaurant because he believed that there was a chance to earn a profit. Profits earned by the business provided money for its growth.

Think about the ways in which the expansion of The Chili House affected the general economy of the town. More jobs were created both directly and indirectly as the business grew. The suppliers who provided the restaurant with equipment and furniture benefited because the business was profitable. If, on the other hand, the business was operating at a loss, investments would have been cut back. The Chili House would have generated less business for the town.

It is important to remember that investments are made with attention to the future. Many investment projects undertaken by business require many years to return a profit. A new building, for example, might take years to build. And it may take many more years until it is profitable to a business. A business that buys a photocopy machine, a computer, or any other equipment does so because there is an indication that the investment will result in profits. In the same way, a business will invest in its staff through training classes and other educational programs only if it can expect to earn profits in the future.

Section Checkups

1. *How does the search for profit lead entrepreneurs to satisfy consumer demand?*
2. *What usually happens if an industry continuously earns lower-than-average profits?*
3. *Why are profits needed for investments?*

Section 3
The Role of Competition

As you know, the main goal of business in a free enterprise economy is to earn a profit. What keeps businesses from raising prices to high levels in order to make a larger profit? First, when prices are raised, consumers buy less. However, competition provides an important check on profit. Competition also brings about efficiency. As you read this section, ask yourself the following questions: *How does competition keep profits at normal levels? Why does competition exist among businesses that offer similar products? What are some forms of nonprice competition?*

The Nature of Competition. Competition is an important force in a free enterprise economy. A large part of this competition grows out of the economic freedom enjoyed by citizens in this system. This freedom makes it possible for individuals to enter business and to compete for profits with other entrepreneurs. Benefits from competition extend to all persons in the economy.

Usually, competition describes the efforts undertaken by businesses to attract customers away from other businesses. There are many forms of competition. In addition, there are different degrees of competition. Some industries have high levels of competition. Other industries have very little competition.

Because competition is an important part of the economy, the government takes steps to maintain it. Antitrust laws are one way in which the federal government acts to preserve competition. These laws are designed to maintain competition by outlawing monopolies and monopoly power. You will read more about antitrust laws in later chapters.

Competition at Work. Competition encourages businesses to be efficient in their use of resources. Through competition, businesses are encouraged to keep prices as low as possible. These efforts lead producers to innovate and to invest.

You have read how profits serve as signals in the economy. When one business is earning an economic profit, other entrepreneurs will enter that line of production. They will attempt to copy or, if possible, to improve on the production methods that brought high profits to the first producer. Competition among businesses will lead these businesses to drop their prices to the lowest-possible level in order to attract customers and sell their product.

Competition will tend to eliminate economic profits. In the end, the buyer benefits because more efficient production methods have been developed. The search for profits benefits the overall economy by encouraging the careful use of scarce resources.

Lines of Competition. In a free enterprise system, businesses face competition from several sources. First, there is competition among businesses within the same industry. The degree of this competition

(Text continues on page 102.)

Innovation and Opportunity
Advertising and problem solving

In 1966, Braniff International airlines faced a problem. They were adding a large fleet of jets to their line of aircraft. With these planes, their passenger and route potential would be greatly expanded. At the time, however, Braniff was not well-known, and company officials decided that Braniff would have to increase its popularity in order to attract more customers.

Wells, Rich, Greene, Inc.

Braniff took its problem to the advertising agency of Jack Tinker & Partners. Three staff members were assigned to the Braniff project. One of them was Mary Wells Lawrence. Lawrence believed that the best way to tackle a problem was to first define it. Once this was done, solutions and innovations could be developed.

The problem, as they defined it, was to separate Braniff from the competition. How could this be done? The idea-making team examined the industry and noted that many things connected with flying were gray and dull looking. The planes, airports, and even the uniforms of flight attendants were all drab.

Lawrence and her co-workers, Richard Rich and Stewart Greene, decided that Braniff should change its appearance. The exteriors of Braniff airplanes were painted in bright colors. The interiors were restyled by a well-known designer and a top fashion designer was commissioned to design new uniforms for the attendants.

These design changes prepared Braniff for an advertising campaign that would distinguish Braniff from the competition. The advertisements focused on Braniff's bright look and new approach to air travel. Before long, a growing number of air travelers preferred Braniff planes, and Braniff grew in popularity and profits.

Mary Wells Lawrence, the innovative advertising expert who played a key role in developing Braniff's campaign, continued to succeed. In 1966 she founded her own advertising agency and has rapidly built it into a multimillion-dollar business. Her creativity and her problem-solving approach to advertising have been important factors in making this agency one of the top companies in advertising.

varies with the number and size of the separate companies in the industry.

Several conditions tend to make one industry more competitive than another. A highly competitive industry is usually made up of a large number of relatively small businesses producing or selling similar products. If many producers are trying to sell the same kind of goods to one group of buyers, there will be a high level of competition. Furthermore, the greatest amount of competition usually occurs in industries that are most easily entered by new firms. Industries that require a large amount of capital, for example, generally contain less competition than those industries where only small investments are needed. The aluminum industry is one example of a field in which there is little competition.

There are many markets that do not fit all of these characteristics. In Chapter 9 you will read about industries that are dominated by a few companies. The American automobile industry is one example of this type of market. Nevertheless, there are other sources of competition that face businesses in these industries.

Businesses must face the competition of foreign producers. Imported automobiles, for example, are in competition with American-made cars. A full range of goods, including cameras, watches, shoes, and toys, is imported to the United States from other countries.

The federal government taxes and regulates imports in order to prevent unfair competition. Even with these regulations, foreign companies present a high level of competition to American businesses.

In many cases, businesses are in competition with firms that are outside of their specific area of business. An airline, for example, competes with other airlines and with bus companies and railroads. Competition from these other transportation companies encourages the airlines to work for greater efficiency and to keep travelers pleased with air travel. In the same way, movie theaters are in competition with other businesses that offer entertainment.

Forms of Competition. Competition among businesses can take many forms. Price competition is only one area of competition. Businesses also undertake what is called *nonprice competition.*

One method of nonprice competition involves product improvement. Businesses compete by changing their products to offer something new and attractive to consumers. A yogurt company, for example, might improve the taste of its product. The company could also compete by offering a new flavor or, perhaps, by designing a new package for the yogurt. The automobile industry has a high level of nonprice competition. Automobile makers change their models each year in order to offer products that meet consumer demand.

Advertising is another form of nonprice competition. Advertising is designed to persuade consumers to buy certain products. As you know, there are many different ways to advertise. Radio, television, newspapers, magazines, and billboards are among the major means used.

Advertisements are a major source of product information for consumers. Because of this, many businesses use advertising to try to convince buyers that their business or their product is in some way better than that of the competition.

Businesses also try to outdo their competitors by offering more services to their customers. A furniture store might provide

(Text continues on page 104.)

Advertising is an important method of business competition. Advertisers use many different approaches to convey their messages. Some advertisements focus on certain qualities of a product, while other advertisements suggest a certain image that is created when an individual uses a product. The advertisements on this page illustrate how competing businesses use advertising to convince consumers to buy their products.

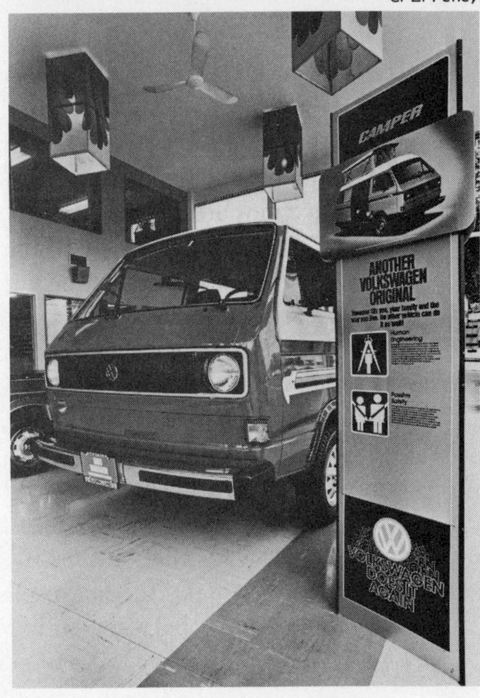

C. E. Pefley

Foster and Kleiser

American Motors Corp.

AMF Harley-Davidson

free delivery service or make credit available to its customers. A car dealer could try to build a good name for its service department. It could stay open more hours than its competitors, promise same-day service, or offer free loaner cars to customers whose cars are in for service. Some stores give their customers trading stamps or chances to win prizes through contests. This service competition often takes place among businesses that offer very similar products. It also is common in industries where only a few large firms produce. The corporations do not want to enter price competition with one another.

Several airlines, for example, might offer daily flights between New York and Los Angeles. Often the fares of competing lines will be quite similar. The services offered by these lines, however, might differ greatly. Airlines often compete through these services. Ticketing procedures, baggage handling, and meals are among these areas of competition.

Section Checkups

1. *What is competition?*
2. *How does competition affect the allocation of resources?*
3. *Why does competition sometimes exist among producers that are making different products?*

Chapter Summary

Profit, or the search for profit, is the driving force of the free enterprise system. Profit is the return for entrepreneurship. Entrepreneurs are willing to take risks, to innovate, and to make investments because of the opportunity to earn a profit. Economists use the term *normal profit* to describe the minimum return that is needed to keep an entrepreneur in a certain business.

Profit performs many functions in our economy. Among other things, profit directs the allocation of resources. Through this system, consumer decisions play a key role in determining how scarce resources will be used. Profitable industries will attract more resources, while unprofitable businesses will be forced to contract, or go out of business.

Profit is held in check through competition. Competition stimulates efficiency. Through competition, buyers tend to get the products that they demand at the lowest-possible prices. Competition exists in many different forms and in varying degrees among the different industries.

Reviewing the Chapter

Identifying Terms

Explain or identify the following:

Innovation	Investment
Risks	Competition
Normal profit	Nonprice competition
Economic profit	Foreign competition

Analyzing Information

1. How does profit lead businesses to innovate?

2. In what ways is profit a return for one factor of production?

3. What are the two ways in which a company can report its profits? Which method is preferred by economists?

4. How does the level of profits affect the amount of resources that are allocated to an industry?

5. What are three conditions that tend to make one industry more competitive than another?

6. How does competition between producers benefit consumers?

7. What factors might indicate that an industry will expand in the next ten years?

8. What are two American industries that must compete with foreign producers?

Analyzing Visual Material

1. Look at the table of profits that is shown on page 94. Which of the listed businesses had the highest rate of profit in 1981? Which of the listed businesses had the lowest rate of profit? How could the information that is provided in this table be useful to an investor who is interested in buying some corporate stock?

2. Examine the advertisements that are shown on page 103. In what ways do these advertisements attempt to convince consumers to buy the products that are shown in the advertisements? Do the advertisements focus on the product or on an image that is supposedly created by ownership of the product? These advertisements illustrate competition between American and foreign producers of similar products. Identify the products that are American made and those that are imported.

Research and Projects

1. Interview a local business owner in order to learn more about profit and competition in a free enterprise economy. If possible, invite a business owner to speak to your class on these topics.

2. Use a classroom bulletin board to post current articles about profit, competition, investments, and other business news. Articles can be found in newspapers, magazines, or other publications.

3. Work in small groups to prepare reports on business competition. Possible topics might include advertising, price competition, product improvement, and service competition.

Camerique

Chapter 7 Income and the Market System

SECTIONS
1. Income and the Overall Economy
2. Personal Income Distribution
3. Income Problems

In the American free enterprise system, people provide productive resources—land, labor, capital, and entrepreneurship—to businesses. In return, we receive income for providing these services. One major reason why the incomes we receive vary is that we provide different amounts and types of resources to production. Wages earned through labor represent the major source of income for most American families. We, as consumers, then use our income to purchase consumer goods and services from business firms.

Section 1
Income and the Overall Economy

Imagine that your family received a check each week from a government office. The check would determine what goods and services your family could buy. The government would also detail each family member's work orders.

As you know, this is not how things work in a free enterprise system. In our economy, the allocation of resources is basically determined by the market forces of supply and demand. In this section, you will examine the importance of incomes in directing the distribution of products. As you read this section, ask yourself the following questions: *How do households earn incomes? Why do some households earn higher incomes than other households? How is national income distributed among the various factors of production?*

What Is Income? *Income* usually describes the payments that are made to households in exchange for the factors of production. As you know, free enterprise is based on private ownership of the factors of production. This means that the households of America control the services and resources that are used in production. That is, land, labor, capital, and entrepreneurship—production *inputs*—all come from households.

Households are willing to supply these inputs because they are paid for them. A cook, for example, spends part of the week working in a restaurant kitchen rather than watching television at home because the job provides income. Incomes allow

H. Armstrong Roberts

Households develop budgets to plan how to use their incomes in ways that will best satisfy their needs and wants.

The circular flow of goods and services

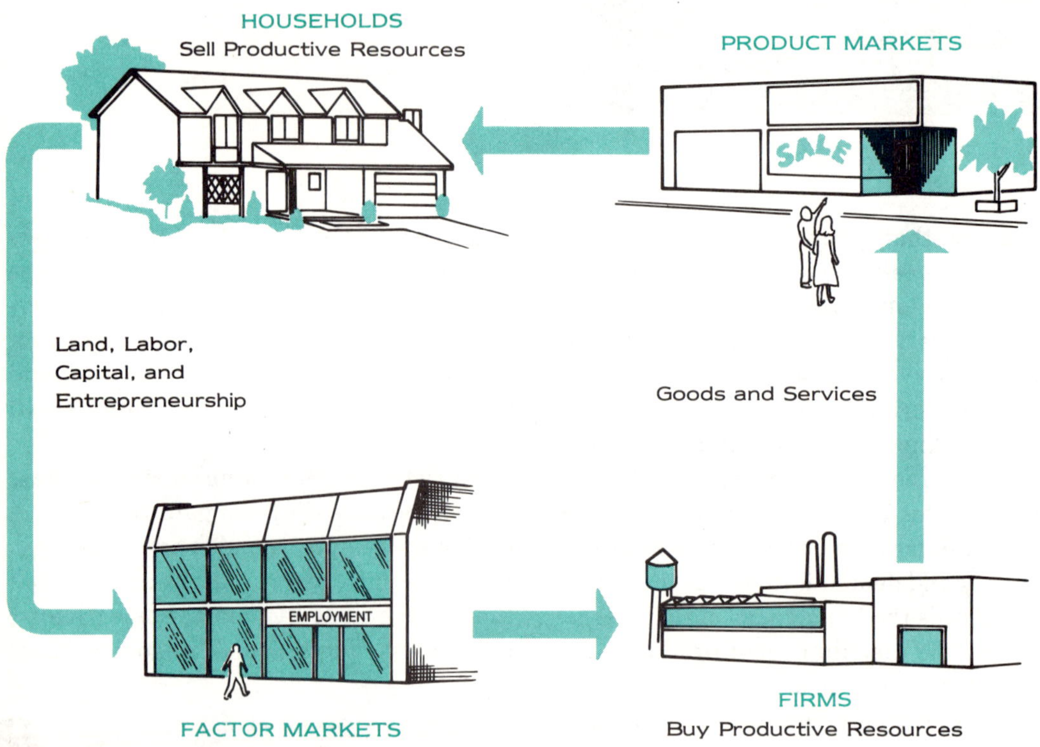

This illustration of the circular flow of goods and services shows how households provide the factors of production that businesses use to produce products for households.

individuals and families to buy the goods and services that are produced in the economy. The illustration on this page shows how income works in the overall economy.

The flow lines on this illustration show how businesses and households are related in the economy. For example, businesses buy services, such as labor and entrepreneurship, from households. In return, households receive incomes. Wages are paid to labor, and profits are paid for entrepreneurship.

Businesses use the factors of production to produce goods and services. Households then use their incomes to purchase the products of business. There is an interdependency between households and business.

Income and Supply and Demand. In general, the size of a household's income is determined through the market forces of supply and demand. Chapter 5 explained how prices are determined through the interaction of these forces. The prices of the factors of production are set in the same way.

Overall, the highest incomes are paid for those services and resources that are the most scarce and the most valuable in production. Households vary greatly in the type and amount of resources and services that they can supply to producers. The wide range in incomes earned by American households reflects these differences. Some households, for example, own rich farmland. These households can earn rent by allowing this land to be used in production.

Most families depend on wages or salaries as their main source of income. Yet there is a wide range in the job skills and occupations of Americans. Wages vary according to the kind of work done and the demand for it. The highest wages are generally paid to those workers whose skills are in short supply and in high demand. Later in this chapter we will take a closer look at wage and income differences.

The Effects of Income. Incomes provide households with buying power. Households are able to share in the nation's output by exchanging their incomes for goods and services.

In general, a household's income is a measure of its contribution to production. The market forces of supply and demand determine the price that is paid for each factor of production. Incomes serve as a force in determining how the nation's resources will be used. For example, high

In our free enterprise economy, most land is owned by private individuals. The owners of land receive rent when their land is used in production.

Harold M. Lambert

wages in one field will tend to draw more workers into that line of work. To explain how incomes function in the overall economy, economists have developed a measure known as national income.

National Income. *National income* is the total income earned through the production of goods and services. It is usually shown as a total for a given year. National income is based on the market prices of the resources that were used in that year's production.

National income shows the combined income of all individuals who contribute to the production of goods and services. If you have a job, your pay is included in this amount. If you have a savings account that pays you interest, that interest income is also included in this amount.

The chart on page 111 lists national income in the United States for selected years between 1930 and 1980. The figures show that the earnings of Americans have greatly increased over these years.

In Chapter 3 you read about several factors that have resulted in our rapid rate of economic growth and rising national income. Normally, as national income rises, the standard of living of citizens also rises. However, *inflation*—the widespread rise in prices—has accounted for part of the increase in national income. But despite the increase in the cost of living, there has also been a great increase in the standard of living for most Americans.

Shares of Income. The chart on page 111 shows how the national income has been distributed among the different productive resources. There are five categories of income.

The first category is called compensation to employees. This represents the percent of our national income that went to those who contributed their labor to production. It includes wages and salaries as well as other compensations and benefits that workers received, such as bonuses, health insurance, and so on.

As the chart shows, labor's share of national income has increased since 1930. Furthermore, labor receives the largest share of national income. By 1980, 75.3 percent[1] of national income—nearly 1,600 billion dollars—was earned by labor in the United States.

The second income group includes the earnings of sole proprietorships, partnerships, and cooperatives. These forms of business organization are explained in Chapter 9. Briefly, these are businesses that are not organized as corporations. Restaurants, repair stores, and farms are common examples of these businesses. Doctors, lawyers, and other professionals who form partnerships are also part of this grouping. A large part of the income that falls under this heading is really a type of salary. It is earned through the labor of the business owners.

The proprietor's share of national income has gone down since 1950. In part, this is because the corporation has become the most important form of business organization. Furthermore, the number of proprietorships has fallen as the number of small farms has decreased.

Rents and Profits. The third and fourth categories on the chart are rents and profits. The earnings that people make for allowing their real property to be used in production are called *rent*. Real property includes land and other natural resources as well as buildings and stores. This category of the national income also includes

1. In 1983, 75.2 percent of our national income—$1,990.1 billion—was earned by labor.

royalty payments from patents and copyrights.

Rental income makes up a small portion of national income. This income group does not include the income of persons or businesses that make real estate their main occupation. Rents paid in those situations are included under the categories of profits and proprietors' income.

Corporate profits are the earnings of privately owned corporations. In 1980,
1 corporations earned 8.6 percent of the national income. This share amounted to about 183 billion dollars.

Interest. The fifth category of national income is interest income. *Interest income* describes the earnings that are paid to individuals who lend money. As you know, businesses often require large amounts of money to purchase capital goods. In most cases, businesses must borrow money to meet their needs of buildings and equipment. These businesses must pay interest in order to obtain the use of money.

As the chart below shows, there has been a rapid and sizable increase of national income in the United States since 1930. The chart also shows the percentage breakdown of how national income has been distributed since 1930.

* In 1983, our national income grew to $2646.9 billion, but the percent distribution remained much the same.

***National income and percent distribution* ***

	1930	1940	1950	1960	1970	1980
National Income, Total*	**73.8**	**79.7**	**236.2**	**412.0**	**798.4**	**2121.4**
Compensation of Employees	63.4%	65.3%	65.5%	71.6%	76.3%	75.3%
Proprietors' Income	15.9	16.1	16.3	11.4	8.2	6.1
Rental Income of Persons	5.9	3.3	3.0	3.3	2.3	1.5
Corporate Profits	8.0	10.9	14.3	11.3	8.5	8.6
Net Interest	6.6	4.1	1.0	2.4	4.7	8.5

*In billions of dollars

Source: U.S. Department of Commerce.

1. In 1983, corporations earned $226.3 billion, or 8.5 percent of the national income.

(Text continues on page 113.)

Looking at Careers
The real estate broker

What does a real estate broker do? Real estate brokers represent buyers and sellers for the sale or rental of property. A family that is interested in buying a home, for example, will usually contact a real estate broker. The broker will assist the family in locating and purchasing property. Brokers also take part in a wide range of other activities concerned with real property.

What qualifications does a real estate broker need? Real estate work requires a great deal of public contact. Brokers must have good communication skills and must be able to work with different types of people. All states require that real estate brokers be licensed. To gain a license, an individual must complete a specified amount of classroom work and must have a certain amount of experience in real estate sales. This experience is usually obtained while the individual works as a salesperson under the direction of a licensed broker. All states also require that brokers pass a written examination on real estate practices and laws.

What about pay and working conditions? Most real estate brokers earn their incomes on a commission basis. Generally, earnings increase as the broker gains experience and makes more contacts in the field. Full-time, experienced brokers generally earn above-average incomes. Brokers must arrange their schedules to the convenience of their clients.

Brent Jones

How does a knowledge of economics help? Brokers must know the current real estate values and should be able to determine the current supply and demand conditions for different types of property. In addition, brokers must be able to counsel clients on tax rates and the availability of mortgages. For more information on careers in real estate, write to **Department of Education, National Association of Real Estate Boards, 155 East Superior Street, Chicago, IL 60611.**

Banks and savings and loan associations pay interest to their depositors. This is possible because these institutions use part of their deposits to make loans or investments. Some of the earnings from these transactions are paid as interest. If you have a savings account, you receive interest income on the money you have deposited. You will read more about interest income in Chapter 8.

The interest category does not include interest that was paid by the government. This means that interest paid on government bonds was not included. Only interest that was paid by private businesses is
1 counted. In 1980, about 180 billion dollars was paid in interest by businesses.

From this information on national income, we can learn how earnings were distributed among the various factors of production. This information, however, does not tell us about the actual incomes that were received by individuals or families in the United States. The following section examines these incomes and how family incomes differ.

Section Checkups

1. *What productive resources must businesses buy from households?*
2. *What are the five categories of income that comprise national income?*
3. *What productive resource earns the largest share of national income?*

Section 2 Personal Income Distribution

In a free enterprise economy, a family's income is largely determined by the forces of supply and demand. Families supply productive services to business. Business pays the highest prices for those resources that are scarce and most valuable to production. This section investigates differences in family incomes. As you read this section, ask yourself the following questions: *What is included in personal income? How do families earn incomes with their property? Why do some occupations offer higher pay than others?*

Personal Income. National income includes money that is not actually received by individuals. For example, a share of corporate profits is paid in taxes. This money is not directly available as income to individuals. Furthermore, the workers' share of the national income includes

1. Businesses paid $247.2 billion in interest in 1983.

money that is not paid to workers as salaries or wages. Money that employers pay for workers' pensions, health insurance, and other benefits is counted as part of the national income but is not included in the personal income of workers.

Personal income refers to the income that is actually received by individuals and families before personal income taxes are paid. It is different from the national income also because individuals do receive income that is not included in national income. Payments from the government—such as social-security income and the interest on government bonds—are not counted in national income. They are, however, counted in personal income.

Differences in Family Income. In the United States, there is a wide range in the incomes earned by families. The table on this page shows the distribution of family incomes in 1980. In that year, the average
family income was $23,974. 1

The table divides families into five different income groups. The first group represents the lowest income level. The families in this level earned less than $5,000 in 1980. As you can see from the
table, over 3.5 million American families 2
were part of this income group in 1980. Or, put another way, 6.2 percent of all American families earned under $5,000 in 1980.

As you use this table, keep in mind that only money income has been counted.

Although most Americans enjoy one of the world's highest standards of living, this is not true for all. As the table below shows, levels of family income vary. However, over 80 percent of all American families earn more than $10,000 a year.

* In 1983, 79.5 percent of all American families had incomes greater than $10,000.

Income levels of American families (latest available figures) *

Income Level	Number of Families	Percent of Total Families
Under $5,000	3,739,000	6.2
$5,000-$9,999	7,659,000	12.7
$10,000-$14,999	8,562,000	14.2
$15,000-$24,999	16,705,000	27.7
$25,000 and over	23,641,000	39.2

Source: U.S. Bureau of the Census.

1. By 1983, the average family income was $23,433.

*2. In 1983, 4.3 million American families—7.3 percent of all American families—earned less than $5,000.

Nonmoney income—such as food or housing aid from the government—has not been included. Because of this, families that appear far below the average income would usually not have been that low if all income had been counted.

1 The table also shows that 16,705,000 families—over one fourth of all American families—earned between $15,000 and $24,999 in 1980. Adding this group to the next category—the families who earned $25,000 or more—we find that over 66 percent of all American families had incomes of over $15,000 in 1980.

Why Incomes Differ. There are several reasons for the differences in incomes among American families. These reasons flow from the basic nature of the free enterprise system. The right to own property and the freedom of choice are key factors in our economy. These factors also influence the incomes of families.

One way that individuals and families earn their incomes is through their property. In the United States, families have the freedom to own as much property as they can legally accumulate. This freedom allows for a wide range in the amount of property owned by families.

Differences in the amounts and types of income-producing property owned by families cause income differences. Some families earn a large part of their incomes from stocks, bonds, and the rental of real property. Overall, the largest property incomes are earned by those families that earn very high incomes. Families in the lower income levels usually do not own income property. Wages and salaries are the main source of income for most families.

Wage Differences. There is a wide range in the wages and salaries of the millions of Americans who make up the country's work force. A physician, for example, might earn many times more money in a year than a clerical worker. The amount of money that workers are paid is influenced primarily by supply and demand.

In general, higher-than-average wages are paid to persons whose talents or skills are relatively scarce and highly useful. Lower wages are paid to persons whose job skills are in great supply or in less demand by our society. Even though Americans generally enjoy freedom of choice in selecting their careers, they do not all enter the jobs that are the highest paying. The supply of workers for these jobs is kept low by a number of different factors.

Many high-paying occupations, for example, require a certain level of skill or natural ability. A great deal of training or education is often needed to qualify workers for these occupations. Only a small percent of all workers, for example, have the ability, skills, training, and desire to become doctors, corporate executives, star athletes, or successful writers.

Some other high-paying jobs are characterized as hazardous or somehow unpleasant. Employers must offer high wages to attract workers to these jobs. For example, many people might not want to work in offshore oil drilling or with radioactive materials. On the other hand, jobs that offer very pleasant working conditions often do not pay high incomes. Many workers may be willing to take these jobs even with low wages.

There are also other conditions that tend to keep the supply of workers for certain jobs low. In some cases, unions or government agencies can restrict workers from entering certain jobs. This control of

*1. In 1983, 17,412,000 families earned between $15,000 and $24,999. About 65 percent of all American families had incomes over $15,000 in 1983.

(Text continues on page 117.)

Using Social Studies Skills
Interpreting statistical tables

Education may be one of the major factors that affect the amount of money that one person may earn. The table below contains statistical information on recent family income. Included is the median number of school years completed by family heads in each income category. Study the table carefully; then answer the questions that follow.

Family income and education

Family Income Level	Number of Families	Median School Years Completed by Head
$2,500-$4,999	2,782,000	9.6
$5,000-$7,499	3,771,000	10.2
$7,500-$9,999	4,127,000	11.4
$10,000-$14,999	9,117,000	12.2
$15,000-$24,999	17,124,000	12.6
$25,000-$34,999	11,210,000	12.9
$35,000-$49,999	6,000,000	13.9
$50,000-$74,999	2,248,000	16.2
$75,000 and over	781,000	16.9

Source: U.S. Bureau of the Census.

1. Based on the table, how many American families earned between $15,000 and $24,999?
2. What was the median number of school years completed by family heads in the income category between $15,000 and $24,999?
3. How many American families earned over $25,000?
4. In which income category did the family heads complete an average of 12.2 years of school?
5. Using evidence from these statistics, what three conclusions can you make about education and income level?

supply is often used to hold wages at high levels. Discrimination also works to limit the number of workers who enter certain fields. In recent years, however, job barriers based on race, sex, or religion have been reduced. As a result, Americans now enjoy more-equal occupational opportunities than in the past.

Wages and Family Incomes. Differences in wages account for the income differences that exist among most American families. The number of wage earners and the types of jobs they hold are important factors that shape a family's income. Some families depend on the wages of one worker, while other families include two or more wage earners.

The actual time of employment of wage earners also shapes the size of a family's income. Some workers are employed for only part of the year. Seasonal layoffs are common in agriculture and shipping. Construction workers are also likely to be unemployed during part of the year.

In general, the size of a family's income depends on that family's contributions to production. Some families earn income through their property. But, most American families depend on the income earned through the labor of family members. In some cases, families cannot earn enough income to meet very basic needs. The following section examines some of the income problems facing Americans today.

Section Checkups

1. *What are two kinds of personal income that are not included in national income?*
2. *What percentage of American families earned over $15,000 in 1980?*
3. *How can the amount of property owned by a family shape the level of that family's income?*

Section 3
Income Problems

Families use their incomes to buy the things that they want and need. There are times, however, when a family's income is not large enough to meet its needs. This section examines such income problems and some attempts to resolve these problems. As you read this section, ask yourself the following questions: *What problems might result in income loss for families? How do changes in the cost of living alter purchasing power? How does the government offer income security?*

The Importance of Income. Income is an important concern for all families. Families use their incomes to purchase the goods and services that they need and want. The spending and saving practices of all individuals and families depend largely upon their incomes.

When families consider their incomes, they are concerned with more than the dollar amount. Above all, they care about the purchasing power of their incomes. This measure of income is referred to as *real income*. Real income is the amount of goods and services that can be bought with an income.

Today, it is estimated that over half of all American families have an income of over $20,000. However, it should be noted that since 1967, inflation has caused the
1 price of living to rise by over 166 percent.
Thus, a $20,000 income buys less than did an income of $10,000 in 1967.

Inflation is one of the most serious problems facing a wage earner. Salaries and wages may not keep up with a high rate of inflation. In 1980, for example, aver-
2 age wages rose by about 9 percent. During
that same year the inflation rate was 12.4 percent. On the average, wage earners suffered a loss in real income. Economic indicators suggest that this problem could become worse in the years ahead.

Problems of Income Loss. A large decrease in income will often present serious problems for families. Families faced with decreased incomes have fewer dollars to spend. A reduction in spending by many families can have a harmful effect on the national economy.

A loss in wages might be caused by one of several possible problems. Illness, for example, can prevent a person from working. Changes in business conditions might also result in unemployment. A business that faces decreased sales may lay off some employees. Workers might also lose their incomes if their jobs are eliminated by technological advances.

Decreases in real income can also occur if wages remain the same while the prices of goods and services go up. As you know, a loss in real income also occurs when wage increases do not keep pace with price increases. When this happens, a family can buy fewer goods and services with its income. This is a common problem during periods of rapid inflation.

To maintain their standard of living, workers seek higher wages during inflationary times. Wage increases that are given to keep purchasing power at the same level are called *cost-of-living adjustments*. Labor unions often ask for contracts that call for automatic cost-of-living adjustments for members. Under these contracts, wages are raised if the cost of living goes up.

During inflationary times, people also make investments to try to keep pace with the rising cost of living. In general, investments in things that rise in price faster than the inflation rate are considered to be good hedges against inflation. There are several kinds of investments that are considered to be financial defenses against inflation. However, in recent years the most successful hedge against inflation for most Americans has been home ownership.

Owning a home is one of the major ways that Americans have used to offset inflation. This is because inflation causes the costs of housing to go up. As housing costs rise, people who rent their living quarters must pay more and more for their housing. This is not the case, however, for homeowners.

1. Between 1967 and 1983, the price of living rose by 198 percent.

2. In 1983, average wages rose by about 5 percent and the rate of inflation was 3.2 percent. On the average, wage earners gained in real income.

Many people continue active lives after retirement. However, fixed-retirement incomes are often inadequate during times of rising prices.

Laimute E. Druskis/Taurus Photos

Homeowners generally pay monthly
1 mortgage payments that remain the same amount over the life of the mortgage. Even when the value of a home goes up, the owner is paying the same mortgage rate that was set when the home was purchased. Therefore, inflation does not affect homeowners in the same way that it affects renters.

Problems of Fixed Incomes. Families and individuals who depend on *fixed incomes* lose real income when prices rise. *Fixed incomes* describes those incomes that are set at a certain amount and are not adjusted with changes in the cost of living. Private retirement pensions and annuities are the most common type of fixed income.

Consider the example of a truck driver who retired in 1970 with a fixed pension of $5,000 a year. Added to this amount was the interest income that he earned on his savings account. He expected to live comfortably on this retirement income. But in 1970 a pound of frankfurters sold for about 83 cents. A pound loaf of white bread was 25 cents.

By 1980, the purchasing power of the dollar dropped severely. As a result, the retired truck driver suffered a loss in real income. The average price for a pound of frankfurters, for example, had climbed to $1.39. Prices of almost all other food items were also higher than they had been in 1970. Price increases in housing, transportation, and medical care had also occurred. As a result, this retiree, along with other individuals on fixed incomes, faced a lower standard of living.

Income Security. The threat of income loss has led many Americans to seek some type of income security. Several different solutions have been suggested as ways to protect families from income loss. These proposals have been aimed at reducing the risks faced by individuals in the free enterprise system.

In many cases, Americans have looked to the federal government for income security. The government has responded in several ways. Through minimum wage laws, the federal government has set a lower limit on the wages paid to most workers. The government has also required that men and women be paid the same wage when they do the same job. Steps have also been taken to give income

1. Due to uncertain economic conditions, lending institutions began issuing adjustable-rate mortgages (ARM)—mortgages whose interest rates are reset after certain intervals of time.

security to individuals who cannot work. The social-security system is an important part of the government's income-insurance program. Social-security and unemployment-insurance payments provide incomes to individuals and families who lose their wage incomes. However, not all workers are covered by these programs. Additional public-assistance programs—called welfare—have also provided income security to those in need. Both the federal government and state governments undertake welfare programs.

Some workers have also sought income security through their labor unions and collective bargaining. (See Chapter 10.) Some labor contracts, for example, protect members from layoffs. Through these agreements and others, unions have attempted to guarantee certain incomes for their members. Furthermore, many labor unions consider income security to be one of their major goals for the future.

Section Checkups

1. *What is real income?*
2. *Why does a loss in real income present problems for families?*
3. *What problems are faced by individuals living on fixed incomes?*

Chapter Summary

Individuals and families earn their incomes by providing productive services and resources to businesses. Businesses use these factors of production to produce goods and services. These products, in turn, are purchased by households spending their incomes.

The size of one's income determines the amount of goods and services that the person can afford. From information on national income, we can learn how buying power is distributed among the owners of various productive resources and services in our economy. In the United States today, over 75 percent of national income is paid to workers. The level of wages paid to each worker is largely determined through the forces of supply and demand. These market forces also set the prices paid for the other productive resources.

Households depend on their incomes to purchase the things that they want and need. Certain problems, however, sometimes cause loss of income. A number of attempts have been made to protect Americans from this economic insecurity. Many of these efforts involve government action.

Reviewing the Chapter

Identifying Terms

Explain or identify the following:

Income	Rental income
Household	Real income
National income	Fixed income
Interest	Social security

Analyzing Information

1. In what ways are businesses and households interdependent in a free enterprise system?

2. What market forces determine the amount of income earned by a family?

3. How do incomes serve to direct the uses of our country's factors of production?

4. What changes in the distribution of national income have taken place since 1930?

5. Why do family incomes differ?

6. How do most American families earn their incomes?

7. What relationship exists between the supply of workers who can do a job and the wage paid for that job?

8. What does a loss in real income mean to a family?

Analyzing Visual Material

1. Look at the national-income chart that appears on page 111. What was the dollar increase in our country's national income between 1930 and 1980? Which category of income accounted for 1.5 percent of national income in 1980? What was the dollar value of that share of national income? How much money was earned as corporate profits in 1980? How much more money was earned as proprietors' income in 1980 than in 1970?

2. Study the table on page 114 that lists the income levels of American families. How many American families earned more than $15,000 in that year? How does this total compare with the total number of American families who earned less than $15,000 in that year?

Research and Projects

1. Prepare a report on the current wage rates being paid for selected occupations in your community. Information can be obtained from newspaper want ads and through interviews with personnel officers or employment counselors. In your report, try to determine how supply and demand influence these wage rates.

2. Do research to learn about the different ways people have attempted to protect themselves against income loss. The local library, local savings institutions, and local social-security offices may serve as resource centers for this information. In a class discussion, evaluate these efforts and possibilities for economic security in the future.

H. Armstrong Roberts

Chapter 8 The Role of the Consumer

SECTIONS
1. **Consumer Demand**
2. **Effective Consumer Decision Making**
3. **Consumer Guidelines**
4. **Savings and Using Credit**

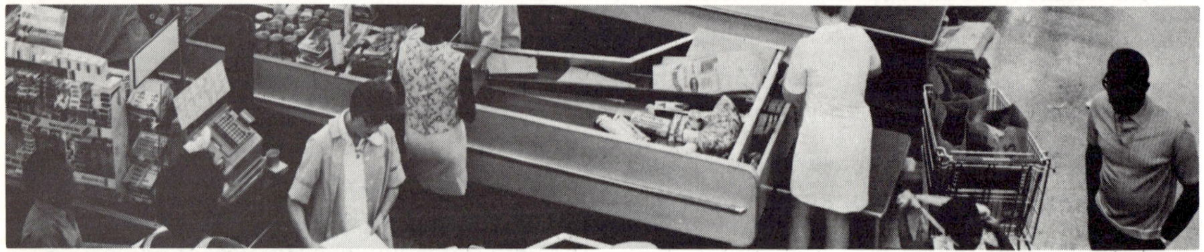

We are all consumers, and in our free enterprise economy, there is a wide range of goods and services available for us to buy and to use. Consider the thousands of food products and other items that are sold in grocery stores. All of us, however, have limited amounts of money to spend. We must determine how to use our limited funds in ways that will best satisfy our needs and wants. Wise consuming involves an overall plan of spending and careful shopping. As consumers, we should obtain all necessary information in order to evaluate different products and to make effective use of our incomes.

Section 1
Consumer Demand

Consumption is what economics is all about. One of the main goals of economic activity is the satisfaction of consumer wants. This section explains consumer demand and its impact on the overall economy. As you read this section, ask yourself the following questions: *Why must consumers make decisions among different products? How does the consumer determine what goods and services will be produced? In what ways does the size of a family's income determine its spending?*

The Goals of Consumers. The major goal of each consumer is to obtain the most satisfaction from his or her limited income. The key in examining consumer actions is to remember that consumers have unlimited wants and limited incomes. When choosing among alternative products, consumers try to select those goods and services that will yield the greatest satisfaction.

Consumers must often make difficult choices. Think about the consumer decisions that you have to make each day. If
1 you buy a record album for 7 dollars, you will not be able to use that money for something else. Or, if you plan to buy a car after you graduate from school, you will have to adjust your purchases of other products to save money for the car. In doing so, you might have to pass up a few concerts or movies that you would like to attend. The choice is yours as a consumer. It is your right to make your choices and to spend your money in ways that meet your needs and wants. This freedom of choice exercised by consumers is a basic part of our economy.

The Effects of Consumer Demand. In a free enterprise system, consumers determine what will be produced. This concept is often referred to as *consumer sovereignty*. It means that the consumer is the ultimate decision maker in determining the uses of resources.

For example, consumers use their sovereignty through their purchases. The dollars that consumers spend can be viewed as votes. Products that are in high demand will get many dollar "votes." On the other hand, products that do not satisfy consumer demand—those that do not sell well—get fewer "votes." Since entrepreneurs seek profits, they will produce those products that are attracting the greatest numbers of consumer "votes."

The growth or decline of an industry is largely determined through the spending of consumers. Furthermore, the level of overall economic activity is also determined by consumer spending. If, for example, consumer spending drops, industries will sell less, fewer workers will be employed, and there will be a decline in overall economic activity. Thus, consumer demand affects employment, investment, prices, and all other aspects of our

1. The value of what you give up to buy the record album is called the *opportunity cost*. If you could have seen a movie with the 7 dollars, the opportunity cost of the record album is not seeing the movie.

Although every consumer is different, some general patterns of consumer expenditures can be drawn. This graph shows the proportional divisions of consumer expenditures in the United States in a recent year.

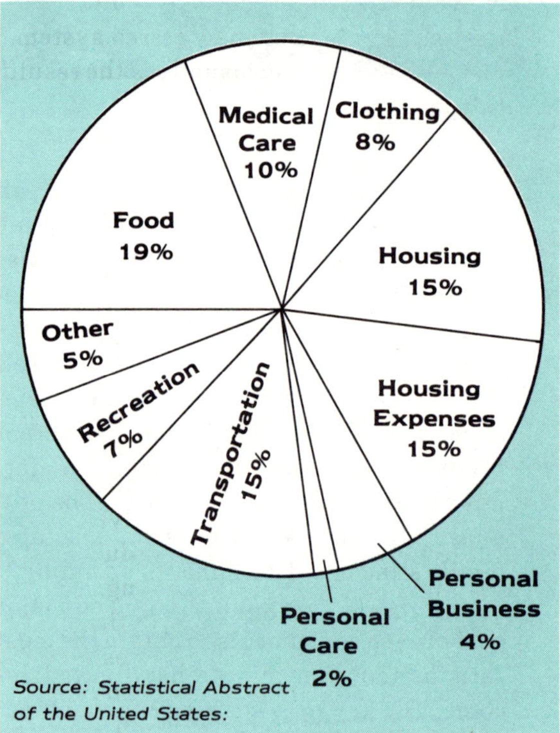

Source: Statistical Abstract of the United States:

economy. Freedom of choice and consumer sovereignty guarantee that our economy tries to meet the needs and wants of the individuals.

Income and Demand. There are several factors that determine the amount and type of products that an individual or family will consume. Above all, consumption depends on the ability to buy. Income provides this ability to buy.

Families with large incomes have more dollars to spend than those with small incomes. Savings and credit—which will be discussed later in this chapter—can be used to increase buying ability. Income, however, remains the major factor because a family's ability to save or to use credit is largely determined by its income. Of course, families do not use their entire incomes to buy goods and services. They must pay federal taxes and, in many cases, state and local taxes on their incomes.

The level of a family's income is important in determining how that family will use its income. In general, low-income families spend most of their incomes on food, housing, and medical care. Families with larger incomes tend to use part of their money for education, recreation, and other expenses. For the most part, as income rises, the proportion of income spent for things other than food, housing, and medical care increases.

The circle graph on this page shows how Americans spent their incomes in a recent year. The breakdown reveals that a large share of all consumption was of products that are not considered to be basic necessities. Furthermore, the basic divisions—those of housing, clothing, and food—usually include spending that is beyond essential needs. Dollars spent for six-course meals in expensive restaurants, for example, are included in the food category. It is the high income of some families that makes it possible for those Americans to spend so much money on nonessentials.

Creating Demand. You have learned that Americans spend a large part of their incomes on things that they do not need to survive. Much of this additional consumption occurs because a demand has been created. For example, your demand for the latest style of jeans, a new stereo system, or a new record album usually is the result of demand creation.

Advertising is a major way of creating demand. Through advertising, businesses try to convince consumers that they should buy certain products. Businesses use many methods to convey this message. Think about the advertisements that you see each day and how they attempt to convince consumers to buy.

There are many different forms of advertising. Magazines, newspapers, television, radio, outdoor signs, and direct mail are among the media used by advertisers. Store-window displays and product packaging are also forms of advertising. Advertising is used by large national firms and by small local businesses. It is estimated
1 that overall, more than 35 billion dollars is spent in the United States each year on advertising.

Advertising and the Economy. Demand creation is important to our economy. A high level of consumption is needed for American business to maintain a high level of activity and employment. The automobile industry, for example, is dependent on new-car sales. Normally automobile makers redesign their cars every year or so, presenting consumers with new options and styles. These changes often make older automobile models less desirable. By making changes, the automobile industry uses product improvement and advertising to persuade people to buy new cars. You should remember that demand creation is important in other consumer industries as well. Furthermore, keep in mind that when consumers lower their level of consumption, economic problems usually occur.

It is also important to remember that consumer wants are relatively unlimited. Even without advertising, most individuals at all income levels have long lists of wants that exceed their purchasing power. Advertising is a form of competition. Producers use advertising to maintain the demand for their goods and services in relation to the other things consumers want and need.

Advertising and product improvement provide many benefits to consumers. Advertising is an important source of product information. A shopper who is interested in buying a television, for example, can learn about available models, features, and prices through advertising. Product improvement makes high-quality goods available. The buyer, however, must remember that advertising and product changes are used by businesses to gain the dollar "votes" of consumers. The wise consumer must be aware of demand creation. To gain the most satisfaction from a limited income, the consumer must consider all purchases carefully.

1. In 1983, about $60 billion was spent on advertising in the United States.

Section Checkups

1. *What is meant by consumer sovereignty?*
2. *How does consumer spending influence the growth or decline of industries?*
3. *Why do businesses try to create demand?*

Section 2
Effective Consumer Decision Making

People buy many kinds of goods and services. Some products, such as peanuts and magazines, cost relatively little; but other things, such as automobiles and homes, cost many thousands of dollars. How do people decide what goods and services to buy? How do they decide where to buy these products? This section investigates consumer decision making. As you read this section, ask yourself the following questions: *What is the purpose of budgeting? Why must consumers analyze advertising carefully? How do public and private groups assist consumers?*

Consumer Decisions. The key to being a wise consumer is sensible decision making. Consumers must first determine what goods and services they want and need. Next, they must decide how to use their limited incomes to obtain these products. Then, consumers must decide when and where they will buy these products.

In many ways, consumers must act like businesses and try to be as efficient as possible in using their limited resources. The market system rewards efficient consumers and penalizes inefficient consumers. Persons who are not well informed and who do not follow sound consumer practices in shopping and *budgeting*—expense planning—will not get as much satisfaction from their incomes as they could.

Budgeting. A budget is a plan for income use. Budgets are used by businesses, governments, and consumers. A budget provides a way of controlling expenses and debts. Budgets help consumers to plan ahead and to choose spending goals. The goal of budgeting is to determine how future income can be used to meet needs and wants. Budgets allow consumers to decide how much of their incomes they need to use for daily, weekly, or monthly expenses. Budgets also allow consumers to plan for larger, less-frequent expenses.

No one budget or budgeting system will be perfect for all individuals and families. As you know, incomes differ greatly. And spending and saving practices differ with income level. Furthermore, people have different interests, goals, values, and wants. Those differences will be reflected in how they spend their incomes. Even budgets planned by your friends will vary. Some of your friends, for example, may plan to spend their money for summer vacations, or they may plan to save their money for college. Other people you know might give a higher priority to spending money on clothes.

One major advantage of using a budget is that it forces an individual or a family to *think* about goals and priorities. It also provides an opportunity to evaluate how

Designing a budget

1. Decide on both short-range and long-range financial goals. Short-range goals should include your immediate goals, such as expenses you will have this week. Long-range goals might include money for college or for a car. Be as exact as possible in determining the amounts of money you will need to meet these goals.

2. Estimate your income. Include only income that you are sure of receiving.

3. Plan your expenditures. Determine exactly how you can use your income to meet your goals. Keep in mind that you have both short-range and long-range goals.

4. Keep track of expenditures and income. This will aid you in evaluating your budget. You might find that your original budget is not realistic, or that your needs and goals change. If necessary, revise your budget.

A budget can help you to make efficient use of your income. Budgeting involves planning expenditures and some record keeping. These guidelines explain the basic steps in preparing a budget.

well income is being used to satisfy needs and wants. The chart on this page lists some guidelines for preparing a budget.

Information for Wise Buying. There are several information sources available to consumers to aid them in making wise decisions. First, all consumers should determine their own preferences. Personal tastes vary. Each consumer should select products that satisfy his or her own wants and needs, rather than buying something because it is popular or in style.

In planning their purchases, shoppers should try to gain information from other people who have firsthand information about the product or business in question. For example, someone who plans to buy a car or have service done on a car should consult with other people who have faced a similar situation. Information from friends or neighbors can be helpful for effective decision making. Other sources of consumer information include federal and local government agencies and private consumer organizations.

Government Offices for Consumers. Consumers can also obtain product information from a number of government offices. Some of these agencies are designed to carry out various local, state, or federal consumer-protection laws. Most cities, for example, have departments that inspect restaurants. Local governments also enforce laws to standardize weights and

USDA

This Department of Agriculture representative (right) supervises the grading of fruits and vegetables for canning and freezing.

measures. Inspectors check scales used to weigh fruits, vegetables, and meats. Some also enforce local laws requiring that unit-price information be available to shoppers.

On the national level, the Federal Trade Commission regulates advertising throughout the country. It is responsible for eliminating false or deceptive advertising. Another agency, the Food and Drug Administration, protects the public from dangerous foods, drugs, and cosmetics. And the Department of Agriculture assists consumers with their food purchases. This office inspects and grades foods that enter into interstate commerce. One of the most common examples is the grading of meat as choice, prime, and so on.

Several federal offices also print booklets that contain consumer information. The Department of Agriculture publishes booklets on food and nutrition. Perhaps one of the most helpful sources for consumers is the federal Consumer Information Center. This government agency distributes hundreds of booklets on a wide range of consumer-interest topics.

Private Consumer Organizations. There are also a number of private organizations that provide information about products and services to consumers. Many communities have agencies known as better business bureaus. These offices are part of a nationwide organization that works to eliminate misleading advertising and unfair treatment of consumers.

There are many other consumer organizations that work to promote the interests of consumers. The largest is the Consumer Federation of America. This group and several other consumer groups test and rate products for consumer use. The results of these tests are made available to consumers in publications. These reports are often considered to be valuable sources of product information.

Section Checkups

1. *How does a budget assist a consumer in determining needs and wants?*
2. *What are three government sources of information for consumers?*
3. *Why should consumers seek product information?*

Section 3 **Consumer Guidelines**

In Section 2 of this chapter you learned how information can be used by consumers in making effective use of income. In this section you will learn about some guidelines that will help you be a wise consumer. As you read this section, ask yourself the following questions: *What are three kinds of home ownership? Why should car buyers do comparison shopping? How can consumers get the most for the money they spend on food?*

Housing. *Housing*—a place to live—is one of the basic needs of all consumers. Furthermore, housing satisfies many consumer wants, such as privacy, recreation, and comfort. For most Americans, buying or renting housing represents the largest expenditure made from their incomes. It is important that consumers make wise decisions when they select housing.

Consumers must consider many factors when they select housing to be sure it will satisfy their needs and fit their budgets.

Everett C. Johnson/De Wys, Inc.

In all cases, consumers must determine whether they will rent or buy their housing. There are advantages and disadvantages in both owning and renting. The chart on this page lists some of these points.

Rental Housing. Most Americans rent housing at some time in their lives. Often, consumers move into their first rental apartments after high-school graduation while they attend college or when they begin full-time jobs. Some people prefer renting to owning and rent even though they could afford to buy their own housing.

In selecting rental property, consumers must consider many factors. Renters must determine how much space they need and what type of building and location will meet their needs. Heating, air conditioning, parking, and laundry facilities are among the other features that renters should consider in their selection.

Most rental housing is *leased*. A lease is a legal contract between the landlord and the tenant. A lease lists the length of time that the agreement will be in effect and the monthly rental rate. Some leases also include clauses covering such things as *liability*—who is responsible—in the case of damage to the property, procedures for ending the lease before it elapses, and the tenants' rights to keep pets. A lease should also list any services that will be provided by the landlord. Because a lease is a legal contract, renters should read the agreement carefully before signing it. As with all contracts, consumers should only sign leases that are completely filled out, leav-

Housing represents the largest single expenditure made by most Americans. This chart lists the advantages and disadvantages both of buying and of renting housing.

A comparison of owning and renting

	Owning a Home or an Apartment	Renting a Home or an Apartment
Advantages	Control over property Greater privacy Mortgage payment an investment Possible increase in value Pride of ownership Tax advantages	Greater mobility Does not require large down payment Less maintenance work Lower maintenance costs
Disadvantages	Possible decrease in value Requires large down payment Owner responsible for maintenance Commitment to long-term mortgage	Less security and stability Rent money not investment Less control over property Less privacy

ing no blank spaces. Renters also should ask the landlord or rental manager to explain any part of the lease that is unclear.

Home Ownership. There are several different kinds of housing that a consumer might own. The most common is the *single-family dwelling*—a building owned and occupied by an individual or a family who lives in it. *Condominiums* are another form of housing. Most condominiums are apartments in multiple-unit buildings. Owners of condominiums own their individual living unit. Unit owners also share in joint ownership of common areas and property. Joint ownership usually applies to the hallways, the elevators, the recreational facilities, and the property lot. Many town houses involve similar ownership arrangements. Town-house dwellers often own their own unit and share in joint ownership of certain common facilities. For both condominiums and town houses, there may be an additional fee charged to cover maintenance of these common facilities. This fee should be figured in with the total cost of the unit.

Some housing involves other ownership arrangements. A *cooperative* describes a form of home ownership in which unit residents buy a share in a corporation that owns a multiple-unit building and the property. The corporation then leases the individual units to the shareholders.

In recent years, condominiums, town houses, and cooperatives have become increasingly popular. In part, this is because high costs have made it difficult or impossible for many families to buy single-family dwellings. The alternative forms of housing, however, are not always less costly than the single-family dwelling. In all cases, consumers must carefully determine their needs and weigh the benefits and drawbacks of available alternatives in selecting their housing.

Automobiles. Next to housing, automobiles are usually the most-expensive things that consumers buy. Furthermore, Americans buy cars far more frequently than they buy housing. Some experts estimate that many consumers buy between 15 and 20 cars in their lifetime.

Consumers must consider many factors in deciding whether or not to buy a car. Transportation needs and wants should be considered along with budget information. Some consumers find the costs of owning and operating a car are too high for their budgets. Some other consumers decide not to own cars because cars are not the best means of transportation for their life-styles. Motorcycles or public transportation, for example, might fit the transportation needs of these consumers.

Deciding what kind of car to buy is not easy. Car shoppers must make many decisions. They must decide between hundreds of new and used cars. The advertising of automakers and dealers generally stresses the glamour, the speed, and the image of their products rather than information about operation and costs. It is possible, however, to find such information.

Information for Buying Cars. There are several sources of information that are valuable to car shoppers. Publications of several consumer organizations and various car magazines often provide information that can be helpful. These publications discuss the results of tests that have been made on new cars, the prices of cars, and the costs of operating cars. They also comment on options that are available in cars and list the costs of these options.

(Text continues on page 133.)

Being a Wise Consumer
Automobile insurance

Everyone who drives or owns an automobile should know about automobile insurance. Automobile insurance provides protection from the risks that are faced by ownership or operation of a car. A wise consumer first checks to be certain that the insurance being considered is adequate. The main types of coverage that should be studied are liability, medical, collision, and comprehensive.

Liability: Many states require that owners and drivers carry two types of liability insurance to protect others from loss. *Bodily injury liability* protects the insured against claims or suits made on behalf of people who are injured or killed by the insured's car. *Property liability* covers damages to property that are caused by the insured's car. The specific amount of liability coverage issued to a person is often expressed in three numbers—such as 100/300/20. Under this coverage, the insurance company would pay a maximum of $100,000 in the case of bodily injury for one person, a maximum of $300,000 for all personal injuries in an accident, and a maximum of $20,000 in property damages.

Medical: This coverage provides for medical services and hospital care made necessary by an automobile accident. It applies to occupants of the insured's car, including the insured and anyone else who, with permission, drives or rides in the insured's car. This coverage pays for injuries regardless of who is at fault for an accident. Generally, payments are limited to medical problems incurred within a year of the accident.

Collision: This coverage applies to damage of the insured's car as the result of collision. Collision insurance can be very expensive, but it can be reduced by selecting a policy that involves a deductible amount. The deductible—often $50 or $100—represents the amount that the insured would pay for repairs. The remainder of the bill would be paid by the insurance company. Policies with high deductibles have lower *premiums*—payments—than those with low deductibles.

Comprehensive: This coverage protects the insured's car against loss that occurs if the car is damaged or stolen, excluding damage from an accident. This coverage usually includes protection against loss by fire, theft, explosion, and vandalism.

Car buyers should also consider recommendations or criticisms made by other consumers. Firsthand information is also valuable for selecting a car dealer. Consumers might also consult with automobile mechanics or other specialists before making decisions about car purchases. This is particularly true when buying a used car. Most consumer consultants strongly recommend that a used car be examined by a skilled mechanic before it is purchased. The small fee charged by a mechanic may well be worthwhile if the consumer is able to avoid buying a car that requires costly repairs. In some states, used cars must also pass a state inspection for safety before they can be legally purchased.

Comparison shopping is very important when buying a car. Car dealers often vary in the services they offer and the prices they charge. They also offer different service warranties. Dealers generally sell new cars below the manufacturer's suggested price, which is listed on the window. Buyers should compare dealers to find the best possible bargain. Used-car buyers can also expect dealers to discount prices to make a sale.

Buying Food. Food costs represent the second-largest expense in the budget of most Americans. Eating a nutritional diet is basic to maintaining good health. However, many Americans from all income levels have poor diets. Their food dollars are not being used in the best way to satisfy their needs and wants.

Choosing food is not easy. There are thousands of different food products offered for sale in a typical American supermarket. Food items range greatly in nutritional value and in price. Furthermore, food advertising and packaging are designed to encourage buying. In some cases, advertising and packaging can be deceptive and misleading. There are, however, some guidelines consumers can follow to get the most for the money that they spend on food.

As in all buying, consumers should first evaluate their needs and wants before they shop. Menu planning is very important for several reasons. Planning gives the consumer an opportunity to take advantage of special sales and to provide for nutritional needs. Shopping lists based on meal plans also help the consumer to avoid impulse buying, which tends to raise food bills. Consumers usually find that they buy more food than they should if they shop when they are hungry. It is a good idea to avoid grocery shopping when you're hungry or if you are with someone who tends to buy too much.

Guidelines for Food Buying. Consumers can get the most from their food dollars by determining exactly what they want for their money and by using all available information in selecting products. This method of buying sounds easy, but it is not always used. Many shoppers do not think about the products they buy or the prices that they pay for the items that they buy.

Consider the example of convenience foods. In general, convenience foods—such as canned spaghetti or frozen dinners—cost much more than items prepared at home. In some cases, these ready-to-eat items are desirable because they save time. It is important, however, for consumers to consider the extra money that they are paying for these convenience items. Furthermore, some convenience foods may not be as nutritious as foods prepared at home. Some convenience foods contain a

Joan Menschenfreund/Taurus Photos

Many stores offer "no brand" or generic products along with more-popular national brands. Consumers can compare these products with other brands to determine which items are the best buys.

high content of salt, sugar, or preservatives, which in large amounts could be harmful to your health.

Consumers also should read product labels to learn about the contents of each item. Many labels list information about the nutritional value of the product. Some labels or packages also state freshness dates. These dates are required on perishable foods in some cities. They aid the consumer in selecting fresh foods.

Consumers should also become familiar with food grades used by the federal government. Meats, milk, eggs, produce, and fish are graded according to quality or size. These grades provide consumers with standard guidelines to use in choosing the item that meets their needs. For example, a top-grade steak might be good for some meals but might not be the best meat to use in a casserole or a stew.

Many stores carry a *private-label* or *generic* line of food items. These items are generally of the same quality or of a slightly lower quality than the more expensive national brands. Consumers can often save money by comparing different brands to determine the best buy.

Overall, consumers find that the key to wise buying is effective use of available information. This is true not only for food shopping but also in shopping for other goods and services. Informed decision making enables consumers to get the highest possible satisfaction from their limited incomes.

Section Checkups

1. *What is a lease?*
2. *What are three sources of information that can aid car buyers?*
3. *Why is planning important to food shopping?*

Section 4
Savings and Using Credit

Used wisely, savings and credit are valuable tools for consumers. This section examines how consumers save and how they use credit to increase their satisfaction. As you read this section, ask yourself the following questions: *Why do consumers save? What factors should consumers consider when deciding what they will do with their savings? Why do some consumers use credit?*

Savings. Personal income that is not spent is called *savings*. Savings provide people with money for future consumption. When people save, they refrain from present spending in order to have money to spend in the future.

There are many reasons why people save. Many people, for example, save in order to have financial security in case of an emergency. An unexpected household or medical expense can be paid from savings. Furthermore, savings can be used to replace income lost during periods of unemployment or between career changes. Many consumers also save for financial security after retirement.

Consumers also save with specific future purchases in mind. Many products cost too much to be paid for from a weekly or monthly income. But through savings, consumers are able to pay for vacations, cars, or other expensive items. Some high-school students save to help pay for at least a part of their college education.

Savings can also provide consumers with additional income. This occurs when individuals allow others to use their savings. For example, savers are paid interest for the use of their money. The most common type of interest is paid to consumers who put their savings in a bank, a credit union, or some other savings institution. Some individuals use their savings to invest in stocks and bonds.

Managing Savings. Consumers who decide to save must also decide where they will put the money that they do not spend. Money can be kept at home in a jar or in a dresser drawer. Or, savings can be put in an interest-earning bank account or a government savings bond. Savings can also be invested in such things as real estate or corporate stock. Savers face many alternatives. Information about these alternatives is important to the consumer for efficient savings management. Much of this information is available at your library. However, there are three considerations that consumers should make before they decide what to do with their savings.

The first consideration is safety. All consumers want their money to be safe. Therefore they must consider the relative safety of the place where they keep their money. Savings kept at home, for example, may not be safe from theft or fire. In contrast, savings accounts in most banks and most savings and loan associations are

Camerique

Most banks and savings and loan associations offer several types of savings plans. This banker is explaining options available to these savers.

insured by the federal government up to $100,000. Other forms of savings vary in safety. Savers should investigate the risks involved in any savings plan they consider.

The second consideration is the amount of return received for the money saved. Money in savings accounts, for example, earns interest. However, not all savings accounts earn the same rate of interest. Furthermore, the actual earnings paid on an account also vary with the ways in which earnings are computed and by the frequency with which earnings are paid. The skill activity on page 137 shows some different returns that would be received at various rates.

The third consideration is how easily the savings can be made available to the consumer to use as money. Savers should always determine how quickly and easily they can get their savings if they need to use their savings. Some ways of saving are more *liquid*—more easily converted into cash—than others. Savings accounts usually allow savers easy access to their money. Yet, some savings plans—often those that offer higher rates of interest—require that money be deposited for a set period of time. When they choose a way to save, consumers must always consider how quickly they may need their money and how accessible it will be.

Savings and the Overall Economy. Savings are important, not only to the individual consumer but also to the health and growth of the economy. By limiting their consumption and by saving, individuals make money available for businesses to improve or to increase their production. These advances in business benefit the overall economy.

(Text continues on page 138.)

Using Social Studies Skills

Computing interest

To earn the most from their money, savers should compare both the interest rates and the method of calculating interest used by different savings institutions. Savers earn higher interest from institutions that *compound interest*—pay interest on accumulated interest as well as on the principal. The *principal* is the money that was deposited.

To determine the interest that will be paid on savings, multiply the interest rate by the amount of money on which interest will be paid. The table below lists the growth of a $100 savings account.* The different columns represent different rates of interest, all compounded annually. Study the table carefully; then answer the questions that follow.

Original deposit of $100

Year	5%	6%	8%	10%
1	$105	$106	$108	$110
2	110	112	117	121
3	116	119	126	133
4	122	126	136	146
5	128	134	147	161
6	134	142	159	177
10	163	179	216	259
20	265	320	466	672

1. How much interest would be earned by the savings account in one year at 8% interest?
2. If this $100 was left on deposit for 10 years, how much more money would be earned at 8% than at 5%?
3. If this $100 was left on deposit for 20 years, how much more money would be earned at 10% than at 6%?
4. How much interest would be earned if $100 was left on deposit for 5 years at 6% interest?

*Amounts have been rounded to the nearest dollar.

To understand the relationship between savings and business development, consider the money that savers deposit in banks. The banks use these funds to make loans to businesses, to buy stocks, or to undertake other types of investment. This investment of savings enables businesses to buy capital and to expand their production. In general, money that savers deposit with savings and loan associations and other savings institutions is used in much the same way. Savings deposited with savings and loan associations provide the money that these institutions lend to home buyers in the form of mortgages. Thus, the income that consumers choose not to spend or choose to delay spending makes business growth possible.

Buying With Credit. Credit can be helpful because it enables consumers to buy goods and pay for them over a period of time. Credit allows consumers to purchase products with borrowed money. Through credit, consumers are able to obtain goods and services in the present and pay for them in the future. A consumer who buys something on credit today is agreeing to use future income to pay for the product. Most American consumers use some form of credit during their lifetime.

There are several different forms of credit. Each form generally involves some interest or other finance charge that must be paid by the consumer for the use of the money. Credit charges can be expensive. It is important for consumers to consider those costs and the limits of their future incomes in the decisions they make concerning credit use.

Charge Accounts. One of the most popular forms of credit is the charge account. This type of credit is offered by thousands of different businesses. Clothing stores, airlines, gas stations, and car rentals are among the many types of businesses that offer charge accounts.

Customers who open charge accounts enter into certain agreements with the business that offers the credit service. The business agrees to allow the customer to make purchases without using cash. The customer agrees to pay for the purchases at some later date, along with a specified finance charge that is added to the account.

Most businesses that offer charge accounts issue *credit cards* or *charge plates* to customers who qualify for credit. These cards are used for identification when a customer charges a purchase. Charge customers are also assigned a *credit limit*—a maximum dollar value of merchandise that can be bought on credit.

Under some charge-account agreements, the customer is expected to pay for all purchases within a set period of time—often 30 days. In some cases, payments are due by the tenth day of the month following the month during which the purchases were made. If, for example, a customer charged a purchase for $40 on May 3 and another purchase for $60 on May 10 at the same store, the store would expect full payment of $100 by June 10.

Under most charge-account agreements, customers must pay a *finance charge* if they fail to pay the full bill when it is due. This charge is a set percentage of the unpaid balance. Some stores also withdraw credit privileges from customers who do not pay their bills when they are due.

Other Charge Accounts. Many stores offer *revolving charge accounts.* Under these plans, customers are not required to

Neil Heilpern/Globe Photos, Inc.

Credit cards have become a very common method of making purchases in the United States. Over 50 percent of all American families use one or more credit cards.

pay their entire balance each month. They must pay only a certain portion of the bill. A finance charge is added to the unpaid balance each month.

Some banks issue another type of credit card. These credit cards—such as Visa and MasterCard—allow customers to charge products at thousands of participating businesses in the United States and in many foreign countries. Individuals who use these cards might pay a yearly service charge as well as a finance charge on any unpaid balance.

Installment Plans and Loans. Many credit purchases are made through installment plans. Under these agreements, buyers are required to make a down payment on the product. The remainder of the purchase pric is loaned to the buyer by the seller or a lending agency. The loan, plus any added finance charges and any service charges, is paid off in a series of monthly payments. Automobiles and furniture are frequently financed through installment plans.

Under an installment agreement, the consumer takes possession of the product at the time of purchase. The consumer is *not*, however, the legal owner of the merchandise until the last installment payment is made. If the consumer fails to make the payments, the lender can *repossess*—take back—the item.

Consumers can also obtain other loans to pay for college expenses, home improvements, or other expenses. There are many sources for these loans. The federal government, for example, sometimes makes low-interest loans to students or owners of small businesses. Also, people in disaster areas can qualify for special loans from the federal government.

Home mortgages are also loans. Mortgages are generally long-term loans, ranging from 15 to 30 years. Homeowners pay off their mortgages in monthly installments. As with other loans, mortgage payments represent both interest payments and money actually repaid on the loan.

Using Credit Wisely. All consumers must use credit wisely in order to get the most for their money and to avoid overwhelming debt. In all cases, it is important to learn the costs of credit and to realistically evaluate future income. With this information, the consumer can decide whether or not a purchase should be made on credit.

More and more Americans each year find that they have used credit to buy more than they can afford. Unwise use of credit can result in higher monthly payments than can be paid for with existing income. To help these consumers, public and private organizations now offer advice to help settle these debt problems.

Consumers who decide to use credit should shop for it in the same way they would shop for other services. For example, different stores often have different finance charges. And banks usually offer loans at lower rates than many finance companies. Consumers should always compare credit plans to get the lowest possible cost and best available terms. Overall, it is important for the consumer to know the cost of credit in order to use credit as an effective consumer tool.

Credit Bureaus. Any consumer who has considered buying something on credit should know about credit bureaus. A credit bureau is a business. It gathers information about people who apply for credit privileges or who are using credit. This information is then furnished, for a fee, to other businesses. This information is used to determine whether or not to grant a loan, a charge account, or some other form of credit to an applicant.

For example, imagine that you want to buy a stereo from a department store on credit. The store might ask a local credit bureau for your financial record. This record would include a history of your employment, outstanding debts, and an account of how you paid your bills in the past. If you had failed to pay some bills on time, your credit record would show this information. The store would use this information to decide whether or not you qualify for credit. You have the right to know what information is included in this report. If the report contains false information, you have the right to have the information corrected. These rights are important to consumers, since many businesses use credit reports to make their credit decisions.

Credit and the Overall Economy. In recent years, credit has become increasingly popular with American consumers. The growth in credit use has had a major impact on the economy. Consumer demand has increased as more buyers have used credit to purchase those goods and services that they otherwise could not afford. Increased consumer demand has led to economic growth.

A high use of consumer credit, however, can also have adverse effects on the overall economy. Overuse of credit can lead to overexpansion of business activity. Inflation then occurs as demand outpaces supply.

The tie between credit use and inflation has led the federal government to control credit during periods of inflation. In 1980, for example, President Carter believed that inflation had increased partly because American consumers had gone into debt too heavily. To fight rising inflation,

President Carter took steps to curb the use of credit. The Federal Reserve Board, for example, was directed to control consumer borrowing. The board placed greater restrictions on lenders and took steps to tighten the use of credit. In addition, President Carter also asked consumers to reduce their use of credit in order to fight inflation. Economists, government officials, and business leaders have recently given a great deal of attention to the effect of widespread credit use on the overall economy.

Section Checkups

1. *What three things should consumers consider in selecting how to save their money?*
2. *How does saving by consumers benefit the development of business and the overall economy?*
3. *Why is it important for consumers to make all payments when they make purchases on installment plans?*

Chapter Summary

One of the main goals of economic activity is the satisfaction of consumer wants. In a free enterprise system, consumers determine the types and quantities of goods that will be produced through their purchases. Consumer sovereignty is a basic part of our economy.

Consumers try to use their limited incomes in ways that will bring about the greatest possible satisfaction. To do this, consumers evaluate their incomes and determine how to use their money to meet their own wants. Budgets assist consumers in planning how income can be used to satisfy both short-term and long-term goals.

The market provides buyers with a wide range of goods and services. To get the most from their incomes, consumers try to become well informed about the goods and services that they can buy. There are many sources of information available to consumers, including public and private consumer information offices.

Consumers also benefit from effective use of savings and credit. Savings provide money that can be spent in the future. Credit makes it possible for consumers to use money before they earn it. Consumer spending, savings, and credit have an important impact on the overall economy. They affect the level of business activity as well as the general health of the economy.

Reviewing the Chapter

Identifying Terms

Explain or identify the following:

Consumer sovereignty	Dividends
Budgeting	Charge account
Lease	Finance charges
Condominiums	Installment loan
Savings	Repossess

Analyzing Information

1. How do low-income families and high-income families generally differ in the ways that they spend their incomes?

2. Why is the creation of consumer demand important in our economy?

3. How does a budget aid a consumer in determining how income should be used?

4. In what ways do certain federal agencies assist consumers?

5. What housing options are available to consumers who want to own their own homes?

6. Why is comparison shopping important to a consumer who plans to buy a car?

7. How can savings provide income for consumers?

8. Why should consumers consider finance charges when they are making decisions about using credit? What other factors should be considered?

9. How does the use of consumer credit affect the overall economy?

Analyzing Visual Material

1. Examine the circle graph that appears on page 124. Approximately what was the combined percent of expenses used for food, medical care, clothing, housing, and housing expenses? What one category of expenses represents the largest single area of expenses for consumers?

Research and Projects

1. Prepare a budget for one month. List all sources of income and how you plan to use this income for spending and saving. Discuss this budget with the class and compare it with the budgets prepared by classmates.

2. Work in small groups to prepare reports on savings. Possible topics include the various forms of savings, the returns and liquidity of various savings plans, and the safety of savings institutions.

3. To learn more about credit, interview local merchants, bank officers, and representatives from consumer protection groups. Inquire about the percentage of purchases that are made with credit, the qualifications that consumers must meet to obtain credit, the applications that must be completed, how finance charges are computed, and the problems that are faced by creditors and debtors.

Unit 2 Reviewing the Unit

Understanding the Unit

1. What factors have accounted for the large increase in productivity that has characterized the development of American industry?

2. Why might a change in the price of gasoline lead to a change in the demand for bicycles?

3. How are shortages and surpluses related to demand and price?

4. How does the opportunity to earn a profit encourage a person to innovate?

5. In what ways does competition encourage efficient use of resources?

6. What factors help to determine the size of a family's income?

7. Why can a family's real income change while its dollar income remains the same?

8. In what ways do consumers influence production?

9. What sources of product information are available to consumers?

Questions for Discussion

1. How do you think our economy would change if the government limited incomes?

2. Do you think income inequality is desirable or undesirable? Explain your answer.

3. In your opinion, should the federal government provide more guidance and protection for consumers?

4. How might business be affected if consumer credit was cut off completely?

Recommended Reading

Allentuck, Andrew J. *Consumer Choice: The Economics of Personal Living.* New York: Harcourt, Brace, Jovanovich, 1977. An examination of consumer decision making in both broad and specific terms.

Brooks, John. *The Game Players.* New York: Times Books, 1980. A book that explores the development of top-level corporate decision making.

Kaye, Marvin. *A Toy Is Born.* New York: Stein and Day, 1973. Accounts of risk taking and innovation undertaken by entrepreneurs in the toy industry.

Porter, Sylvia. *New Money Book for the 80's.* Garden City: Doubleday, 1979. A comprehensive guide to personal finance. Contains valuable information and guidelines on a wide variety of current consumer problems.

Rees, Albert. *The Economics of Work and Pay.* New York: Harper and Row, 1979. A study of wage levels and labor force participation.

Walker, Glen. *Credit Where Credit Is Due.* New York: Holt, Rinehart, and Winston, 1979. A guide to the use of credit in the United States today.

Economics at Work

Making economic choices: Financing a used car

Imagine that you plan to buy your first car after graduation when you begin a full-time job. You will be earning $180 in take-home pay each week. You have saved $1,000.

After several days of car shopping, you find that you cannot afford a new car. However, you have looked at used cars and have found one that you like. It costs $3,000. To buy it you must arrange financing. You consult 2 banks and 2 finance companies to get the best deal. The banks require either 20 percent or 33 percent of the selling price as a down payment. They both offer the loan for 24 months. The finance companies will accept a lower down payment—$300—and one will give you the loan for 36 months. There is, however, a significant difference in the interest rates charged by the lenders. Your finance options are listed below.

Source	Down Payment	True Annual Interest	Term of Loan	Monthly Payment
Bank A	$ 600.00	14.00%	24 months	$105.66
Bank B	1000.00	14.00	24 months	95.00
Finance Company A	300.00	21.23	24 months	136.38
Finance Company B	300.00	21.04	36 months	90.78

Examine these plans and determine which one you will select. Write an explanation of your decision. Be sure to explain how the cost of the loan, the size of monthly payments, budget considerations, and other factors affected your choice. Be certain to take into consideration any new expenses you will incur as an owner and operator of an automobile.

Next, assume that you receive a surprise graduation gift of $500. Will this affect your finance choice? Will you choose a different finance plan than the one you had originally selected?

Photri

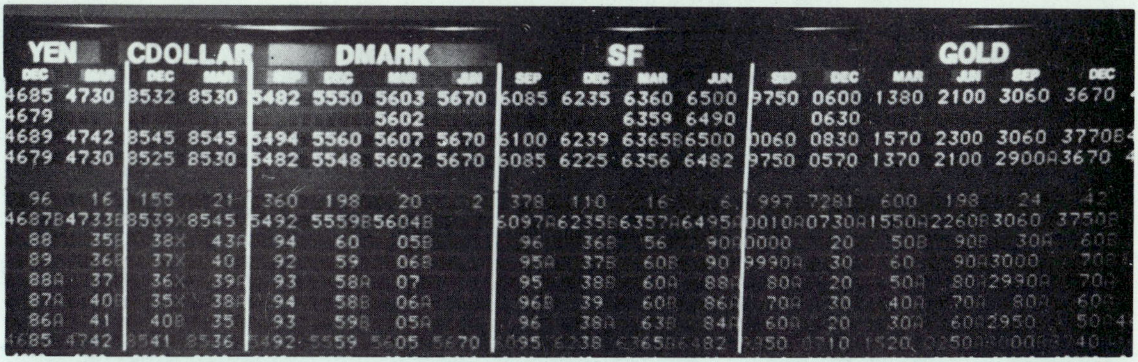

Unit 3 The Organization of American Capitalism

Bethlehem Steel Corp.

Chapter 9 Business Organizations

SECTIONS
1 Types of Business Organization
2 Corporations in America
3 The Role of Business in America

In the past, individuals were able to provide for many of their own needs and wants. People built their own houses, made their own furniture, and grew their own food. But today, in our modern and complex society, very few of us are able to be self-sufficient. For the most part, we depend upon others to produce many of the goods and services we need to satisfy our needs and wants. In return we produce goods and services needed by others. Business organizations play an important part in this process. Business organizations provide the framework for the bringing together of consumers and producers of goods and services.

Section 1
Types of Business Organization

In a market economy like that of the United States, individual businesses are important centers of economic decision making. Individual business companies vary greatly in size and the way they are organized. Basically, there are three forms of business organizations. These are sole proprietorships, partnerships, and corporations. The goal of most businesses is to make a profit. However, nonprofit organizations also play a part in the economy. The most important of these is the cooperative. As you read this section, ask yourself the following questions: *What are the advantages of sole proprietorships? In which professions are most partnerships found? How do corporations obtain their funds?*

Sole Proprietorships. A sole proprietorship is a business owned and controlled by one person. It is the most common form of business organization in the United States. Nearly 80 percent of the 13 million businesses in our country are sole proprietorships. However, sole proprietorships account for only 10 percent of the total yearly sales of all American businesses. For the most part, sole proprietorships are the smallest businesses. Examples of sole proprietorships are television-repair stores and barbershops.

Sole Proprietorships—Advantages. The sole proprietorship has a number of advantages. First, it is fairly easy to organize. Government puts few restrictions on the sole proprietorship. People may need a license to take part in certain business activities, such as the selling of liquor. But, compared to other kinds of business organization, the sole proprietorship is fairly free of restrictions. Second, the sole proprietorship can be profitable. Any profits that are made—less taxes—go to the sole owner. The owner of a sole proprietorship has no partners or stockholders with whom to share the profits. Third, the sole proprietorship has a number of personal advantages. Many people find it difficult to work for another person. They would much rather be their own boss. As owners of sole proprietorships, these people enjoy freedom of choice in making business decisions. And running the business *their* way may give them great personal satisfaction. For many people, freedom and personal satisfaction are the most important advantages of a sole proprietorship.

Sole Proprietorships—Disadvantages. The sole proprietorship does have some drawbacks. One drawback is that many sole proprietorships have very limited resources. The money available for the business amounts to the owner's savings and what the owner is able to borrow. Places from which to borrow are limited. About

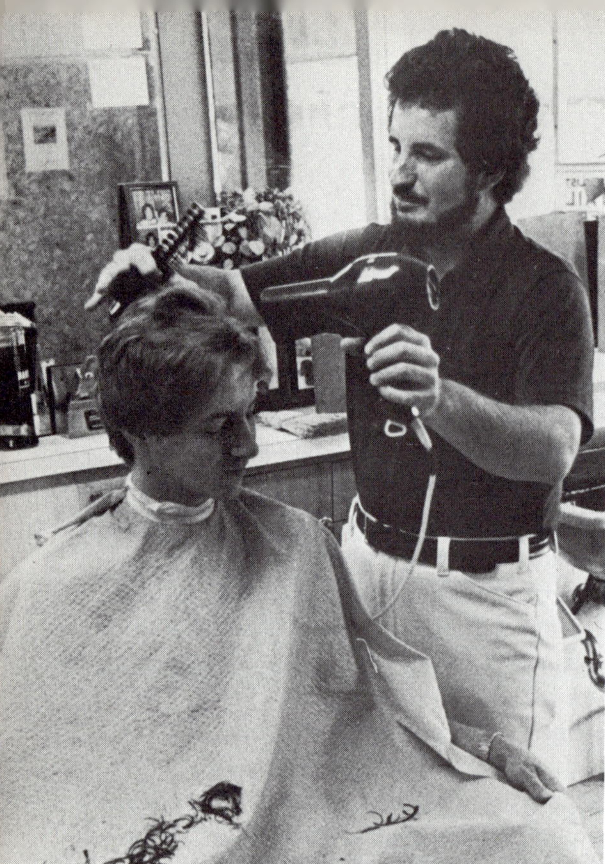
Pat Kelly

The most commonly found form of business organization in the United States is the sole proprietorship. Although sole proprietorships present some disadvantages, most owners enjoy being their own boss and running the business their way.

1 10,000 American businesses fail each year. Most of these are sole proprietorships. Because of this, commercial banks sometimes do not like to take the risk of lending to sole proprietorships.

Another drawback is that the owner has total responsibility for the business. The owner, therefore, must be involved in management, production, and sales. This lack of specialization could make the business less efficient. A third drawback is that the sole proprietorship has a *limited life*. On the death of the owner, or if the owner sells the business, the sole proprietorship no longer exists. This often makes future sales and purchases uncertain.

Perhaps the most important disadvantage of the sole proprietorship is that the owner has *unlimited liability*. This means that the owner is responsible for all business debts. The possessions and all sources of income of the owner can be attached to pay business debts. So, if the business fails, the owner may lose savings, house, car, or other personal possessions.

Partnerships. A partnership is an agreement between two or more persons to own and operate a business together. Each partner agrees to provide some part of the work or capital, or both, and to take a share of the profits or losses. A business partnership is generally established in a written contract. Certain important matters are spelled out in this *partnership contract*. For example, how profits and losses are to be shared and the duties of each partner would be included. The procedure to follow on the death or withdrawal of one or more of the partners would also be mentioned. Partnerships are not a common form of business organization in the United States. Less than 10 percent of all American businesses are partnerships. But this form of organization is widely used by some professional workers, such as accountants, architects, doctors, and lawyers.

Partnerships—Advantages. As with a sole proprietorship, there are few legal barriers to the setting up of a partnership. However, nearly all such businesses are

1. By 1983, business failures averaged 18,000 per year.

established by a written contract. Compared to the sole proprietorship, finances are more readily available with a partnership. A number of partners are able to bring more funds to the business. And partnerships are better able to borrow money, as they often have more possessions with which to secure loans. The partners often bring specialized skills to the business. For example, in a medical partnership one doctor might be a general practitioner, another might specialize in child care, and a third might specialize in eye surgery. This specialization can bring more business and make the partnership more efficient.

Partnerships—Disadvantages. The disadvantages of a partnership are similar to those of a sole proprietorship. Although funds are more available with a partnership, they are still somewhat limited. This could prevent the business from growing. Like the sole proprietorship, the partnership has a limited life. On the death or withdrawal of one or more of the partners, the partnership is ended, and a new partnership agreement has to be drawn up. Unlike the sole proprietorship, the partnership could have problems in the making of business decisions. With a number of partners involved in management, there could be disagreements over how to run the business.

As with the sole proprietorship, the biggest drawback of the partnership is that each partner usually has unlimited liability. Each partner is liable for all business debts, even if the debts are the result of the actions of another partner. If the business fails, partners could lose their personal possessions.

Efforts have been made to change the liability aspect of the partnership. The Uniform Limited Partnership Act allows for people to invest in a partnership without risking all their possessions. As *limited partners* their liability for business debts is limited to the amount of money they have invested in the business. Nearly all states have now adopted some form of limited-partnership law.

Corporations. Today, the corporation is certainly the most important form of business organization in the United States. Only 14 percent of American businesses are corporations. However, corporations account for about 85 percent of the business in America. They also produce most of America's goods and services and employ most American workers.

Compared to the sole proprietorship or the partnership, the corporation is fairly difficult to set up. People who wish to *incorporate*—form a corporation—must get the permission of the government of the state in which they wish to be headquartered. When the state gives this permission, it issues a *corporate charter*. This charter makes the corporation a legal entity—a person separate and apart from the people who own it. The affairs of the corporation are set apart from the noncorporation activities and funds of the owners. This means that the owners of a corporation have *limited liability*. They can lose only what they have put into the business. Their personal assets cannot be attached to pay corporation debts.

The Organization of a Corporation. When a corporation is established, the ownership is divided into a number of equal parts or *shares*. The corporate charter specifies how many shares there will be. The shares are held by *stockholders*, or shareholders. Stockholders are the owners of the corporation. They have the right to vote in the election of the corporation's board of directors. Voting rights are given on the basis of one vote per share of common stock owned. Stockholders with only a few shares have little influence in the election.

The board of directors selects certain corporation officers, such as the president, the treasurer, and so on. These officers are responsible for the smooth running of the corporation. (See diagram on this page.)

The election for the board of directors is generally held at the yearly stockholders' meeting. Stockholders not able to attend often vote by *proxy*—written authorization for another person to vote for them. If the year's business has been good, the board is normally returned for another year. However, if a majority of stockholders are not pleased with the board's performance, a whole new board could be voted in.

Raising Corporate Funds. A major advantage of the corporation is its ability to raise funds. Corporations raise funds by selling new shares of ownership and also by borrowing.

Basically, there are two kinds of ownership shares: *common stock* and *preferred stock*. Common stock carries the right to vote for the board of directors and to re-

The organization of a corporation

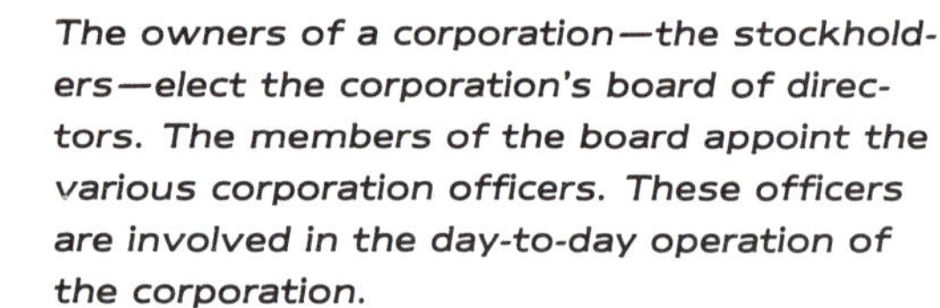

The owners of a corporation—the stockholders—elect the corporation's board of directors. The members of the board appoint the various corporation officers. These officers are involved in the day-to-day operation of the corporation.

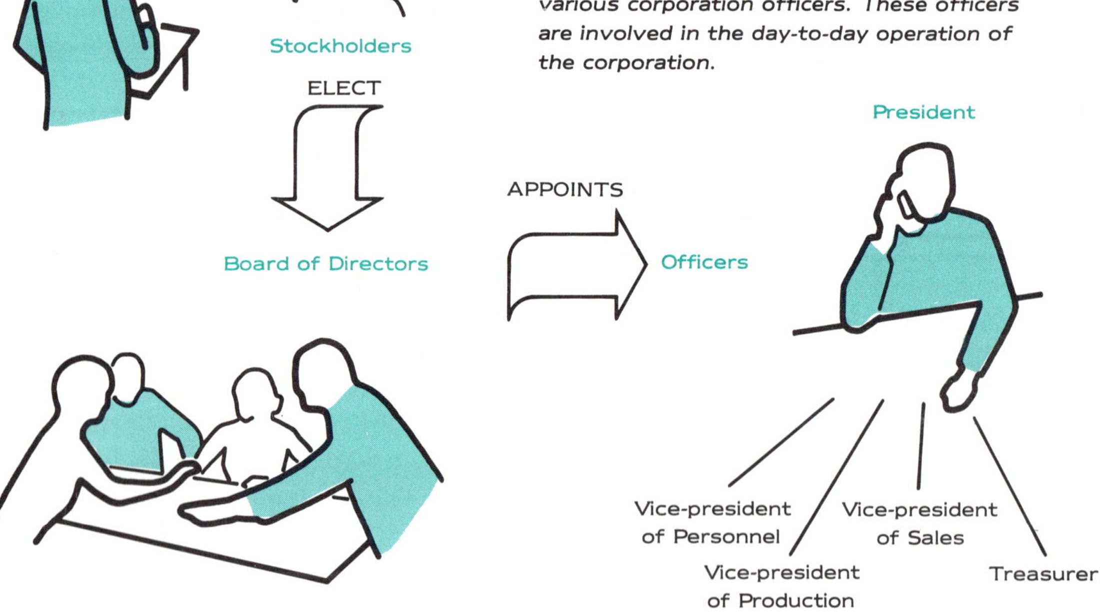

ceive a *dividend*—a share in any profits, paid in return for investing. When investing, common stockholders take the greatest risk. If business is very good, they could receive a big dividend. However, if business is poor, they may receive nothing. Holders of preferred stock do not have the right to vote for the board of directors. In return for their investment they receive a fixed dividend. This is paid before any dividends are given to common stockholders. But, regardless of how great the corporation's profits may be, preferred stockholders receive the same set dividend.

Corporations can also raise funds by borrowing. In return they issue *bonds.* A bond is a written promise to pay back the money borrowed at a later date. A bond also contains a promise that the corporation will pay *interest*—a fixed amount of money paid at regular intervals—for the use of the borrowed money. Rates of interest on bonds are fixed, no matter what profits the corporation makes. But the interest must be paid, even if the corporation suffers a loss. Corporations are not the only organizations to raise funds in this way. This method of raising money is often used by federal, state, and local governments.

Cooperatives. Although the sole proprietorship, the partnership, and the corporation are organized differently, they do have one thing in common. The main goal of each one is to make a profit. But many nonprofit organizations play a part in American business. The most important of these is the cooperative.

A cooperative is a business whose owners are also its customers. The general goal of a cooperative is to provide its owners with some kind of advantage. *Consumer* cooperatives try to get products for their members at lower prices. *Producer* cooperatives try to sell their members' products at higher prices. And *service* cooperatives try to offer members special services, such as insurance or credit, on better terms than are generally available.

In some ways the organization of a cooperative is similar to that of a corporation. People can buy ownership shares. These shares give them the right to vote for the board of directors. Members of a cooperative also have limited liability. But there are a number of differences.

The goal of a cooperative is to try to make or save money for its members, not to make a profit. Cooperative members receive one vote no matter what their investment, not one vote per share owned. And a cooperative issues *patronage dividends.* This means that earnings or savings are shared according to the amount of business a member has done with the cooperative. Corporation profits, on the other hand, are shared according to the number of shares owned.

In terms of the amount of business done, the cooperative is not as important as the sole proprietorship, the partnership, or the corporation. Even so, the cooperative is still important in many areas of American business life, especially in agriculture.

Section Checkups

1. *What advantages does the partnership have over the sole proprietorship?*
2. *How is a corporation organized?*
3. *How does a cooperative differ from a corporation?*

Section 2
Corporations in America

Corporations have played an important part in the American economy. The first English settlers held corporate charters from the English government. Since that time, corporations have grown in size and power. This growth is due to the many advantages corporations have over other forms of business organization. Even so, they also have some important disadvantages.

Stocks and bonds issued by corporations are traded on the securities market through stock exchanges. New issues of stock are underwritten and sold by investment bankers. This trade in securities is regulated by the Securities and Exchange Commission. As you read this section, ask yourself the following questions: *How have corporations increased and consolidated their power? Where and how are securities traded? How are new issues of corporate stock sold?*

Origins and Early Growth. The corporation is not an American invention. Many early English business corporations were founded during the reign of Queen Elizabeth I. These corporations were interested in investment in overseas exploration and were funded mainly with private capital. Their methods of operation were set down in public charters issued by the government.

Corporations played an important part in the early development of America. The first English settlers in Virginia, Massachusetts, and Pennsylvania held corporate charters from the English government. Most of the colonies chartered their own corporations to build bridges, canals, and roads. And the Thirteen Colonies continued this practice even after winning their independence.

In the early 1800's states began to pass new laws to regulate corporations. The first came in 1811, when New York State passed a general incorporation act. Under this act, any group filing the correct papers and promising to follow state laws could become a corporation. Other states soon followed New York's lead. After this, the corporate form of organization spread in all businesses.

The Large Corporations. With growing industrialization in the second half of the nineteenth century, the size and number of corporations in America grew rapidly. As the corporations grew in power, they often formed pools, trusts, and holding companies to fix prices and limit competition. (See diagram on page 153.) This led to great industrial empires in such industries as the railroads, steel, oil, and coal mining. These empires were founded by business leaders like Andrew Carnegie and John D. Rockefeller.

Efforts were made to limit the growing power of the corporations. The Sherman Antitrust Act was passed in 1890. This act

Major forms of business combinations

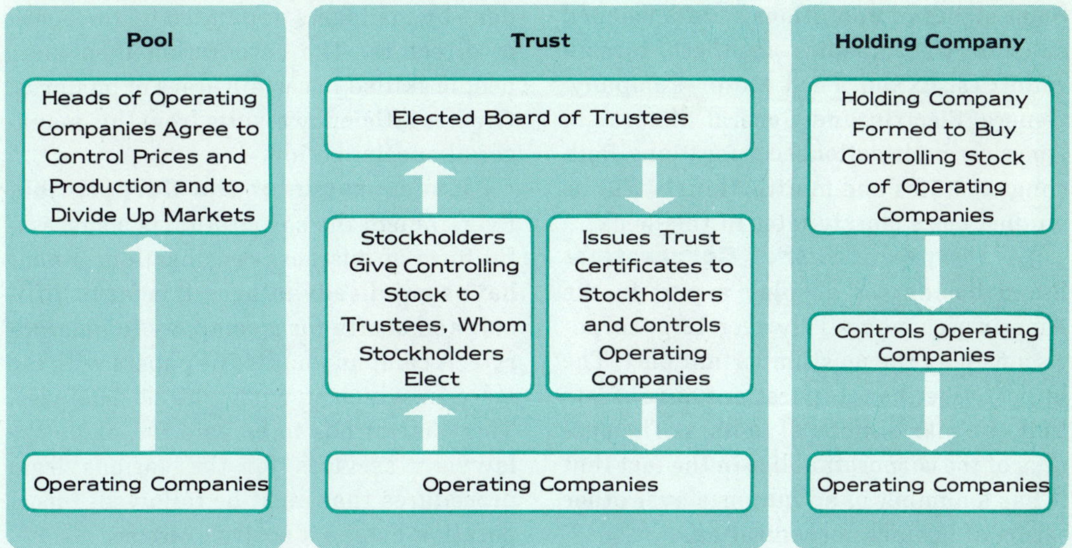

The diagram above shows the ways in which the major forms of business combinations—pools, trusts, and holding companies—were organized. In the late 1800's, some American business leaders built huge industrial empires by using such methods of business consolidation.

outlawed the restraint or the monopolizing of trade. However, the act could not stop the continued consolidation of big business. Through such methods as the *merger*—one business company combining with or buying up another—new and larger corporations were formed in the early 1900's.

But antitrust laws did not fail completely. They did limit the worst abuses of the big corporations. They also kept the American economy fairly competitive. And they have kept many small companies from being pushed out of business by the big corporations.

Large Corporations Today. American corporations have continued to grow and consolidate their power. Several new forms of business consolidation—such as the *conglomerate* and the *multinational*—have been used.

A conglomerate is the outcome of a merger of companies in different industries. The advantage of a conglomerate is that its holdings are diversified. This protects the business against possible changes in consumer demand for certain goods or services. A conglomerate could have holdings in such different industries as telephone equipment, publishing, car rentals, and hotel supplies.

A multinational is a company with holdings in a number of countries. In recent years many large corporations have increased their sales in foreign countries. Some of these corporations have developed subsidiary companies in these foreign countries. Exxon, Ford Motor Company, General Electric, and General Motors are American multinational corporations. Both conglomerates and multinationals will be studied more closely later in this book.

Advantages of the Corporation. Small businesses do play a part in the American economy. However, large corporations play the most important part. The largest American corporations have assets that run into billions of dollars. The success of the corporation lies in the fact that it has a number of advantages over other forms of business organization.

As you know, a major advantage of a corporation is its ability to raise funds. By selling shares of stock and issuing bonds, a corporation can raise funds. This availability of funds means that the corporation does not have the growth problems of the sole proprietorship or the partnership.

A corporation's stockholders have limited liability. The law views the corporation as an entity separate from its owners. As such, it is responsible for its debts. A stockholder who has invested $1,000 in stock can lose only that amount. Managers and employees of corporations also are generally not liable. Owners of sole proprietorships or partnerships, however, are liable for all business debts.

The death or withdrawal of any of the stockholders does not affect the life of the corporation. Transfer of ownership is fairly easy. Ownership is transferred simply by the owner's selling his or her stock. Neither the sole proprietorship nor the partnership has this continuity.

In most corporations, the stockholders do not run the business directly. This is done by managers appointed by the board of directors. The corporation then hires people skilled in certain areas of business. Greater efficiency results from this managerial specialization.

Disadvantages of the Corporation. Even though the corporation is a successful form of business organization, it does have some disadvantages. It is fairly difficult and costly for a company to incorporate. A company has to file papers with the state in which it wishes to do business. This charter has to be paid for, as do the lawyer's services for the various legal procedures that must be followed. Incorporation can be a costly exercise.

Another problem is the separation between ownership and management. Although most stockholders have the right to vote for the board of directors, they often have very little say in the running of the business. But, for the most part, the interests of the stockholders are served. The basic goal of the corporation is to make as much money as possible for its owners. Even though professional managers rather than the owners run the corporation, the profit motive is usually very powerful.

A further problem is that corporations are subject to many government restrictions. A merger or other form of business consolidation must comply with federal antitrust laws. Federal and state laws regulate the sale of stock. And the corporation is heavily taxed. The corporation has to pay federal income tax. Tax rates on corporate earnings range from 17 percent on [1]
the first $25,000 to more than 45 percent on earnings over $100,000. Taxes also have to be paid to the state in which the company is

1. Tax rates on corporate earnings range from 15 percent on the first $25,000 to 46 percent on earnings over $100,000.

incorporated. And stockholders have to pay federal income tax on dividends of
1 more than $100.

Large corporations have proved to be a necessary and efficient form of business organization. They can, however, lead to great concentrations of economic and political power. But this power can be abused. The actions of corporations affect many people who have no direct ties to them. So government keeps a close watch on corporate activity. This will be discussed further in Chapter 12.

The Securities Market. You have already learned that corporations issue certificates of ownership, or stock, and that the ownership of stock is transferable. But where and how are stocks transferred from one person to another?

The general term for a certificate issued by corporations is *security*. Securities are bought and sold in the *securities market*. This is an economic market in which buyers and sellers of securities get together to trade. Trading is done in places called *stock exchanges*. These may be organized on a national level, such as the New York Stock Exchange or the American Stock Exchange. Or they may be organized on a regional level, such as the Midwest Stock Exchange or the Pacific Coast Stock Exchange. Stock exchanges do not buy securities; they provide a place where trading for securities can be done.

One way in which corporations raise money is by selling shares of ownership. Buyers of these shares are issued certificates of ownership, usually referred to as stock.

INCORPORATED UNDER THE LAWS OF THE STATE OF NEW YORK

COMMON SHARES

CERTIFICATE NUMBER

COMMON SHARES

SHARES

AMERICAN TELEPHONE AND TELEGRAPH COMPANY

CUSIP 030177 10 9

SEE REVERSE AS TO ABBREVIATIONS

This Certifies that

SPECIMEN

is the owner of

FULL PAID AND NON-ASSESSABLE COMMON SHARES OF AMERICAN TELEPHONE AND TELEGRAPH COMPANY,

Witness the seal of said corporation and the signatures of its duly authorized officers.

Chemical Bank (NEW YORK)

AUTHORIZED OFFICER.

REGISTRAR.

AMERICAN TELEPHONE AND TELEGRAPH COMPANY

TRANSFER AGENT

TREASURER

CHAIRMAN OF THE BOARD

201- 0686889

AT&T

1. Federal income tax now must be paid on dividends of more than $400.

(Text continues on page 157.)

Using Social Studies Skills

Reading the stock exchange list

Below is an annotated extract from an imaginary stock exchange list. All prices for stocks are quoted in dollars. Study the list very carefully; then answer the questions that follow.

Annotations:
- High / Low (first two columns): Highest and lowest price per share paid so far during year
- 100s: Number of shares traded during day, in 100s
- Net Chge: Net change from previous day's closing price
- Stocks: Name of stock
- Div: Most recent annual dividend paid per share
- High / Low / Close (day): Prices per share paid for stock during day—highest, lowest, and price at closing of trading

High	Low	Stocks	Div	100s	High	Low	Close	Net Chge
2½	1	ABCInt	. . . .	1	1½	1½	1½	. . . .
9½	7	BamCo	.36	31	9	8½	8½	- ¼
48½	38½	CorpInt	1.66	42	45½	44¼	44½	- ¼
9	4	DDInt	. . . .	6	5½	5½	5½	- ¼
42¼	25½	EdInc	2.20	13	39	38½	39	+ ½
288½	223½	FEnt	9	771	272	268	269	-2¼
28½	19	GICorp	.44	1195	21½	21¼	21½	+ ¼
33	22½	HapCo	1.85	446	32¼	32	32	- ¼
42¼	32½	IntEnt	2.40	219	40½	40	40	- ¼
15	6¼	JolCo	.40	26	14¼	13½	13½	- ½

1. What is the lowest price per share paid for ABCInt stock so far during the year?
2. How many shares of IntEnt stock were traded on the day of listing?
3. If you owned 100 shares of GICorp common stock, what would your most recent dividend payment have been?
4. What was the previous day's closing price for FEnt stock?
5. If you bought CorpInt stock at its lowest price during the year, then sold it at the day of listing's closing price, what profit per share would you make?

Stock exchanges allow only listed securities to be traded through their facilities. To have its securities listed with an exchange, a company must meet certain requirements. Basically, a company has to be fairly large and be able to show financial stability. Smaller companies and companies doing business in a certain area tend to be listed with a regional exchange. However, most securities are unlisted. These are traded in the *over-the-counter* market.

To buy or sell securities, a person seeks the services of a *brokerage firm.* Brokerage firms normally have a *seat* on a stock exchange to make the trading of listed securities easier. Owning a seat means you are a member of the exchange. Only members are allowed to trade on the exchange. Seats on exchanges are very expensive. National-exchange seats can sometimes cost more than a quarter of a million dollars.

Trading in the securities market involves the transfer of existing securities. The corporation whose stock is being traded receives no money. For example, when stock in General Motors is traded on the New York Stock Exchange, the money goes to the person selling the stock, not to General Motors. A corporation must sell a new issue of stock to receive funds.

Investment Banking. New issues of securities are not sold through stock exchanges. Rather, they are bought by securities specialists, known as *investment bankers.* Before buying a corporation's new issue, an investment banker looks very carefully at that corporation. If it looks financially sound, the banker may offer to *underwrite* the new issue. This means that the banker buys the issue from the corporation at a negotiated price. The banker assumes the risk of selling the issue

Alan Reininger/De Wys, Inc.

Stock exchanges provide a place where brokers can trade stocks. The stocks of more than 2,000 corporations are listed with the New York Stock Exchange, shown above.

to the general public at a profit. Having been assured of receiving its funds, the corporation is not directly concerned with the resale of the issue.

The Work of the SEC. As in other areas of the economy, government plays a part in the trading of securities. The Securities and Exchange Commission (SEC), set up by the Securities and Exchange Act of 1934, tries to protect the public when buying securities. All but a few stock exchanges must register with the SEC. The SEC requires that sellers of securities give certain financial information to the public. And the SEC regulates the sale of securities and the activities of investment bankers.

However, the SEC does not offer advice on investments. Nor does it offer guarantees that certain securities are sound.

Why Do People Buy Securities? In general terms, there are three reasons why people are willing to buy securities. First, they hope to make some income on their investment. Some part of a corporation's profits may be used to pay dividends to stockholders. And interest on bonds is paid regularly. Both dividends and interest offer income for investors.

Second, some people buy securities because they think the price will go up in the future. If this happens, the securities will have a better resale value, and owners will make a profit. This increase in value is called *capital appreciation*. Anything that makes a corporation's securities look more attractive—an increase in the corporation's earnings, or an important innovation in the corporation's business—will cause a rise in the price of the security.

Third, some people buy securities for speculation. The prices of securities often change from day to day. Some people—*speculators*—try to predict these changes, and buy or sell securities accordingly. By buying and selling at the right time, speculators can sometimes make large profits.

There are no set guidelines for investing in securities. Each investor must look at his or her financial standing and objectives. The key to all investment is *risk*. Investors can make a loss as easily as they can make a profit.

Section Checkups

1. *Where were the first business corporations founded?*
2. *How are existing securities bought and sold?*
3. *Why do people buy securities?*

Section 3
The Role of Business in America

The major goal of businesses is to make profits. In trying to reach this goal, businesses perform certain functions and meet a number of obligations.

Competition acts as an important regulatory force in the American economy. In some economic situations competition is limited. In others, such as in the case of monopolies, there is no competition. In the American economy government works to protect competition. As you read this section, ask yourself the following questions:

What are the functions and responsibilities of businesses? How does competition benefit both businesses and consumers? How do oligopolies and monopolies differ?

Households and Businesses. The two most basic units in the American economy are the individual household and the business firm. These economic units are on opposite sides of the market. Households, in an economic sense, provide productive resources—land, labor, capital, and entrepreneurs—to business firms. With these productive resources, business firms make goods and services. In return for productive resources, households receive income—rents, wages, interest, and profits. This income is used to buy goods and services from business firms. Because of this, we say there is a circular flow of goods and services and income between households and businesses. (See diagram on page 108.)

You have already seen that the ways in which businesses are organized are varied. In the same way, households differ greatly. Some households may only have one person; others may have five, six, or seven persons. And household incomes may vary. But all households face the same problem. They try to *maximize*—get the most—satisfaction from their incomes. In the same way, businesses try to maximize their profits.

Businesses Play Two Roles. In trying to maximize profits, businesses play two economic roles. First, businesses are *producers*. Private businesses are the main source of America's total output of goods and services. To produce all these goods and services, businesses use most of America's resources. So, businesses are also *consumers*.

Size of households in the United States, 1980

Persons	Number of Households
1	18,936,000
2	25,787,000
3	14,569,000
4	12,768,000
5	6,117,000
6	2,549,000
7 or more	1,643,000

Source: U.S. Bureau of the Census.

The chart above shows that the size of households in the United States varies. There are less than 2 million households of 7 persons or more. However, there are over 59 million households of 3 persons or less.

About 70 percent of the total output of private businesses is made up of consumer goods. The remaining 30 percent of output is divided equally between capital goods for further production and goods and services for our government. To a large extent the output of businesses is determined by consumer demand. In fact, American businesses make few decisions without giving thought to American consumers.

Functions of Businesses. American businesses perform a number of important functions when trying to satisfy consumers. Businesses buy available resources and through the process of production turn them into goods and services that are useful to consumers. To this end, businesses are always trying to make new and better products. Businesses spend millions of dollars every year in their efforts to satisfy the demands of consumers.

As a direct result of production businesses provide employment for workers. By producing goods and services to satisfy consumers, businesses create jobs. As businesses increase their activity, more jobs become available. In providing jobs, businesses also provide income for workers. This income helps pay for goods and services workers desire.

Businesses also help pay for the cost of
1 government. About 15 percent of federal income comes from taxes paid by business organizations. State and local government also collects taxes from businesses. These tax dollars help to pay for the many services offered by all levels of government. Without the taxes paid by businesses, government would have to cut services or raise the level of personal taxes.

Responsibilities of Businesses. The responsibilities of businesses take many forms. Businesses have a responsibility to their workers. This is usually met by providing safe working conditions, job security, and fair wages. Businesses also have a responsibility to their owners to make the greatest profits possible. However, profits cannot be pursued without thought for other things. Certain standards of behavior have to be followed. Some of these standards are set by businesses themselves; others are set by government. Most businesses feel that they have a social obligation to follow these standards closely.

Businesses in competition must also try to give consumers value for their money. This includes giving consumers true information—through labeling and advertising—needed to make wise economic decisions. It also means giving limited guarantees that products are in good working order. Businesses are led to do these things through laws and also through the desire to help themselves. Giving good service and high quality products attracts more customers.

The social responsibility of businesses involves even more than this. Nearly all businesses are working to better the so-

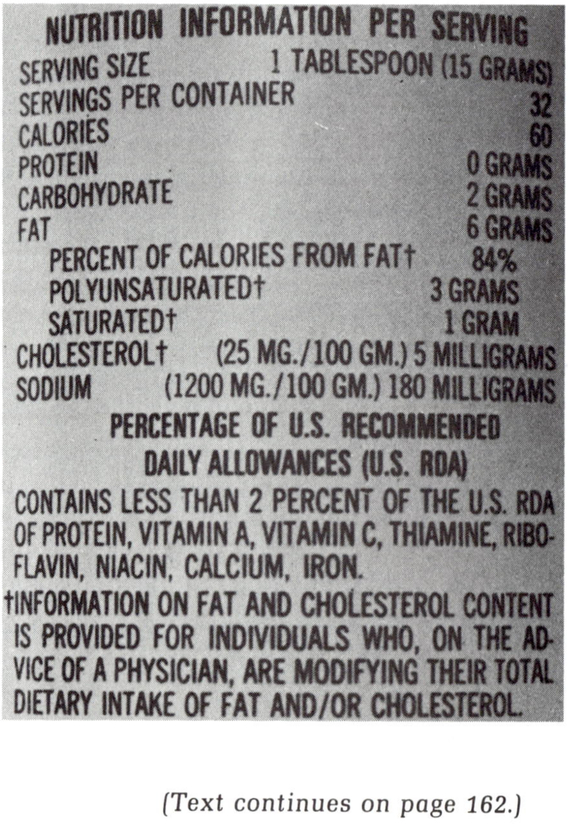

Jerry Sloan

NUTRITION INFORMATION PER SERVING

SERVING SIZE	1 TABLESPOON (15 GRAMS)
SERVINGS PER CONTAINER	32
CALORIES	60
PROTEIN	0 GRAMS
CARBOHYDRATE	2 GRAMS
FAT	6 GRAMS
PERCENT OF CALORIES FROM FAT†	84%
POLYUNSATURATED†	3 GRAMS
SATURATED†	1 GRAM
CHOLESTEROL†	(25 MG./100 GM.) 5 MILLIGRAMS
SODIUM	(1200 MG./100 GM.) 180 MILLIGRAMS

PERCENTAGE OF U.S. RECOMMENDED DAILY ALLOWANCES (U.S. RDA)

CONTAINS LESS THAN 2 PERCENT OF THE U.S. RDA OF PROTEIN, VITAMIN A, VITAMIN C, THIAMINE, RIBOFLAVIN, NIACIN, CALCIUM, IRON.

†INFORMATION ON FAT AND CHOLESTEROL CONTENT IS PROVIDED FOR INDIVIDUALS WHO, ON THE ADVICE OF A PHYSICIAN, ARE MODIFYING THEIR TOTAL DIETARY INTAKE OF FAT AND/OR CHOLESTEROL.

An important responsibility that businesses fulfill is to provide consumers with information about goods and services being offered for sale. Food labels, for example, contain important information that can be helpful to consumers.

1. In 1983, 6 percent of federal income came from taxes paid by business organizations.

(Text continues on page 162.)

Being a Wise Consumer
Warranties

A warranty is a promise by manufacturers or sellers to stand behind their products. Generally, there are two kinds of warranties—written and implied. A written warranty can be either full or limited. A full warranty is the most complete promise a manufacturer or seller will give. A limited warranty promises less than a full warranty. A full warranty may promise to repair defective products free of charge. However, a limited warranty may promise only parts free of charge, not labor.

An implied warranty is a right created by state law. The most common form is the "warranty of merchantability"—a promise that a product is fit for its ordinary uses. For example, a consumer can expect a toaster to toast. Implied warranties need not be written down; they come automatically with every sale.

At the right is an example of a written limited warranty. This warranty includes (1) the duration of the warranty, (2) what is covered for repair or replacement, (3) what is not covered, (4) what has to be done to get service, (5) the limits of the warranty, and (6) a statement that the buyer is legally protected.

A ONE-YEAR
LIMITED WARRANTY

(1) The Plumpton-Minimax Company guarantees this product for one (1) year against defects in material and workmanship.

(2) This product will be repaired or parts replaced free of charge during this period.

(3) This guarantee applies only to parts that are defective. It does not cover repairs made necessary by normal wear, misuse, accidents, or negligence.

(4) If service is required, send this product prepaid to the nearest Plumpton-Minimax Company branch or authorized service station.

(5) There is no other express warranty. All implied warranties are limited to the duration of the express warranty.

(6) This warranty gives you specific legal rights, and you may also have other rights which vary from state to state.

If a product is defective and the seller fails to honor the warranty, the buyer should

1. Write to the manufacturer.
2. Get in touch with the local consumer protection office.
3. Go to small claims court.
4. Inform the Federal Trade Commission.

ciety in which they operate. This entails such things as offering equal opportunities for women and minorities, safe working conditions, and so on. Another responsibility is the protection of the environment from industrial pollution. In many cases businesses have done these things voluntarily. However, the social responsibility of businesses has been underlined by government legislation.

Voluntary safety programs by businesses, and federal and state laws, ensure that workers in hazardous occupations have the correct protective equipment and clothing.

Eric Kroll/Taurus Photos

Competition. As you have read, competition is a major characteristic of the American economy. Competition is all the things businesses do to attract customers. So competition makes businesses listen very carefully to consumers. In this sense, competition is a regulatory force in business.

In competing to attract customers, businesses will try to make better products in a more efficient way. This will allow businesses to sell products to consumers at lower prices. In this way competition benefits both businesses and consumers. The most competitive businesses will survive and make profits. Those that cannot compete will go out of business. So, in a truly competitive market, consumers are able to get the highest quality products at the lowest possible prices.

The way in which competition benefits both businesses and consumers can be seen in the pocket-calculator industry. Some years ago market research showed that many consumers were interested in machines that could help them to calculate their everyday mathematical problems. In response to this, companies in the electronics field introduced pocket calculators. Although these first calculators were expensive, rather large, and sometimes unreliable, they sold fairly well. A number of companies made sizable profits. This led other companies to enter the field. Millions of dollars were poured into research as these companies competed to make more efficient models. Prices fell rapidly as new and better calculators were made. Some companies made huge profits. Other, less-efficient companies did not survive.

Today, pocket calculators are fairly cheap, often no bigger than a credit card, and highly efficient. Technological ad-

Competition has led the makers of pocket calculators to try to produce high-quality products at low prices. For the most part, the result has been pocket calculators that are small, inexpensive, and efficient.

Joan Menschenfreund/Taurus Photos

vances have given us calculators that can handle complex problems. Obviously, consumers have benefited. They are now able to buy a high quality product at a low price.

Oligopoly. In any discussion of competition it is also important to note that competition might be limited in certain situations. One such case is an *oligopoly*—a market situation where there are only a few sellers of a product. Oligopolies occur in industries where only a few large companies are dominant. They are most often found in the manufacturing industries. An example of an oligopoly is the United States automobile industry, which, for the most part, is dominated by Ford, Chrysler, General Motors, and American Motors.

One reason why oligopolies develop is that entry into manufacturing industries is difficult. Most manufacturing industries require large amounts of capital goods—factories, machinery, tools, and so on. These capital goods often cost a great deal of money. The return on such an investment is likely to be small at first. It might take years to make a profit. Therefore, very few companies can afford to enter the field. The few that can become an oligopoly. As these companies grow in size, they may also come to control the natural resources needed to produce their product. So, other companies find it even more difficult to enter the industry and compete.

One outcome of an oligopoly is that price competition may be greatly limited. Such large companies do not want to risk a "price war" with one another. However, there is nonprice competition. In real terms there may be little price difference in the automobiles made by Ford, Chrysler, General Motors, and American Motors. But these automobile companies compete by using brand names, styling, personal sales methods, and advertising. In this sense there is competition in an oligopoly.

Monopoly. Even in a free market economy there are certain situations that are noncompetitive. These occur when monopolies exist. As you have read, a monopoly exists when one company has control of the production and supply of certain goods or services. Most monopolies are harmful to the economy. Competition forces businesses to be more efficient and to respond quickly to consumers' wants. In a monopoly these conditions may be absent.

Monopolies can limit production to create an artificial scarcity. This allows monopolies to raise prices. Without competition to force monopolies to be efficient, valuable resources will be wasted. And, as they gain control of economic resources, monopolies gain political power. In this way, they are sometimes able to make government do their bidding.

But all monopolies need not be an economic danger. As you read in Chapter 3, some industries, such as public utilities, may be better run as monopolies. However, the benefits of competition usually outweigh the benefits offered by a monopoly. In the American free enterprise economy, efforts are always being made to protect competition. These efforts will be studied more closely in Chapter 12.

Section Checkups

1. *What functions do businesses perform?*
2. *How does competition act as a regulatory force in business?*
3. *Why are most monopolies an economic threat to consumers?*

Chapter Summary

The forms of business organization vary. Basically, there are three legal forms: the sole proprietorship, the partnership, and the corporation. These business organizations strive to make profits. But nonprofit organizations, such as the cooperative, also play a part in our economy.

Corporations have played a part in the American economy since colonial times. They have steadily grown in size and power, due to the advantages they have over other forms of business organization. Corporate stocks and bonds are traded in the securities market. Existing stocks and bonds are traded through stock exchanges. New issues are sold by investment bankers. This trade in securities is regulated by the Securities and Exchange Commission.

In striving to make profits, businesses are both producers and consumers. They also strive to fulfill certain responsibilities. Competition ensures that many of these responsibilities are met. But in certain economic situations, such as in oligopolies and monopolies, competition is limited.

Reviewing the Chapter

Identifying Terms

Explain or identify the following:

Unlimited liability	Bond
Limited liability	Interest
Proxy	Security
Common stock	Stock exchange
Preferred stock	SEC
Dividend	Oligopoly

Analyzing Information

1. What are the advantages and disadvantages of the sole proprietorship?

2. How does a corporation raise funds?

3. In what way are new issues of securities sold?

4. How does the SEC regulate the trading of securities?

5. In what ways do businesses try to improve the society in which they operate?

6. How do oligopolies and monopolies limit competition?

Analyzing Visual Material

1. Carefully study the chart on page 153. What was the purpose of these business combinations? Do you think that such business combinations were necessary for industrial growth in the late 1800's?

2. Study the table on page 159 carefully. What was the total number of households in the United States in 1980? How many households of two persons were there? How many households of seven or more persons were there? What do these figures suggest about life-styles in the United States in 1980?

3. Look carefully at the picture on page 160. What does the picture show? In what ways does the information shown in the picture help consumers? What other information might be included on a food label? Do you think that this kind of food labeling serves a useful purpose?

Research and Projects

1. Imagine that you have $5,000 to invest in the stock market. Study the financial section of your newspaper carefully; then choose the stocks in which you wish to invest. Follow your investments closely for one week. At the end of the week, present a report to the class on how your investments fared.

2. Select a cooperative that is in operation in your area. Using the information on page 151 of this book as a guide, write a report on this cooperative. Your report should include how the cooperative is organized and the services it offers its members. Present your report to the rest of the class.

3. Design and draw a stock certificate for an imaginary corporation. You may use the illustration on page 155 as a guide.

Chapter 10 The Role of Labor in America

SECTIONS 1 Labor and Production
2 The Growth of Labor Organizations
3 Collective Bargaining

H. Armstrong Roberts

American workers play an important part in our economy. They make up the labor force that provides the labor needed to produce goods and services. Throughout the history of our nation, the American labor force has been changing. And over the years, American workers have organized labor unions. Early unions often excluded certain groups of our society. But today, union membership reflects all segments of the American labor force. A major purpose of many labor unions today is to negotiate collective-bargaining agreements with management.

Section 1
Labor and Production

Labor is an important factor of production. Labor is supplied by workers—a country's labor force. The nature of the labor force may be different from country to country. Over the last 200 years, the American labor force has undergone a number of changes.

Members of the labor force receive payments for work. These payments are called wages. Decisions on wage levels are influenced by supply and demand. As you read this section, ask yourself the following questions: *In what ways might the labor force differ from country to country? What changes have taken place in the American labor force? How do money wages and real wages differ?*

The Nature of Labor. As you learned earlier, labor is one of the four factors of production. Labor is used to produce goods and services that consumers demand. Both physical and mental work are needed for this. The group of people available in a country to do this work is called the *labor force.*

In general terms, the labor force is that part of the country's population that is working for pay or is looking for paid work. This group is very important to a country's economy. It accounts for the production of nearly all a country's goods and services. In this way, what the labor force does directly affects a country's economic growth.

The nature of the labor force is not the same in all countries. The size of a country's labor force is related to the size of its population. A larger population will generally mean a larger labor force. The United States has a population of more than 200 million and a labor force of about 1
100 million. A country with a much smaller population would also have a much smaller labor force.

Labor forces may also be different in terms of quality. The American labor force, for the most part, is efficient and highly productive. This is because most American workers have received a good education and are healthy. Some underdeveloped countries have very large labor forces. However, these labor forces are not always very productive. Workers in underdeveloped countries rarely receive an education equal to that received by American workers. And many workers in underdeveloped countries do not enjoy a healthy, balanced diet or good medical care.

The American Labor Force. Our government views the labor force in a distinct way. The labor force is made up of people aged 16 or older who have civilian jobs or who are looking for work. Members of the military services are generally viewed as being apart from the labor force. Full-time students, homemakers, retired workers, and people under 16 years of age are not

1. In 1983, the population was 234.2 million and the civilian labor force was 111.6 million.

viewed as part of the labor force. People in prison and people in certain hospitals and institutions are also not included.

Over the last 200 years, our labor force has changed. To begin with, it has grown. In the late 1700's, our labor force numbered about 2 million people. By the 1980's, this number had grown to nearly 100 million. The kinds of work done by the labor force have also changed. In the early years of our country, nearly all American workers were involved in agriculture. Today, only about 3 percent of American workers have jobs in farming. More and more workers have moved into manufacturing and service occupations.

The American labor force is also changing in terms of the people in it. In recent years, minorities have come to play a more important part. And with the growing importance of service industries, more women have entered the labor force. In 1900, less than 20 percent of the labor force was made up of women. Over the last 80 years, this percentage has more than doubled.

Over the last few years, laws to end discrimination in hiring have opened up new areas of employment to many Americans. And women have begun to enter occupations that were traditionally held by men.

Betty Medsger

Betty Medsger

The way in which the labor force operates has also changed. In the early years of our country, goods were made by craft workers who were responsible for all stages of production. But technological advances and assembly-line techniques have given us mass-produced goods. Although efficient, mass-production methods may make working conditions unpleasant. At one time, workers spent many hours a day working at unsafe machines. But today, largely through the efforts of organized labor and government legislation, working conditions have improved.

Wages—The Price of Labor. Earlier in this section you read that the labor force is made up of people working for pay or looking for paid work. The payments received by workers are known as *wages*. In economic terms wages are the price of labor's services.

The labor force is made up of workers who do many different kinds of jobs. The types of wages these workers receive are also different. One form is wages paid on an hourly rate. Workers who are paid an hourly rate of $5 will receive $5 for each hour they work. In some cases, workers are paid on a piecework basis. For example, fruit pickers might be paid a set amount for each box of fruit they pick. Some workers are paid on a monthly or yearly rate. This kind of wage is called a salary.

A number of workers receive wages above their base rate. Some receive extra pay if they increase their productivity. Others receive a bonus if their companies' profits have been good. People who work in dangerous conditions, such as miners, often receive higher wages. In the same way, people who have to work night shifts often receive more money. It should be remembered that wages are subject to deductions. Such things as taxes will be taken out before workers receive their paychecks. Some workers also have social security and insurance payments deducted.

Most workers receive payments that are not shown in their paychecks. Many companies offer their workers paid vacations, medical insurance, and contributions to pension funds. For the most part, unlike regular wages, these benefits are not taxed. *Psychic wages* are also not shown in a paycheck. But to some people the satisfaction of doing a certain job or working in a certain part of the country is as important as making more money.

The dollars in a worker's paycheck are called *money wages*. But, over time, *real wages* are more important. Real wages are linked to the cost of living. They show the buying power of the workers' wages. In times of inflation, money wages may rise, but real wages may remain steady or even fall. For example, during the 1970's, the average weekly wage of American workers rose by about 50 percent. But the cost of living also rose by about 50 percent. So, in terms of real wages, most American wage earners made few gains.

Wage Differences. Members of the labor force do many different jobs. At one end of the scale of jobs are those that require little skill or training. At the other end are those that need a high level of skill and years of training.

Not all workers receive the same wages. But how are decisions concerning wages made? Supply and demand influence these decisions. For example, let us assume that highly skilled workers are scarce. But at the same time, there are large numbers of unskilled workers. Demand for highly skilled workers may be great compared with the relatively few workers to fill the available jobs. On the other hand, unskilled workers may be in plentiful supply compared with the number of jobs available. When demand is high and supply is low, prices will tend to be high. Because of this, skilled workers can, and generally do, receive higher wages.

Different wages for different kinds of work are not unusual. But in some cases workers doing the same jobs receive different wages. In some industries there is *wage discrimination.* Women are often paid less than men for doing the same work. For many years, blacks and other minorities received little more than a living wage. Such inequalities have been a major concern of many important federal laws since the early 1960's.

Section Checkups

1. *What is the labor force?*
2. *How has the American labor force changed over the last 200 years?*
3. *Why do skilled workers usually receive higher wages than unskilled workers?*

Section 2
The Growth of Labor Organizations

The first labor unions in the United States were formed by craft workers in the late 1700's. In the second half of the 1800's, attempts were made to organize on a national level. The most notable was the American Federation of Labor (AFL).

The growth of organized labor was helped by a number of laws passed in the first half of the 1900's. However, a split in the leadership of the AFL led to another national labor organization, the Congress of Industrial Organizations (CIO), being formed in 1938. Growing opposition to labor led to the merging of the AFL and the CIO in 1955. As you read this section, ask yourself the following questions: *What is craft unionism? Why did union leaders object to the Taft-Hartley Act? How do the goals of the AFL-CIO differ from those of the AFL?*

The Bettmann Archive

In their early years, labor organizations stressed the need for unity among workers as a way to attain their goals.

Early Organization. The first labor unions in the United States were formed in the late 1700's. Printers, shoemakers, and carpenters living in the big cities organized to fight pay cuts. These first unions were small, and membership of each was limited to workers in one particular craft or trade. Their chief concerns were pay, working hours, and working conditions.

During the first half of the 1800's, the labor movement faced strong opposition. Many employers fought bitterly against the organization of unions. There were also a number of laws that denied workers the right to organize. Even so, workers continued to try to form unions. But no set pattern of organization appeared.

Many unions formed during this time followed the lead of the earliest unions. They kept membership to workers in a particular craft. A few unions, however, were open to all workers, regardless of craft or industry. Most unions were interested only in the problems of pay, hours, and working conditions. But some had political goals, such as changing the money system and setting up public education. The course of labor organization before 1850 was far from smooth. But some patterns of organization began to emerge in the second half of the nineteenth century.

National Organization. American workers made a number of efforts to organize on a national scale after 1850. The first national union was formed by printers in 1852. The rise of national unions led, in turn, to the formation of national federations—organizations of various unions.

In 1869, a number of Philadelphia garment workers founded the Knights of Labor. It was a secret society until Terence V. Powderly became its leader in 1879. Under Powderly, the Knights of Labor was open to all workers, skilled or unskilled, black or white, male or female. The Knights of Labor grew rapidly during the early 1880's. By 1886, membership was estimated at 700,000 workers. But Powderly was not a strong leader. And the labor unrest of this time, such as the Haymarket Riot of 1886, set public opinion against unions. Because of this, the Knights of Labor declined rapidly in the late 1880's.

As the Knights of Labor faded, a new national federation emerged. In 1886, a group of labor leaders from a number of craft unions formed the *American Federation of Labor* (AFL). Its first president was a cigar maker named Samuel Gompers.

Gompers felt that unions should be open only to workers with a defined skill or craft. This is called *craft unionism.* Gompers felt strongly that there should be a countrywide federation of individual unions, such as the AFL. However, he thought that each individual union should be in charge of its own affairs. Gompers also thought that government should stay out of labor problems. These should be settled by employers and unions themselves. In the same way, he felt that unions should not get directly involved in politics by forming their own political party. The ideas of Gompers and the AFL dominated American labor for many years.

A Different View of Unionism. The approach of the AFL to unionism was very different from that in other countries. In nearly every other industrialized country a form of political party grew out of the labor movement. In these countries, the labor party wanted government to play a large and direct part in employer-union issues. And in these countries, semiskilled and unskilled workers also played a part in the labor movement.

In the United States, as well as in other countries, there were labor leaders who differed with the AFL approach. These leaders tried to organize workers in unions according to their industry rather than their craft. This is called *industrial unionism.* Under this, all workers in one industry—such as the steel industry or the automobile industry—belong to one union. Employers were against this kind of organization. They feared that this kind of union would become too big and powerful. Generally, early efforts to form industrial unions failed.

Setbacks for Labor. During the late 1800's and early 1900's, unions suffered a number of setbacks. The labor unrest of this time turned public opinion against them. The American people began to tire of the violence that often followed union activities. Radicals who had little to do with the unions sometimes took part in these violent incidents. Soon, many Americans began to fear that all union members were interested only in the overthrow of the government.

In these years, employers took steps to lessen the power of the unions. Many workers were made to sign *yellow-dog contracts*—promises that they would not join a union. Many employers drew up *blacklists*—lists of union members who were not to be given work. And employers sometimes used immigrant workers as *strikebreakers*—people brought in to take the place of striking workers.

Culver Pictures, Inc.

In the late 1800's, the labor movement in the United States was marked by unrest and violence. In 1894, federal troops were used to end the strike against the Pullman railroad car company in Chicago.

Federal laws also limited the power of the unions during this time. The Sherman Antitrust Act, passed in 1890, outlawed practices that monopolized or restrained trade. Labor unions were not mentioned in this law. Even so, it was used against them in the courts on a number of occasions. One case in point was the United Hatters Union. In trying to organize felt-hat makers, the union called a strike against a Danbury, Connecticut, hat firm. To speed things up, the union also tried to get stores to *boycott*—refuse to buy—the hat firm's goods. The hat firm took the union to court. In 1908, the Supreme Court found the union to be in restraint of trade. This was a serious setback for the labor movement.

The Clayton Antitrust Act of 1914 was designed to remove unions from prosecution under the Sherman Antitrust Act. However, the wording of the Clayton act was unclear. As a result, the courts ignored the Clayton act and continued to use the Sherman act against unions.

New Legislation Helps Labor. After the Clayton Antitrust Act, a number of laws were passed that proved helpful to the unions. In 1926, the Railway Labor Act was passed. This applied only to the railroads. It called for *collective bargaining*—the negotiation of contracts by employers and unions. It also called for the end of yellow-dog contracts in the railroad industry. Six years later, the Norris-LaGuardia Act outlawed yellow-dog contracts in all industries.

Then, in 1935, Congress passed the National Labor Relations Act. This is better known as the Wagner Act. It gave workers the right to organize and set up procedures for collective bargaining. Before the Wagner Act, the only way workers could form a union was to get their employer to recognize the union through a strike or a threat to strike. The Wagner Act set up the National Labor Relations Board. The board was empowered to hold elections for workers to decide if they wanted to form a union.

By 1935, there was a renewed interest in industrial unionism. But the AFL remained a craft union. As a result, a split within the leadership of the AFL developed. A number of unions formed the Committee for Industrial Organization. The unions making up the committee were thrown out of the AFL. In 1938, the members of the committee formed a rival federation, changing the name to the Congress of Industrial Organizations (CIO). The first president of the CIO was John L. Lewis of the United Mine Workers.

With the forming of the CIO, union membership grew rapidly. Union membership almost doubled as many unskilled workers were organized for the first time. And during World War II (1941–1945), both the CIO and the AFL gained many new members. By the end of the war, more than 35 percent of all nonagricultural workers were union members.

The Taft-Hartley Act. After World War II, unions continued to grow in size and power. Strikes broke out as workers tried to get higher wages and better working conditions. Many Americans began to feel that the unions had become too powerful. These people blamed some postwar problems, such as rising prices, on the unions. In response to this feeling, Congress passed the Labor-Management Relations Act in 1947. This is better known as the Taft-Hartley Act. It gave the government greater control over the unions.

Among other things, the Taft-Hartley Act outlawed the *closed shop*—a situation where only workers belonging to the union could be hired. It also stopped unions from making direct contributions to candidates in national elections. And the Taft-Hartley Act set up special ways to deal with strikes that threatened the country's safety.

Most labor leaders were opposed to the Taft-Hartley Act. They called it a "slave-labor law." However, other Americans saw the act as setting a balance of the power between labor and management.

The AFL-CIO. As opposition to organized labor grew, the AFL and the CIO began to think of joining together. In 1955, AFL President George Meany and CIO President Walter Reuther signed an agreement forming the American Federation of Labor and Congress of Industrial Organizations (AFL-CIO). Its first president was George Meany. He kept this position until 1979, when at the age of 85, he retired. On his death in 1980, many people hailed him as one of the greatest American labor leaders.

Courtesy of the AFL-CIO

George Meany (center, left) and Walter Reuther (center, right) joined hands to acknowledge the unification of the American Federation of Labor and the Congress of Industrial Organizations. The AFL-CIO is now one of the most powerful labor organizations in the world.

Courtesy of the AFL-CIO

In their struggle to have their union recognized, members of the United Farm Workers of America organized boycotts of farm products, such as grapes and lettuce.

While Meany was president, the AFL-CIO retained many of the characteristics of the AFL. However, it did undergo some change as a result of the changing times and the greater interest in industrial unionism. For example, the political goals of organized labor have changed. The AFL often opposed minimum-wage laws and, until the 1930's, opposed unemployment insurance. But now the AFL-CIO supports a number of programs dealing with such things as health care, education and training, and minimum-wage laws.

The AFL-CIO is a very powerful lobbying force in national and state governments. And the AFL-CIO often endorses political candidates who it believes will represent the interests of labor. However, the AFL-CIO has remained separate from any political party.

The AFL-CIO has continued to stay out of the business of individual member unions. The member unions set their own policies and do their own organizing. Today, the AFL-CIO rarely becomes involved in the labor disputes of member unions. These things are considered to be the business of the individual unions.

Recent Developments. In recent years, some workers who have never been organized before have joined unions. During the 1960's, Cesar Chavez, a Mexican American labor leader, began to organize migrant farm workers in California. Chavez was opposed not only by employers but also by a union, the Teamsters Union. Chavez overcame this opposition and founded the United Farm Workers of America (UFW). The UFW is now a member of the AFL-CIO.

(Text continues on page 177.)

Using Social Studies Skills
Interpreting graphs

Over the last 100 years, organized labor has come to play an important part in the American economy. The two graphs below provide information on American organized labor. The pictograph shows total union membership for the years 1930 to 1980. The bar graph shows union membership as a percentage of the nonagricultural labor force. Study the graphs carefully; then answer the questions that follow.

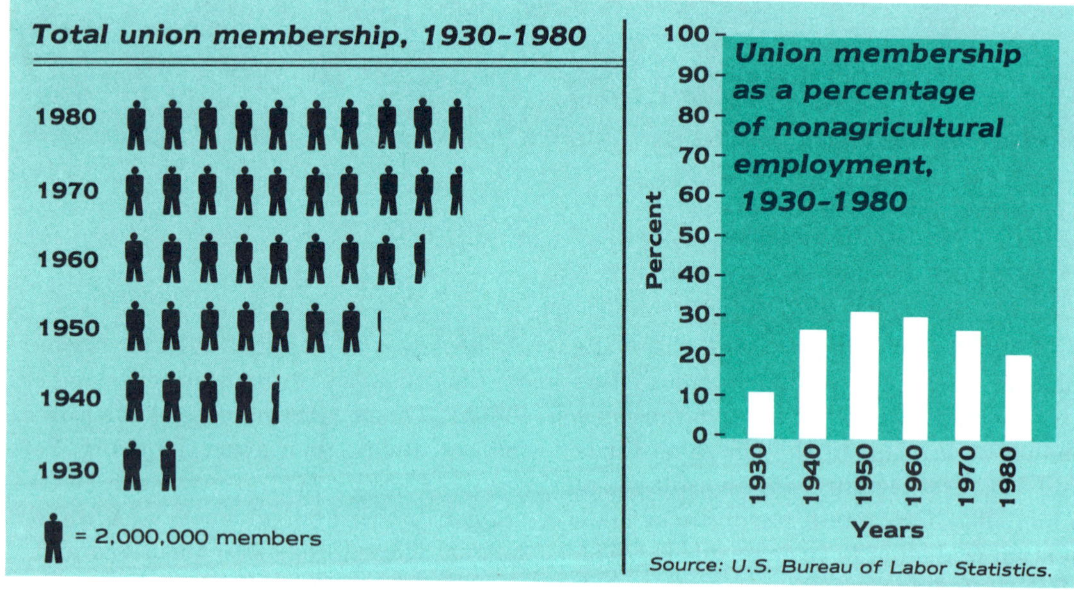

1. In which year was union membership at its greatest?
2. About how many workers became union members between 1940 and 1950?
3. Between which years was there the greatest growth of union membership as a percentage of the nonagricultural labor force?
4. In 1950, approximately what percentage of the nonagricultural labor force was unionized?
5. What conflicting trends do the graphs show for the years 1950 to 1970?
6. What general trends do you think the two graphs show?

In the early 1960's, federal government workers were given the right to organize, but not to strike. Since that time, many state government workers have won similar rights. As a result, membership in public-workers' unions has grown rapidly.

The number of American workers who are union members has been growing steadily. However, the percentage of the total work force that is unionized has fallen. As you recall, by the end of World War II, more than 35 percent of all nonagricultural workers were union members. But this figure has now fallen to nearly 21 percent. Some people argue that fewer American workers are joining unions because organized labor has become outdated and too big. But many union members do not agree. They feel that American workers would not have gained so much without unions.

Section Checkups

1. *What were the chief concerns of the first unions?*
2. *How did the approach of the AFL to unionism differ from that of unions in other countries?*
3. *What was the cause of the split that developed in the leadership of the AFL during 1935?*

Section 3 Collective Bargaining

Collective bargaining is the process of unions and employers negotiating contracts. Many people view it in terms of pay raises only. In fact, it settles many important issues.

It is very hard to measure the impact of collective bargaining. In terms of free enterprise, its greatest impact is that it involves many people in economic decision making. As you read this section, ask yourself the following questions: *What is the importance of the no-strike clause? How are worker-management grievances settled? What are the advantages and disadvantages of the union-security clause?*

The Importance of Collective Bargaining. In the past, workers formed unions to protect their interests. A united group of workers was better able to get employers to meet demands. As you recall, the process of unions and employers working out contracts is known as *collective bargaining*. But how important is this process?

Most American workers enjoy high levels of pay and a high standard of living. Many union leaders state that these things have been made possible by the unions. Some business leaders do not agree. They state that union demands for higher pay and a voice in the running of business have brought economic problems. Both points of view exaggerate the way in which unions affect the economy. The price of labor, like other prices, is basically determined by supply and demand.

During the 1970's, pay levels for most groups of workers rose steadily. This was the case whether or not they were represented by a strong union. But pay raises that are the result of collective bargaining are highly visible. The raises themselves, and the process through which they were gained, often get a lot of coverage in the newspapers and on television. However, market forces set limits on the possible pay raises for both union and nonunion workers. Within these limits, collective-bargaining agreements spell out the details of pay raises.

The importance of collective bargaining should not be overlooked. But it should be viewed as more than just a way to get pay raises. It also spells out such fringe benefits as vacation time, certain kinds of insurance, and retirement plans. And it settles a number of important issues in labor-management relations.

No-Strike Clause. Collective bargaining in America covers certain things that are not often found in other countries. Most major American labor contracts have a no-strike clause. This means that the workers agree not to strike during the lifetime of the contract. Most labor contracts last from two to four years. This kind of clause gives businesses and workers the economic stability they need to be productive and competitive. This also makes it possible to carry out the long-term planning that is needed in an industrial economy.

It is hard to measure the importance of the no-strike clause for the American economy. However, it is certainly very great. It is surprising, then, that few other countries in the world use the no-strike clause in collective bargaining.

Grievance Procedures. Clauses dealing with workers' complaints during the life of a contract are also found in nearly all American labor agreements. Again, this is not the case in many other countries. These clauses offer a step-by-step procedure for handling disputes between workers and management.

When labor disputes arise in America, union and management representatives try to solve them quickly. If possible, higher-level officers are not brought into the process. Most grievance procedures follow a set pattern. The worker must set down the complaint in writing. If the management representative involved agrees that the complaint is justified, the problem can be worked out at this level. If both parties fail to agree, higher-level officers are brought in. And if no agreement can be reached, an outside arbitrator is brought in. The arbitrator's decision settles the matter once and for all.

Such procedures are important because they offer workers protection. By agreeing not to strike, workers give up an important bargaining weapon. But grievance procedures protect them against unfair treatment while they do their day-to-day tasks at work.

(Text continues on page 180.)

Looking at Careers
The personnel officer

What does a personnel officer do? Generally, personnel officers act as a link between workers and management. This involves a number of tasks. Personnel officers interview, select, and hire new workers. They are responsible for the various processes involved in the payment of wages and the organization of fringe benefits. Personnel officers often organize education and training programs for workers. And personnel officers help to solve any problems that might arise in worker-management relations.

What qualifications does a personnel officer need? Many employers require personnel officers to be college graduates. Some employers look for people with degrees in business subjects. Other employers prefer people with a more general education. However, not all personnel officers are college graduates. Some enter personnel work as clerks and are promoted on the basis of work experience. All personnel officers receive on-the-job training to help them develop certain skills, such as interviewing.

What about pay and working conditions? Salaries and working conditions will depend upon educational background and experience. Whether the personnel officer works in government service or private industry may also affect salary levels. There is opportunity for advancement, but the field is very competitive. Most personnel officers work from 35 to 40 hours a week, usually in an office.

H. Armstrong Roberts

How does a knowledge of economics help? Personnel officers must hire the best workers and match them to the jobs they can do best. Detailed knowledge of business organization is helpful here. An understanding of the forces of supply and demand and how they affect the labor market is also useful. Personnel officers need to have knowledge of taxation and federal regulations to fulfill their administrative tasks. An understanding of economics is important in the everyday work of personnel officers. For more information on careers in the personnel field, write to **American Society for Personnel Administration, 19 Church Street, Berea, Ohio 44017.**

Seniority Clause. A number of controversial issues are often covered by collective bargaining. One of these is the seniority clause. Unions often want to include such items as seniority clauses in contracts. These clauses state that benefits and promotions will be given according to the length of time workers have been with the company.

Union leaders want these clauses because they feel that seniority is a simple and fair way to decide promotions. In this way, workers are protected against such things as favoritism and discrimination. Management representatives are often against this way of deciding promotions. They feel that this may allow less-qualified workers to be promoted. So, seniority clauses are sometimes modified. Workers with seniority are promoted when they are at least as qualified as any other worker.

Seniority clauses clearly have both benefits and costs. Using seniority as a reason for promotion is simple and fair. It also tends to encourage loyalty to the company. But it could cause inefficiency. If seniority is the only reason used for promotion, less-qualified workers may be promoted.

Union-Security Clause. Perhaps the most controversial issue covered by collective bargaining is that of union security. As you will recall, the Wagner Act of 1935 set up the National Labor Relations Board. When a majority of workers in a company vote to form a union in an election set up by the board, they are allowed to unionize. The Wagner Act states that the union must represent all workers in the bargaining unit. Even workers who voted against the union and those that choose not to join must be represented.

Because of this, unions try to negotiate a union-security clause. This states that management may hire whom they want. But all workers may be required to join the union after they have worked for a period of time. This period of time is usually 30 days. This kind of arrangement is known as a *union shop*. *Closed-shop* arrangements—where workers must be union members before they can be hired—were outlawed by the Taft-Hartley Act of 1947. A number of agreements include *agency-shop* clauses. These clauses state that workers do not have to join the union. However, they have to pay union dues to cover the cost of the services provided by the union.

Right-to-Work Laws. Federal legislation allows individual states to outlaw union-security clauses if they so wish. Twenty states, mostly in the South, now have *right-to-work laws*. These laws make union-security clauses illegal.

People who defend the right-to-work laws state that workers should not have to join unions to keep their jobs. These people also state that union-security clauses increase the economic and political power of the unions.

Those people who are against right-to-work laws state that union-security clauses may be needed because many workers get a "free ride." Union leaders work hard to settle collective-bargaining agreements. But these agreements also benefit workers who are not union members. Some people view right-to-work laws as a restriction of freedom. These people say that even if both union and management want to include a union-security clause, they are not free to do so. And other opponents of right-to-work laws say that in states that have these laws, government plays too great a part in decision making. In states without these laws, decisions, for the most part, are left to the private sector.

The discussion of right-to-work laws against union-security clauses raises strong feelings. There is some truth on both sides of the argument. Because of this, the issue is likely to remain a controversy for a long time.

Collective Bargaining—Impact. It has been said that "where political democracy exists, industrial democracy will be inevitable." In other words, if people are allowed some voice in how their country is run, they will want to be involved in what affects them most directly—their jobs. In the United States, industrial democracy is offered through collective bargaining. Other free countries depend more on labor-based political parties and the law. Labor unions and collective bargaining, as we in the United States know them, do not exist in communist countries like the Soviet Union. There are unions in the Soviet Union. But they carry out the dictates of the Communist party. They do not represent workers.

Our system of collective bargaining in the United States generally works fairly well. But sometimes we run into problems. Through the no-strike clause, many of the problems connected with strikes have been eliminated. However, when unions and management are working out a new contract, American workers are free to withdraw the labor. Today, there are about 200,000 collective-bargaining contracts in effect in the United States. About 50,000 of these are renegotiated in any one year. We usually have between 4,000 and 5,000 strikes a year. This means that more than 90 percent of all contracts are renegotiated without any kind of work stoppage. In fact, American industry loses more time through coffee breaks than through strikes.

Bruno Torres/UPI

Many people are against giving the right to strike to public employees, as this could endanger the public safety.

Even so, strikes mean a loss of income for some people and inconvenience for others. And some strikes can be a major threat to the economic stability of the country. But it should be remembered that strikes play a part in industrial democracy. And some workers have made major gains by withdrawing their labor. However, through collective bargaining, every effort should be made to lessen the number and impact of strikes.

Many Americans view collective bargaining as having something to do with setting wages. But it should be remembered that market forces will set the range of pay levels. And collective bargaining should be viewed more broadly than in terms of its direct economic effects. When free enterprise is considered, perhaps the most important impact of collective bargaining is on who makes the decisions. With collective bargaining, many people share the economic decision-making power. This might not be the case if industrial-relations issues were directly handled by the government.

Section Checkups

1. *What is collective bargaining?*
2. *How do the union shop and the agency shop differ?*
3. *Why do union leaders oppose right-to-work laws?*

Chapter Summary

Labor is one of the factors of production. The labor force is the group available to provide this factor. The American labor force has undergone many changes in the last 200 years. Members of the labor force receive wages for their work. The levels of these wages are influenced by the forces of supply and demand.

American workers have formed unions since the late 1700's. During the late 1800's, the AFL, a national federation of craft unions, was formed. The AFL dominated the American labor movement for many years. In the 1930's, a split developed in the leadership of the AFL. This resulted in the formation of the CIO, a federation of industrial unions. In the 1950's, with opposition to organized labor growing, the AFL merged with the CIO to form the AFL-CIO. Labor unions continue to play a part in the American economy today.

Collective bargaining is the process by which union and management representatives settle contracts. Because of the image presented by television and newspapers, many people think that collective bargaining deals only with wages. In fact, it settles many important issues. The use of no-strike clauses and grievance procedures promotes industrial stability and provides protection for workers. In terms of the free enterprise system, collective bargaining is very important as it involves many people in economic decision-making.

Reviewing the Chapter

Identifying Terms

Explain or identify the following:

Labor force	Wagner Act
Money wages	Taft-Hartley Act
Real wages	George Meany
Craft unionism	No-strike clause
Industrial unionism	Closed shop
Blacklist	Union shop
Boycott	Agency shop

Analyzing Information

1. How might the labor force differ from country to country?

2. What forces influence decisions regarding wage levels?

3. In what ways did the National Labor Relations Act of 1935 benefit the American labor movement?

4. In what ways are the goals of the present-day AFL–CIO similar to those set down by Samuel Gompers?

5. What are the benefits and the costs of using seniority as a reason for promotion?

6. What arguments against union-security clauses are advanced by supporters of right-to-work laws?

Analyzing Visual Material

1. Look closely at the illustration on page 173. What is shown in the illustration? Why do you think troops are being used? In your opinion, should striking workers have the right to picket?

2. Carefully study the picture on page 175. What type of industrial action is being taken by the workers in the picture? Why do workers use this kind of industrial action? How does this type of industrial action differ from that shown in the illustration on page 173? What other forms of industrial action might be used by workers to air their grievances?

Research and Projects

1. Two speakers could be chosen from the class. One speaker could make a presentation showing why workers should join unions. The other speaker could make a presentation showing why workers should not join unions. After the presentations have been made, each member of the class could write a report detailing the arguments put forward by each speaker.

2. Using newspapers and current-affairs magazines, find out as much as you can on strikes involving civil servants—firefighters, police, teachers, and so on. With this information, write a report for presentation to the class on whether you think civil servants should have the right to strike.

3. Draw two cartoons concerning the Taft-Hartley Act. One should show the view of the unions; the other should show the view of management.

Camerique

Chapter 11 Money and the American Banking System

SECTIONS 1 Money and Its Functions
2 The American Banking System
3 The Federal Reserve System

In primitive societies, trade was carried out by exchanging one item for another. Corn, for example, could be exchanged for fish, furs, or tools. But as societies grew more complex, a medium of exchange—money—became necessary. The nickels, dimes, quarters, and dollar bills with which we are familiar are very different from many of the things that have served as money in the past. And our system of central banking differs greatly from the banks of the Middle Ages. Money and our banking system play an important part in our everyday life. Money and banks also perform an important function in our economy.

Section 1
Money and Its Functions

Money is an important part of economic life in the United States. But people have not always used money to buy goods and services. In the past, goods and services were exchanged through barter. Today, money serves as a medium of exchange, a standard of value, and a storehouse of value. To perform these functions, money must have certain physical and economic characteristics.

In the past, many different things were used as money. In the United States today, the money supply is made up of coins, paper currency, and checking accounts. As you read this section, ask yourself the following questions: *How does the barter system operate? What functions does money perform? What physical and economic characteristics should money possess? How do money and near-money differ?*

The Barter System. Nearly every day, there are stories in the newspapers about companies making million-dollar profits. At other times, there are stories about workers getting pay raises. And advertisements in the newspapers and on television claim that money can be saved by buying a certain product or by shopping at a certain store. Money is an important part of most people's lives.

Money is anything that people will accept in payment for goods and services. In the past, many different things have been used for money. The history of money can be traced back about 3,000 years. To the best of our knowledge, money was not used before that time. Even today, some primitive societies do not use money.

Without money, goods and services are exchanged through *barter.* Under the barter system, goods and services are exchanged for other goods and services. If you had a pig to sell and you wanted corn, you would exchange the pig for the corn.

In a society, barter will work as long as the economy is fairly simple. As the economy becomes more complex, problems arise. If there are only two kinds of goods to exchange, calculating their worth is easy. For example, if only pigs and corn were available to exchange, ten pigs could be worth one ton of corn. However, as the kinds of goods increase, barter becomes difficult. How many fish would be needed to buy a pig? Or how many pairs of shoes would be needed to buy a ton of corn?

Another problem with barter is that there has to be a *coincidence of wants.* That is, a person with fish to sell who wants to buy shoes must find a person with shoes to sell who wants to buy fish. So, business transactions might become rather awkward.

As a society becomes more complex, people begin to specialize in certain activities. People are no longer able to provide for all their own needs themselves. It soon becomes clear that the barter system no

Some things that have been used as money

Animals	Food	Metals	Other Items
Cattle	Corn	Brass	Cowrie shells
Chickens	Fish	Copper	Paper
Goats	Rice	Gold	Stone
Horses	Salt	Iron	Tobacco
Pigs	Spices	Lead	Wampum
Sheep	Tea	Silver	Whale teeth

Throughout history, many different things have served as money. The coins and paper currency that are widely used today are fairly recent innovations. Above is a chart showing a few of the many things that have been used as money.

longer works. A *medium of exchange* becomes necessary.

Money as a Medium of Exchange. The most important function of money is that it serves as a medium of exchange. With money, the problem of the person who has fish to sell and wants to buy shoes is solved. That person can sell the fish for money. The money can then be used to buy shoes. The money will also be accepted for buying corn, gloves, pigs, or anything else.

As a result, money is sometimes called *generalized purchasing power*. This term means that the use of money allows freedom of choice. When a person exchanges goods or services for money, that money can be used to buy many things. And these things need not be bought at the place where the original exchange was made. Goods and services can be bought from the place offering the best bargain.

Money as a Standard of Value. Another function of money is that it serves as a standard of value. The monetary unit—the dollar, the franc, the mark, and so on—of a country serves as a unit in which the value of all goods and services can be measured and expressed. In this way, the value of a good or a service can be shown as a price. For example, the value of an automobile might be $9,000, the value of a pair of shoes might be $50, and the value of a paperback book might be $3.

Money also provides a standard by which the values of different goods and services can be compared. A record album that sells for $7.50 is equal in value to 10 hamburgers that sell for $0.75 each. All goods and services can be measured by the yardstick of money.

Money as a Storehouse of Value. A third function of money is that it serves as a storehouse of value. This means that people can save their money, or generalized purchasing power, for future use. They know that it will be accepted at any time in exchange for goods and services.

However, money is not always an efficient storehouse of value. In times of rising prices, the value or purchasing power of money falls. But money is not the only available storehouse of value. Anything of value can be used. For example, stocks and bonds, works of art, houses, and land can all be used as storehouses of value. In some cases, these items may be more efficient storehouses of value than is money. Stocks and bonds may provide dividends and interest. Works of art may increase in value. And land might be used to provide income.

Nevertheless, many people prefer to use money as their storehouse of value. One major reason is that money is readily available to pay bills and to buy food. Stocks and bonds or works of art are not normally accepted as payment for grocery bills. And turning them into money quickly may result in a loss of value.

Physical Characteristics of Money. To perform its various functions, money should have certain physical characteristics. First, money should be durable and not likely to deteriorate when used. Second, money should also be portable. That is, it should be small, light in weight, and easy to carry. Third, money should be divisible. In other words, it should be possible to make change.

Perhaps the most important physical characteristic of money is that it should be easy to recognize as money by all those who use it. Money also should have distinctive markings to make forgery difficult.

At this point it should be noted that physical characteristics alone do not make money important. Money must also have economic characteristics.

Economic Characteristics of Money. The most important economic characteristic of money is its acceptance. Money must be accepted *as money* by all those who use it. For example, when you provide your labor as a baby-sitter or a gardener, you probably accept money in return. This is because you are confident that other people will, in turn, accept it in exchange for goods and services.

Many people are willing to accept paper money because it is backed by law. If you look closely at a dollar bill, you will see the words "This note is legal tender for all debts, public and private." People are willing to accept paper money, such as dollar bills, because the government has stated that it is money. However, it should be noted that the government has not declared checks to be legal tender. But most people are willing to accept them in exchange for goods and services. They are reasonably sure that checks can be exchanged for currency.

As with other economic goods or services, money must be scarce to have any value. Like other commodities, money is subject to the forces of supply and demand. When the supply of money increases more rapidly than does the demand, the value or purchasing power of the money falls. If the purchasing power continues to fall, fewer and fewer people will be willing to accept the money. Eventually, the money may become worthless.

Money supply in the United States, January 1980 *

	Billions of Dollars	Percent of Total
Currency	107.4	28
Checking Accounts	272.9	72

Source: Federal Reserve Statistical Release.

Although the amount of money in circulation in the United States changes from month to month, the balance between currency and checking accounts usually remains the same.

What Is Money? As you read earlier, money is anything that people will accept in exchange for goods and services. In the past, many things were used for money. (See chart on page 186.) But what do we in the United States use for money today?

1 The supply of money in the United States is made up of *currency*—coins and paper money—and *demand deposits*—checking accounts—in banks. Credit cards, although accepted when buying goods and services, are not regarded as part of the money supply. This is because debts are incurred when credit cards are used. Money is required to pay these debts.

Coins are the smallest part of our money supply. They make up about 2 percent of the total money supply. Paper money makes up about 20 percent of the total supply. By far the largest part of our money supply is in checking accounts. These accounts make up more than 70 percent of the American money supply. (See chart on this page.) In fact, more than 90 percent of all payments in the United States are made by transfers from checking accounts.

Savings accounts at financial institutions such as commercial banks, savings and loan associations, and credit unions are not considered to be part of the money supply. They are called *near-money*. Gov- 2
ernment bonds held by families and businesses are also regarded as near-money. Near-moneys can easily be changed to currency or transferred to checking accounts. However, they are not thought to be part of the money supply since normally they are not used as a means of exchange. For example, grocery bills are not commonly paid with government bonds.

Checking accounts and near-money both play an important part in our economy. To better understand this, you will need to know something about financial institutions in the United States. This subject will be covered in the next section.

Section Checkups

1. *What is the barter system?*
2. *How does money serve as a standard of value?*
3. *Why is near-money not considered part of the money supply?*

*1. Time deposits on which checks may be written are now part of the money supply.

2. Money-market accounts are considered to be near-money.

Section 2
The American Banking System

Banking has a long history. The first bankers were money changers and goldsmiths who stored other people's valuables in strongboxes. In time, the receipts they issued for the valuables were used as money.

Banking in the United States dates from early colonial times. But our current national banking system was not established until the early 1900's, when the Federal Reserve System was set up.

There are a number of important financial institutions in the United States. They all provide useful services. As you read this section, ask yourself the following questions: *How did banking begin? What kinds of financial institutions are there in the United States? What services are offered by banks? What are the assets and liabilities of banks?*

The Beginning of Banking. The history of banking goes back to early civilizations. The early bankers were money changers and goldsmiths. These people had safe and secure strongboxes. In time, merchants began to leave their money and other valuables in these strongboxes.

Banking as we know it today developed in Italy during the Middle Ages. Then, as in earlier times, goldsmiths stored the money and other valuables of merchants. These goldsmiths gave each merchant a receipt for the money or property deposited. The goldsmiths promised to return the money or property *on demand*—whenever the receipt was presented. In time, these receipts began to be accepted by people as payment for goods and services. In other words, the receipts were used as money.

As this practice spread, the goldsmiths soon found that not all the merchants came to withdraw their deposits at the same time. The goldsmiths found that they only needed to keep a small part of the deposits on hand to cover withdrawals. The remaining money could be loaned out. The goldsmiths were eager to do this, as interest could be earned on the loans that were made. This process became known as the *fractional reserve banking system.*

Banking in the United States. During colonial times, efforts were made to set up banks. But, due to bad management and unstable business conditions, many of these banks failed. After independence, a number of successful banks were opened, such as the Bank of New York. Then, in 1791, Congress passed a bill founding America's first national bank—the Bank of the United States. Although it was a private bank, the federal government owned 20 percent of the bank's stock.

The Bank of the United States grew in power and came to dominate American banking. The owners of many small banks were opposed to the Bank of the United States. Their opposition prevented the bank's charter from being renewed in 1811.

Congress chartered the second Bank of the United States in 1816. But this bank lasted only until 1836. The United States went without a national banking system until the Federal Reserve System was set up in 1913. (See Section 3 of this chapter.)

During the early years of the 1800's, many *wildcat*—unreliable—banks were set up. These banks issued large amounts of paper money, or bank notes, far in excess of the deposits of gold and silver they held. Often, when these bank notes were presented to the banks, they could not be met. The banks did not have enough reserves of gold and silver to redeem the notes. As a result, the bank notes lost their value very rapidly. This contributed to a serious financial panic in 1837.

Congress tried to end banking abuses by passing national bank acts in the 1860's. Then, in 1913, the Federal Reserve System was established. Since that time, the American banking system has been closely regulated in order to control the money supply and to protect depositors.

There are about 14,000 banks in the United States today, and they play an important part in our economy. Therefore, it is important to know about the kinds of banks there are and how banks operate.

Financial Institutions in America. There are many different kinds of financial institutions in America. Probably the most familiar is the *commercial bank.* As you will recall, about three quarters of the American money supply is in the form of checking accounts. Checking accounts are
1 maintained by all commercial banks.

Savings and loan associations accept savings deposits on which they pay interest. *Mutual savings banks* also accept savings deposits on which they pay dividends. Commercial banks also offer savings accounts on which they pay interest. These savings institutions use the money on deposit to make loans. Savings institutions may ask depositors to give a few days notice if they intend to withdraw their deposits. Because of this, savings accounts are called *time deposits.*

One kind of financial institution that has grown in recent years is the *credit union.* Members of a credit union can deposit money with the credit union. In return they receive shares that earn interest. Members are often able to borrow from the credit union at low interest rates.

Services That Banks Provide. Banks offer a wide range of services to their customers. They offer a safe and secure place to store money and valuables that if kept at home might be lost or stolen. Valuables and important papers can be stored in safe-deposit boxes in banks.

Another service is that money can be deposited in banks. These deposits are protected by insurance. The Federal Deposit Insurance Corporation (FDIC) insures bank deposits. The Federal Savings and Loan Insurance Corporation (FSLIC) insures deposits in savings and loan associations. An added attraction of savings deposits is that they earn interest.

Banks also make loans. Without this service many businesses would not have been able to expand. And without mortgage loans, many Americans would not have been able to buy their own homes.

Most of these services are offered by all financial institutions. But only commercial banks may provide checking accounts. However, many financial institutions offer

1. All financial institutions may offer checkable time deposits—time deposits on which checks may be drawn.

(Text continues on page 192.)

Being a Wise Consumer
Writing a check

Demand deposits, or checking accounts, make up the largest part of our money supply. The use of checks to pay for goods and services has increased over the years. Today, more than 90 percent of business transactions in the United States are completed through checking-account transfers. The following information will help you in handling your own checking account:

1. Your checks should carry your name and correct address.
2. Each check has a number. This number helps you to keep accurate financial records.
3. Your bank identification number is also carried on your checks.
4. When writing a check, always put the correct date.
5. After the words "Pay to the order of," write the payee's name.
6. Write the amount of the check clearly in numerals after the dollar sign. On the line below, write the amount of the check in words. Finish the space with a line. This will prevent words being added that will increase the amount of the check.
7. Your signature should match the one put on file at your bank.
8. Each check should have two sets of code numbers. The first set is your bank's code number. The second set is your account number. These numbers help with the processing of checks.
9. Some checks have a space where you can write what the check is for. This information will help you to keep accurate records.
10. The name and address of your bank is usually on each check.

Your checkbook will have a place where you can keep a continuing record of your account balance. If you make a mistake when writing a check, destroy it and start a new one. And *never* lend your checkbook to other people.

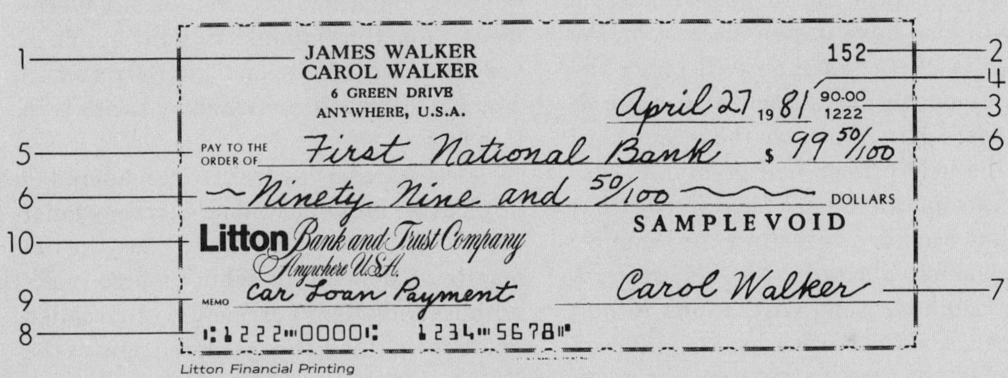

Litton Financial Printing

1 negotiable order of withdrawal (NOW) accounts. NOW accounts are savings accounts from which money can be withdrawn by check. They are checking accounts in everything but name.

How Banks Create Money. By making loans, commercial banks can actually create money. To understand this process, let us assume that you have been offered a very good part-time job. The job requires that you have your own car. You have seen exactly the model you want for $800. However, you do not have $800. So, you go to a bank and ask for a loan. Banks have loan officers who process loan applications. The loan officer will ask you a number of questions. First, the loan officer will want to be sure that the car is worth *more* than $800. A bank may loan you $800 if the car is worth $1,000 or more.

The loan officer will want to be certain that you will be able to repay the loan. You will be asked questions about your income, expenses, and debts. You may also be asked to provide references from your employer, your teacher, or a family friend. These references will give the loan officer some idea of your character, your work experience, and your school activities.

If the loan officer agrees to the loan, you will probably be asked to sign a promissory note—a promise to pay—for $800. You will also have to pay interest on the loan. It is likely that you will repay the loan in monthly installments over one or more years. After you sign the promissory note, the loan officer will give you a deposit receipt for $800. This shows that $800 has been deposited in your account.

Everyone is pleased with this arrangement. You have $800 with which to buy your car. And the bank is earning interest on $800 that it was not earning before. But this loan also has important implications for our economy. When the bank agreed to the loan and put $800 in your checking account, it was creating money. When you left the bank with your deposit receipt for $800, there was $800 more money in circulation than when you entered the bank.

The Bank's Balance Sheet. A closer look at banks will help you better understand this process of creating money. All banks have *assets* and *liabilities*. (See chart on page 193.) Assets are things that you own, and liabilities are things that you owe.

Among the assets of banks are buildings, furniture, parking lots, and so on. Loans are also assets of banks. Like other firms, banks must earn profits to stay in business. The main way banks earn income is by receiving interest on loans they make. Loans are considered assets because they represent claims on funds banks have loaned to businesses and individuals.

Another kind of asset held by banks is investments in the form of securities. Banks prefer investments that will earn some interest and can easily be converted to cash. Short-term bonds of the federal government are well suited to this purpose. Banks also invest in longer-term bonds of federal, state, and local government. Sometimes, banks buy the bonds of very secure corporations. But only a small part of the securities owned by banks is in this form.

Cash and reserves are also considered to be an asset of banks. Some currency must be kept on hand by banks to meet the demands of depositors who wish to make withdrawals. This currency is often called *vault cash*. It is not considered part of the

1. NOW accounts are now referred to as checkable time deposits and are considered part of the money supply.

Simplified balance sheet for all commercial banks in the U.S, 1979

Assets (in billions of dollars)		Liabilities (in billions of dollars)	
Securities	288	Demand Deposits	435
Loans	814	Time Deposits	674
Cash and Reserves	199	Capital Stock and Surplus	98
Other (buildings, furniture, etc.)	137	Other	231
Total	1438	Total	1438

Source: U.S. Federal Deposit Insurance Corporation.

The simplified balance sheet above is a statement of the financial situation of commercial banks in the United States in 1979.

money supply. Only the money in the hands of the general public is counted in the money supply. The amount of currency a bank may need to hold changes from day to day. On days when people cash their paychecks, there are heavy demands for cash. The Federal Reserve System requires all banks to keep some level of reserves on deposit with their Federal Reserve bank. This requirement is the key factor in our monetary system.

Deposits are the major liability of banks. Deposits represent the money that belongs to depositors. Checking accounts are called demand deposits because checks are payable on demand. If you write a check to someone and you have enough funds in your account, your bank is obligated to convert the check into cash when
1 it is presented. Banks normally do not pay interest on checking accounts. But banks offer savings accounts on which they do pay interest.

1. Some interest-bearing checking accounts are now available.

Capital stock and surplus are also considered to be liabilities of banks. Capital stock represents what has been invested in the banks by stockholders. Surplus is any profits kept by the banks and not paid to stockholders in the form of dividends.

Banks provide many useful services. The most important service offered by banks is the making of loans. In making loans, banks create money. How the creation of money is regulated is the subject of the next section of this chapter.

Section Checkups

1. *What services do banks provide?*
2. *How do banks create money?*
3. *Why are deposits considered to be a liability of banks?*

Section 3
The Federal Reserve System

The Federal Reserve Act of 1913 set up the Federal Reserve System. This is our country's central banking institution. Federal Reserve banks do business with financial institutions, not with the general public.

The Federal Reserve System offers these financial institutions a number of important services. It also serves as banker for the federal government. But its most important function is to control the supply of money in the economy. As you read this section, ask yourself the following questions: *How is the Federal Reserve System organized? How is a check cleared through the Federal Reserve System? What methods are used by the Federal Reserve System to control the money supply?*

Origins and Purpose. The history of banking in the United States has been far from smooth. As you read earlier in this chapter, two attempts to set up a central banking system failed. And a number of financial panics began with bank failures. People in government saw that if the United States wanted economic stability, there would have to be a stable banking system.

In 1913, Congress passed the Federal Reserve Act. This act set up the Federal Reserve System, the central banking institution of the United States. The Federal Reserve System is often called the bankers' bank, because it does business with the banks rather than with the general public.

An important function of the Federal Reserve banks is to hold reserves of cash for commercial banks. These reserves play a key role in setting limits on how much money can be created through the banking

Federal Reserve Bank of Chicago

The Federal Reserve Bank of Chicago serves the needs of District 7 of the Federal Reserve System. More than 2,500 financial institutions in the states of Illinois, Indiana, Iowa, Michigan, and Wisconsin use the services of this Federal Reserve bank.

system. Also, if banks are hit with a large number of withdrawals, they can borrow from the Federal Reserve banks. By holding reserves for banks, the Federal Reserve banks could prevent the failure of any bank.

The Federal Reserve System is also charged with providing currency for circulation. If you look at a dollar bill, you will notice the words "Federal Reserve Note." The Federal Reserve System has to regulate the supply of currency in the economy. And it also must take steps to make sure that our country's money retains its value.

Organization. The Federal Reserve System is run by a 7-member Board of Governors. Members of the Board of Governors are appointed by the President, and they serve one 14-year term. Appointments are set up so that there is a vacancy to be filled every 2 years. Although the Board of Governors was originally established to run the Federal Reserve banks, it now is involved in the whole banking system of our country.

The Federal Reserve System has 12 district banks in various regions throughout the United States. (See map on this page.) Most of these district banks have branch banks to help them carry out their work. All *national banks* must belong to the Federal Reserve System. National banks are those chartered by the federal government. Most banks are chartered by their state. These state banks do not have to belong to the Federal Reserve System, but they may do so if they wish. About 6,000 of our country's 14,000 banks are members of the Federal Reserve System. These member banks do most of our country's banking business. They hold about 85 percent of all demand deposits.

The Federal Reserve System is divided into 12 separate districts. Each district has its own Federal Reserve district bank.

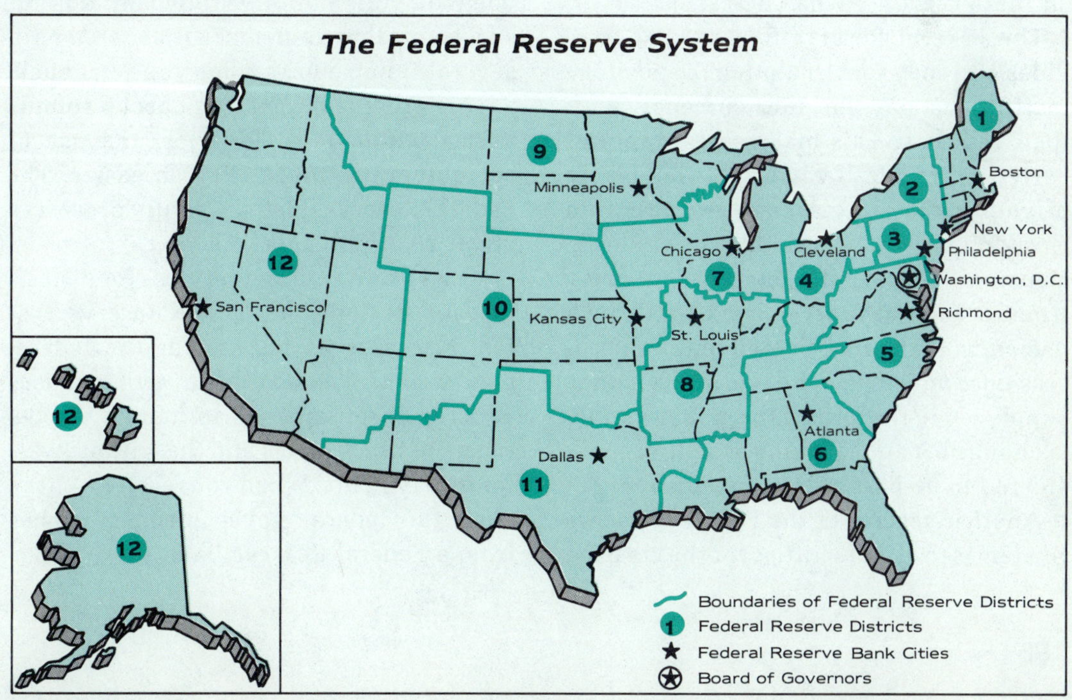

To become a member, a commercial bank must buy stock in its Federal Reserve district bank. Thus, the member banks own their district bank. But the goal of the Federal Reserve System is not to earn profits for its owners. Rather it is to serve the needs of our monetary system.

Services Offered. Until recently, the services offered by the Federal Reserve System were available, free of charge, to only member banks. However, the Depository Institutions Deregulation and Monetary Control Act of 1980 ended this practice. Now, Federal Reserve System services are available to all *depository institutions*—member and nonmember commercial banks, savings banks, savings and loan associations, and credit unions—at competitive prices.

The Federal Reserve System offers many services. One service is that depository institutions may keep reserves on deposit with their Federal Reserve district bank. These deposits are like checking accounts. Depository institutions may draw on these accounts when necessary.

The Federal Reserve System also provides currency for circulation. Depository institutions pay for this currency with their reserves. This makes the supply of currency flexible. If you want to hold more of your money in currency and less in a checking account, you simply cash a check. Your commercial bank gets more currency from its Federal Reserve bank to fill such demands. It should be noted that this process does not change the size of the money supply. Only the form of the money supply is changed. Your checking account is considered to be part of the money supply.

Another service of the Federal Reserve System is to offer facilities for the clearing of checks. Today, most business transactions in America are handled through checking accounts. Very efficient procedures have been developed that make this possible. (See diagram on page 197.)

Let us assume that you live in New Orleans and have a checking account with Whitney National Bank. While on a visit to New York, you write a check for $25 to a Mr. George Jones. He deposits your check in his checking account with Chase Manhattan Bank. Your check is then transferred by the Chase Manhattan Bank to the Federal Reserve Bank of New York. The Chase Manhattan Bank will receive a $25 credit in its reserve account. Your check will then be transferred to the Federal Reserve Bank of Atlanta, or possibly to its branch bank in New Orleans. From there, your check will be sent to the Whitney National Bank, and $25 will be removed from its reserve account with the Federal Reserve Bank of Atlanta. The Whitney National Bank will remove $25 from your checking account and return your check to you with your monthly statement. It is not surprising that your check is covered with several stamp marks when you get it back!

This process of clearing checks sounds very complicated. However, the use of computers has made it much easier. The Federal Reserve System usually processes about 20 billion checks a year.

As well as providing services for depository institutions, the Federal Reserve System also acts as banker for the federal government. The federal government uses Federal Reserve banks to handle the deposits of its revenues and the withdrawals for its payments. When you receive a check from the federal government, it comes from a Federal Reserve bank.

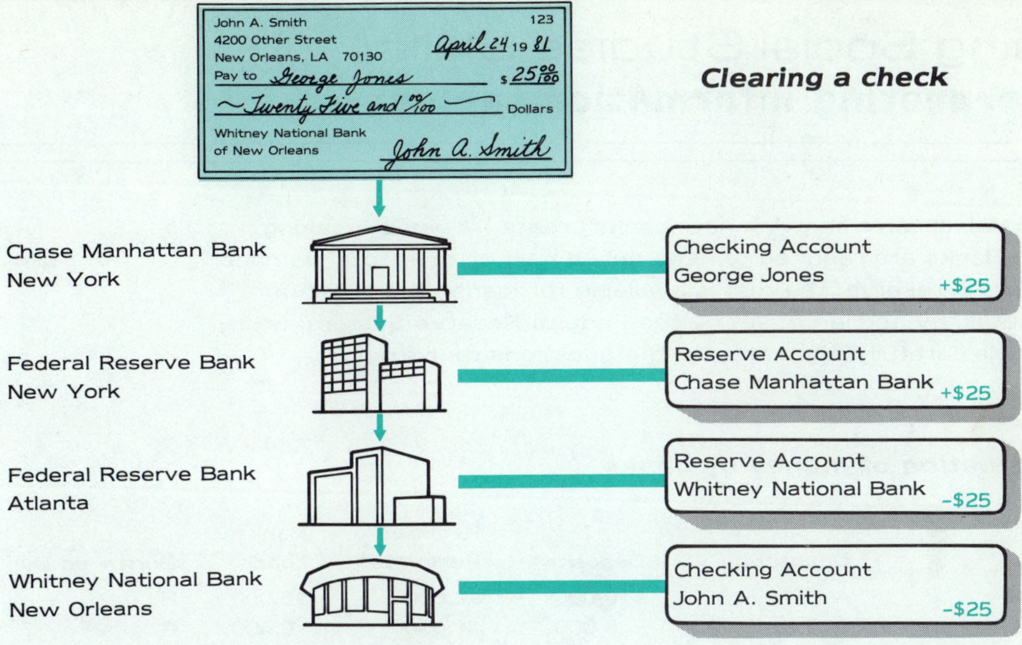

The diagram above illustrates how the Federal Reserve System clears a check. On average, the Federal Reserve System clears about 20 billion checks each year.

Controlling the Money Supply. The major function of the Federal Reserve System is the control of the money supply. As you recall, banks can actually create money by making loans. But banks cannot create limitless amounts of money. This creation of money is regulated by the Federal Reserve System. This can be done by controlling the amount of reserves in the banking system.

All depository institutions are required to keep reserves with the Federal Reserve System equal to some part of their deposits. By raising or lowering the amount to be kept in reserves, the Federal Reserve System can regulate the ability of the banks to create money.

The Federal Reserve System can also control the supply of money by buying and selling government securities. By buying government securities, more money can be put into circulation. Money can be taken out of circulation by selling government securities. The Federal Reserve Bank of New York acts as the Federal Reserve System's agent in all such transactions.

Another way in which the Federal Reserve System can control the money supply concerns interest rates. One service offered by the Federal Reserve System is the making of loans. By changing the interest rate on these loans—the discount rate—the Federal Reserve System can change the money supply. If the interest rate is raised, depository institutions will have to pay more to borrow from the Federal Reserve System. This will tend to make the depository institutions raise the

(Text continues on page 199.)

Using Social Studies Skills

Interpreting information tables

Below is a table showing how banks create money by making loans. Banks are required to keep only a part of their total demand deposits in reserve; the rest is available for loans. The reserve amount is, by and large, set by the Federal Reserve System. Study the table carefully; then answer the questions that follow.

The creation of money by banks

	Deposited By	Deposits*	Required Reserves*	Bank Loans*	Borrowed By
Bank 1	A	$10,000	$2,000	$8,000	B
Bank 2	B	8,000	1,600	6,400	C
Bank 3	C	6,400	1,280	5,120	D
Bank 4	D	5,120	1,024	4,096	E
Bank 5	E	4,096	819	3,277	F
Bank 6	F	3,277	655	2,622	G
Bank 7	G	2,622	524	2,098	H
Bank 8	H	2,098	420	1,678	I
Bank 9	I	1,678	336	1,342	J
Bank 10	J	1,342	268	1,074	K
Bank 20	T	145	29	116	U
Transactions by All Other Banks		5,222	1,045	4,177	
Total		50,000	10,000	40,000	

*Figures rounded to nearest $1.00

1. What was the amount of the initial deposit?
2. What was the total additional money created after all banking transactions?
3. What percentage of demand deposits was kept in reserve?
4. If the reserve requirement is set at 10 percent of demand deposits, what amount of A's deposit would be kept in reserve?
5. With a reserve requirement of 10 percent, how much money would be available to loan to B?
6. Assuming that the reserve requirement is set at 10 percent, how much money would be created by the time a loan was made to F?

By increasing the pressure on reserves, the Federal Reserve System can reduce the money supply. By lessening the pressure on reserves, the Federal Reserve System can increase the money supply.

interest rate on the loans they make. Households and businesses are normally less likely to borrow at high interest rates. So this will limit the amount of money in circulation.

Monetary Policy. All the things that the Federal Reserve System does to make it harder or easier for banks to create money are called *monetary policy*. By raising interest rates and increasing the reserve requirement, the Federal Reserve System "tightens" the pressure on the banks. (See illustration on this page.) This is called a *tight* monetary policy. With a tight monetary policy less money is in circulation, so less is available to be spent or invested. The Federal Reserve System eases the pressure on banks by lowering interest rates and the reserve requirement. This is called an *easy* monetay policy. Under this policy more money is in circulation and is available to be spent or invested.

It is not necessary for you to understand the minute details of how monetary policy works. But you should understand that the Federal Reserve System does have ways to control the money supply. It can increase the money supply and lower interest rates if it wants households and businesses to spend more. And the Federal Reserve System can slow down the spending in the economy by limiting the money supply and raising interest rates.

The Federal Reserve and monetary policy

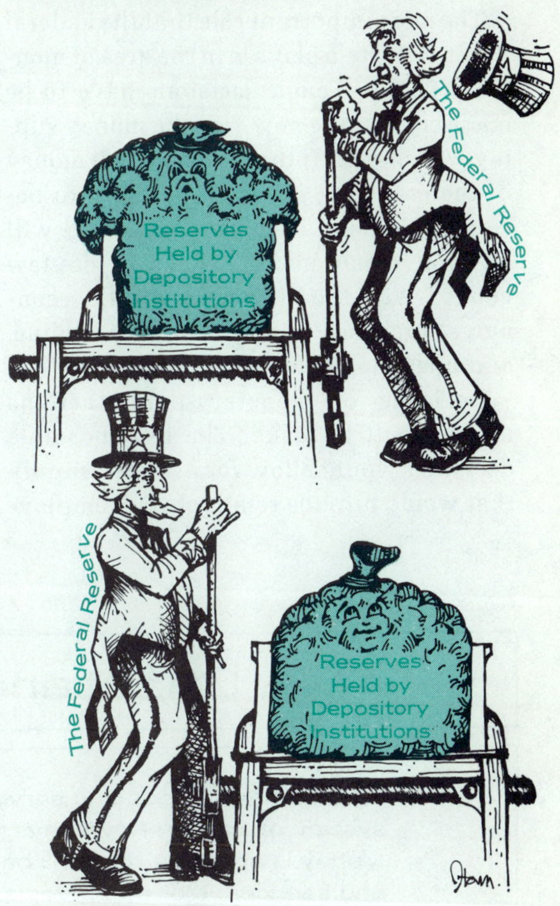

The Importance of the Federal Reserve System. Humorist Will Rogers once said, "There have been three great discoveries in the history of man: fire, the wheel, and central banking." The Federal Reserve System may not be *that* important. But it does allow for a flexible money supply. People are able to choose whether to hold their money in the form of currency or checking accounts. And the Federal Reserve System has helped to develop a banking system in which the American people have confidence.

The most important role that the Federal Reserve System plays is in the area of monetary policy. Tough decisions have to be made concerning how fast the money supply will change. If there is too much money in the economy, inflation is likely to become a problem. This is because there will be "too much money chasing too few goods." With too little money in the economy, purchases of products may decline, and unemployment is likely to go up.

Decisions on monetary-policy actions are difficult to make. The best possible decisions would allow for a money supply that would provide relatively full employment with relative price stability. This will be covered in greater detail in Chapters 12 and 13.

Section Checkups

1. *What services are offered by the Federal Reserve System?*
2. *How does the Federal Reserve System control the supply of money in the economy?*
3. *Why are the actions of raising the interest rate and increasing the reserve requirement called a tight monetary policy?*

Chapter Summary

In the past, goods and services were exchanged through a system of barter. Nowadays, most countries use money. Money is anything that will be accepted in payment for goods and services. Money serves as a medium of exchange, a standard of value, and a storehouse of value. In the United States, currency and checking accounts are used as money.

Banking began in early times, when money changers and goldsmiths stored other people's valuables in their strongboxes. In America, banking has played a part in the economy since colonial times. In the United States during the last 200 years, the number of financial institutions, and the services they offer, have grown. Today, the most important function of banks is to create money by making loans.

The creation of money is regulated by the Federal Reserve System. The Federal Reserve System provides a number of important services to depository institutions. It also acts as the banker for the federal government. But, more importantly, the Federal Reserve System decides upon monetary policy—all the things it does to regulate the money supply.

Reviewing the Chapter

Identifying Terms

Explain or identify the following:

Barter	Time deposit
Money	FDIC
Currency	National bank
Demand deposit	Discount rate
Near-money	Monetary policy

Analyzing Information

1. How are goods and services bought and sold in societies that do not use money?

2. What are the differences between money and near-money?

3. How did the practice of banking begin?

4. What service does a commercial bank offer that other financial institutions do not?

5. What actions can the Federal Reserve System take to make it easier for banks to create money?

Analyzing Visual Material

1. Study the map on page 195 carefully. How many Federal Reserve districts are there? In which city is the Federal Reserve Bank of District 10? Which is your Federal Reserve district? In which city is your Federal Reserve district bank?

2. Carefully study the illustration on page 199. Which drawing represents a tight monetary policy? Which drawing represents an easy monetary policy? What actions can the Federal Reserve System take to implement a tight monetary policy?

Research and Projects

1. Write a report on how United States currency—both coin and paper—is made. Your report should include such things as where currency is made, what materials are used, what methods are used to prevent counterfeiting, and what happens to worn-out currency. Information can be found in encyclopedias, or it can be obtained from the U.S. Department of the Treasury.

2. On page 186 you will find a chart listing some of the many things that have been used as money over the years. Using this as a guide, make an illustrated chart of all the things you can find that have been used as money. Finished charts can be displayed on the bulletin board.

3. Obtain as much information as you can on the Depository Institutions Deregulation and Monetary Control Act of 1980. Such information can be found in business and finance journals, or it can be obtained by writing to your Federal Reserve district bank. Using this information, interview one or more local bank managers to find out how they feel the act will affect their banking operations.

Keith Jewell

Chapter 12 Government and the Economy

SECTIONS
1 The Role of Government
2 Government and Economic Stability
3 The Impact of Government

In all modern industrial economies, government performs certain economic functions. But what part does our government play in the American economy? The very term we use to describe our economic system—free enterprise—suggests that the role of government is limited. However, all levels of government—federal, state, and local—in the United States do perform important economic functions. Government is both a producer and a consumer of goods and services. Government also regulates some of the economic activities of our society. And government has the power to tax and to spend.

Section 1
The Role of Government

Throughout our country's history, government has played a part in the economy. Today, government performs a number of important functions. It takes steps to maintain competitive markets. It provides public goods and services. And it works to maintain economic stability. To pay for all its functions, government collects taxes. As you read this section, ask yourself the following questions: *What steps does government take to support the basic institutions of the economy? What actions does government take to ensure economic stability? What is the difference between a progressive tax and a regressive tax?*

What Part Should Government Play? Since the early days of our country, the federal government has helped some American businesses by imposing tariffs on imported goods. In the mid-nineteenth century, state and federal governments made land grants to railroad companies to help establish a countrywide transportation system. And during times of economic crisis, such as the Great Depression, government has stepped in to restore economic stability.

Today, all levels of government—local, state, and federal—play some part in the economy. But how big a part should government play? The term used to describe our economic system, *free enterprise*, suggests that government's part should be limited. The exact functions that government should perform have long been a subject of discussion. And there are questions as to how well government fulfills those functions it does perform. Even so, most people in the United States would agree that government does have a part to play in our economy.

Maintaining the Market System. In the United States, government takes certain steps to support the basic institutions of our economy. These steps include such things as protecting private property and preserving freedom of choice and free enterprise. In this way, the market system is given a chance to work.

Government has established a legal and social framework within which business can take place. Certain laws protect buyers from business fraud. Government has set up a national system of weights and measures. Government also organizes national defense and ensures domestic security. And government issues currency and regulates the money supply.

All these things make it possible for markets to work. Within this framework, individuals and private businesses are allowed to own and use scarce resources as they see fit.

Maintaining Competition. To make sure that the market system will keep working efficiently, government takes steps to maintain competition. For the most part, this means stopping the devel-

Carnegie Library of Pittsburgh

Andrew Carnegie was one of the major business leaders of the late 1800's. By using a system of vertical organization—owning or controlling each step in production—Carnegie was able to dominate the American steel industry.

opment of monopoly power. One way government has done this is by passing antitrust laws. In some cases, such as public utilities, government directly regulates industry to limit monopoly power. (See Chapter 3.)

Competitive markets have a number of attractive features. Competition makes producers more efficient and responsive to the wants of consumers. Initiative and enterprise are encouraged and often rewarded with success. And with competition, many people take part in the economic decision-making process.

However, the *logic* of competition must be considered. People compete in order to win. When some people win, it might become impossible for other people to compete on an equal basis. For example, if a company is successful, it might begin to receive favorable treatment when buying raw materials. If other companies wish to enter the area of business, they may be less able to compete on an equal basis. This is because they may be unable to buy the raw materials at such favorable rates. Maintaining *effective* competitive markets is something that government must handle.

Antitrust Legislation. In the late nineteenth and early twentieth centuries, people in the United States found that when markets were left alone, they often became less competitive. During this time, monopolies grew in some industries, oligopolies in others. (See Chapter 9.) Output was restricted, and products were sold at higher prices. In time, economic power became concentrated in the hands of a few very rich business leaders. These "giants of industry" helped the United States become a great industrial country. But the successes of these leaders caused problems.

To deal with these problems, Congress passed the Sherman Antitrust Act in 1890. This act was later strengthened by the Clayton Antitrust Act. (See Chapter 9.) These measures, and other laws passed later, were meant to stop private business from becoming too large and powerful. However, most businesses are still allowed to expand. American antitrust laws have been designed to make sure competition remains the basic regulating force in the economy.

Providing Public Goods. Government offers certain goods and services directly to consumers. These goods and services include highways, schools, police and fire protection, and national defense. Such goods and services are called *public goods.*

There are reasons why these goods and services are not provided by private business. Some goods and services, such as national defense, are available to everyone. This is true whether or not people pay for them. No private firm could provide a system of national defense and be able to make a profit. There is no way that the firm could be sure of receiving payment from all those who benefit from the system.

In some cases, goods must be produced and consumed in such large amounts that private business could not hope to produce them and make a profit. An example of this is our country's highway system. Such goods are called *indivisible goods.*

Spillover Benefits and Costs. Sometimes government adjusts the amount of a good or service produced or consumed. This is because all of the benefits or costs connected with the use of the good or service are not reflected in the market. When one person buys and uses certain goods and services, people other than the buyer and the seller may be affected. For example, when a person buys some smallpox vaccine, that person receives some benefits. But other people also receive benefits. They are much less likely to be infected by that person. There are spillover benefits connected with the production and use of such goods as vaccines. But the market will show only the personal benefits received by consumers and producers. Therefore, the government subsidizes such goods to make sure that enough are produced.

There are also spillover costs connected with the production and use of some products. Water and air pollution caused by factories affects many people. This often includes people who do not use the goods produced by the factories. Many people, not only those who use the goods, will have to pay to clean up the pollution. Or they may have to drink polluted water and breathe polluted air. In a case such as this, government expects the owners of factories to recognize all the costs of producing their goods. Sometimes government imposes extra taxes on factories that pollute. At other times, government requires factories to clean up the pollution they cause.

Maintaining Economic Stability. Another function of government is to take steps to ensure the stability of our economy. By and large, the level of business activity in an economy increases when households, businesses, and government agencies spend more. When they spend less, the level of business activity declines and the level of unemployment rises. To stabilize the economy, government tries to achieve relatively full employment at a relatively stable price level.

Government uses *fiscal policies*—taxation and spending—and *monetary policies*—controlling the supply of money and credit—to achieve economic stability. If the level of business activity is low, the federal government might increase its spending, cut taxes, or increase the money supply. To fight inflation, government might cut its spending, increase taxes, or reduce the money supply. In a modern industrial society, achieving economic stability is a troublesome task. However, achieving economic stability is a task our government feels it must fulfill.

The National Debt. Maintaining economic stability is almost entirely the task of *federal* government. Only federal government can vary its budget to suit the needs of the whole economy. However, in trying to stimulate the economy, it may spend more money than it collects in taxes. To cover this difference between spending and taxes, government has to borrow. It does this by selling bonds and other securities. As you read in Chapter 9, a bond is a written promise to pay back the money borrowed with interest at a later date. The amount of money federal government owes is known as the *national debt*.

Our national debt originated shortly after the Revolutionary War, when the national government took over the war debts of the states. In fact, wars are the major cause of increases in the national debt. For example, the national debt increased by more than $150 billion in the 10 years of the Vietnam War. Other causes for increases in the national debt include social-welfare programs and public improvements, such as highways, bridges, and dams.

Characteristics of the National Debt. The national debt has certain special characteristics. First, the national debt is largely owned by the American people. (See table on this page.) Government has borrowed money by selling securities to various government agencies, banks, savings institutions, and individuals. To pay off this part of the debt would not make our country any richer or poorer.

Second, the national debt is made up of government securities that serve a useful

By late 1981, our country's national debt stood at more than 1,005 billion dollars. About one third of this total was owed to government agencies, and slightly more than one fourth was owed to banks and the Federal Reserve System.

* In 1983, the national debt stood at $1,382 billion. Estimates suggest that this will rise to $1,828 billion by 1985.

Ownership of the National Debt*

Government Agencies (all levels)	$293.2 billion
Banks and the Federal Reserve System	$239.8 billion
Other Corporations	$ 57.8 billion
Individuals	$141.0 billion
Other Investors (including foreign and international agencies)	$273.3 billion
Total (as of October 1981)	$1,005.1 billion

Source: U.S. Department of the Treasury.

(Text continues on page 208.)

Using Social Studies Skills
Interpreting graphs

Below are a line graph and a bar graph dealing with the national debt and the GNP in current dollars for the years 1940 to 1980. The line graph shows national debt and GNP totals. The bar graph shows the national debt as a percentage of GNP. Study the graphs carefully; then answer the questions that follow.

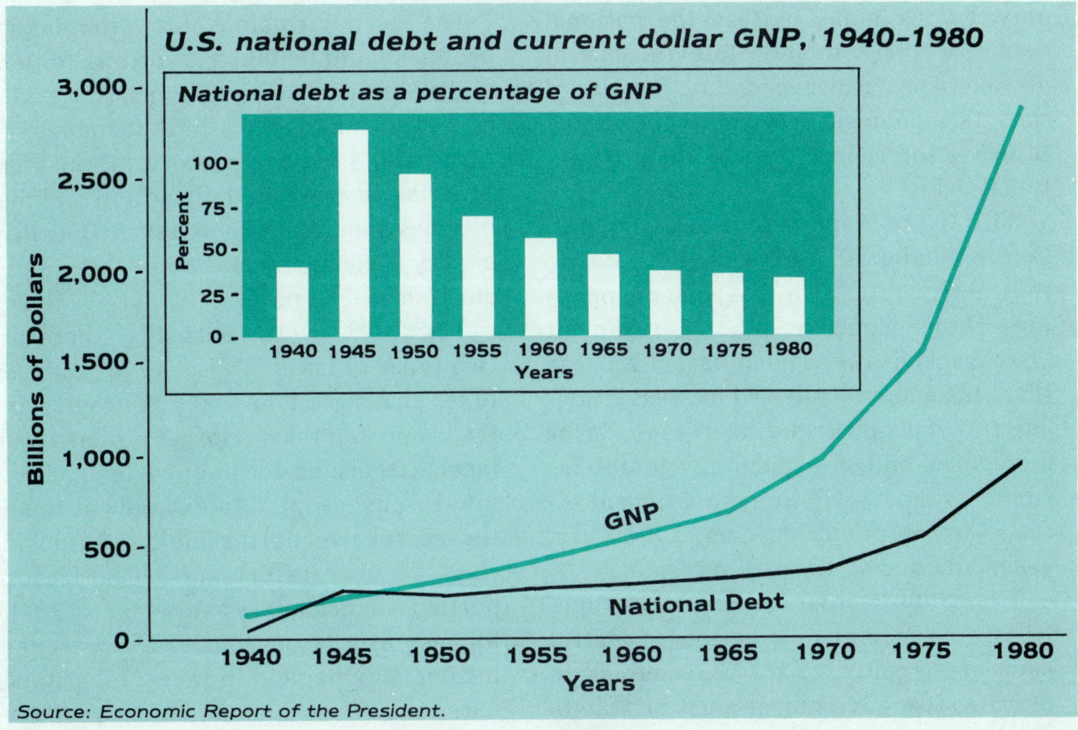

Source: Economic Report of the President.

1. In which year was the national debt greater than the GNP?
2. What historical incident could have caused the national debt to be greater than the GNP at this time?
3. Between which years was there the greatest increase in the GNP?
4. In which years did the national debt represent more than 50 percent of the GNP?
5. In your opinion, what trends do the national debt and the GNP appear to be following?

purpose for many people. When people buy government bonds, they are lending money to the government. However, they are also making a safe investment that pays them interest. Certain investors, such as banks, often have a need for a safe investment that can be turned into cash quickly. Government securities are such an investment.

Finally, it is true that the national debt has been growing over the years. But it has not grown as rapidly as the overall econ-
1 omy. For example, in 1946 the national debt was greater than the total incomes of all Americans. However, today the value of the total incomes of everyone in the United States is three times greater than the national debt.

2 With the national debt over $1,005 billion, a number of Americans have called for tighter controls on government spending. These people feel that government should spend only as much as, or even less than, the amount collected in taxes. However, other people argue that these calls for a *balanced budget*—spending equal to income—will severely limit government efforts to maintain economic stability, especially during times of recession.

Taxation. In order to carry out its functions, government must be able to control some of our country's scarce resources. In other words, government must be able to tax both households and businesses. All levels of government collect taxes. And households and businesses have very little choice in the matter of paying them. As Benjamin Franklin once said, "In this world nothing is certain but death and taxes."

There are two general principles of taxation. The first principle is that people should be taxed according to the benefits they receive from the government programs paid for by taxes. But it is hard to judge how much each person benefits from such programs as national defense or urban renewal. So, this principle of taxation is used only when it is easy to see who benefits from a government program. An example of this is the tax on gasoline. Revenue gained from this tax is usually used to build or maintain roads that are used by those people who buy gasoline.

The second principle of taxation is that people should be taxed according to their ability to pay. In simple terms, those with higher incomes can afford to pay more taxes and should pay more taxes. Most Americans agree that those with higher incomes should pay more taxes. But there is very little agreement about *how much* more should be paid.

Types of Taxes. Basically, there are two types of taxes. These are *progressive taxes* and *regressive taxes.* A progressive tax is one that takes a larger proportion of income from high-income people than from low-income people. An example of this is the federal personal income tax. As income rises, the tax rate increases, so larger proportions of income are paid as taxes. At the highest tax rates, as much as 50 percent of income may be paid in taxes. Inheritance taxes and excise taxes on luxury goods are other examples of progressive taxes.

A regressive tax is one that takes a smaller proportion of income from high-income people than from low-income people. The state sales taxes are examples of a regressive tax. Sales taxes are regressive because high-income people pay a smaller proportion of their income on goods and services subject to these taxes. Because of this, attempts have been made to make the

1. In 1983, total incomes were about two times greater than the national debt.

2. In 1983, the national debt stood at $1,382 billion.

sales taxes more progressive. A number of states do not collect sales taxes on food and medicine.

Income Redistribution. Even competitive markets may lead to inequalities in wealth and income. To limit these inequalities, government has tried to provide some means of income redistribution. Using tax revenues, government has developed certain welfare programs. Such programs provide people who are not able to work or who cannot find work with a limited income. Government programs in education, housing, and health care also help to remove income inequalities. Ability-to-pay taxes also help to limit inequalities in income.

Most Americans agree that taxation is necessary. But there is little agreement as to how heavily individuals and businesses should be taxed. And some people are against government's using taxation as a way to redistribute income. However, many people feel that income redistribution is necessary to make sure that economic power remains widespread.

Section Checkups

1. *What steps does government take to maintain competition?*
2. *Why are public goods not provided by private firms?*
3. *How do the two general principles of taxation differ?*

Section 2 Government and Economic Stability

Throughout our country's history, our economy has been growing. However, this growth has been marked by ups and downs in business activity. These ups and downs are known as business cycles. Although most business cycles differ greatly in length and severity, they do have some things in common.

Business cycles have important effects on our economy. Government often uses its fiscal and monetary policies to control these effects. As you read this section, ask yourself the following questions: *What are the four phases of business cycles? What are the causes of business cycles? What fiscal and monetary policies does our government use to try to control business cycles?*

Gross National Product. As you recall, one function of government is to take

The overall trend of GNP and the phases of a business cycle

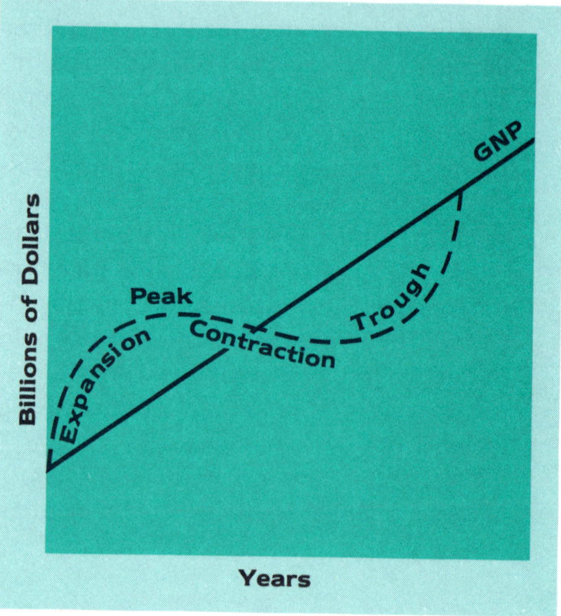

Business cycles have four phases—expansion, peak, contraction, and trough. Even though business cycles may occur, in a growing economy the overall upward trend of the GNP may continue.

steps to ensure a healthy and stable economy. But government needs to have some measure of economic activity to know if the economy is healthy. For most people, the best indicator of economic growth and stability is a country's total yearly output of goods and services. This output is called the *Gross National Product,* or *GNP.*

A country's GNP is the market value of all the final goods and services produced in that country during a given year. Only *final* goods are counted. For example, the production of tires, steel, upholstery, and so on that are used to make a car is not counted. Only the final good, the car, is counted in the GNP. The exact role of the GNP in measuring the economy will be looked at more closely in Chapter 13.

The overall trend of the GNP in the United States has been upward. In the last 50 years, our country's GNP has risen from [1] about \$100 billion to about \$3,000 billion. But this has not been a steady growth. It has been marked by periods of growth and decline.

Business Cycles. The ups and downs in economic activity are known as *business cycles.* The word *cycle* suggests that there is some uniform pattern to these ups and downs. But individual business cycles differ greatly in detail. However, most business cycles do have four phases.

The first phase of a business cycle is often called the *expansion phase.* (See graph on this page.) This phase occurs when business activity, or actual GNP, is greater than the overall trend of the GNP. The second phase comes when this growth in business activity reaches its *peak.* After this peak has been reached, the third phase, *contraction,* begins. During this phase, business activity is in decline. However, it may remain above the overall trend of the GNP for some time. When the decline in business activity reaches its lowest point, the fourth phase, the *trough,* occurs. If business activity is at a very low level during this phase, the economy is said to be in a *depression.* If the level is not quite so low, it is called a *recession.*

1. In 1983, the GNP stood at \$3,309.5 billion.

Business cycles are often different. Some are more severe than others. Some are longer than others. Certain business cycles may last as long as ten years. The reasons why business cycles happen also vary greatly.

External Causes of Business Cycles. A number of people believe that changes in business activity are a result of things *external* to—outside of—the economy. These people feel that such things as the weather, technological innovations, and population changes affect business activity.

In the past, the weather was often given as a cause of business cycles. Good weather led to an increase in agricultural output. This, in turn, led to greater demand for farm machinery. As a result, there was an upswing in business activity. Poor weather would have the opposite effect. This view of business cycles is not widely accepted today. Agriculture now plays a much smaller part in the economies of modern industrialized countries.

Technological innovations have also been given as a cause of business cycles. Entrepreneurs who are willing to invest in innovations are often repaid with increased profits. New products often increase a company's sales. And new methods of production often cut a company's costs. Greater profits bring more investment. An increase in business activity will follow. After the innovation becomes a familiar part of the industry, investment will decrease. And a falloff in business activity will follow unless other innovations are developed.

Some people state that population changes cause business cycles. An increase in population will lead to greater demand for goods and services. As a result, there will be increased business activity. A decrease in population will have the opposite effect.

Internal Causes of Business Cycles. Another view of business cycles states that they are the outcome of *internal* causes—things within the economy itself. Internal causes are such things as psychological factors, the flow of money and credit, and changes in total spending.

Some people feel that business cycles are caused by psychological factors. The optimistic outlook of certain business people might cause a change in business activity. These business people might sense an upturn in the economy. For this reason, they will increase investment and production. Other business people will follow this lead, and business activity will be further increased. Increased business activity will, in turn, increase employment and personal income. This will encourage greater consumer spending.

On the other hand, business people might sense a downward turn in the economy. A downward trend will cause them to limit investment and production. Other business people will follow. And workers, uncertain of the future of their jobs, will limit their spending. All this will lead to a decrease in business activity.

A number of people feel that business cycles are caused by changes in the supply of money and credit. As you recall, commercial banks are able to create money by making loans. An upward trend in the economy may be caused by banks making more loans. On the other hand, it is believed that banks may start a recession by limiting the number of loans they make.

Another internal cause of business cycles involves changes in total spending.

People may choose to save their money rather than spend it. This will cause a falloff in business activity. Too few goods and services will be bought. As a result, money will be taken out of circulation and will not be available for investment.

The Effects of Business Cycles. The effects of a business cycle depend upon which phase the cycle is in. In the first stage of expansion, there is greater demand for goods and services. Businesses increase output to meet this demand. To do this, businesses use more and more resources. More people are employed and earning wages and are therefore able to buy more goods and services. This, in turn, leads to an increase in business profits, as sales are increased.

However, at any point in time there are only so many resources available. If consumer spending continues to rise after all these resources are being used, then prices can only continue to go up. This excess spending causes *inflation*—a rise in prices that reduces the buying power of each dollar. Inflation will be studied more closely in Chapter 13.

The contraction stage of a business cycle usually begins with a falloff in sales. In response, businesses cut production. As production is reduced, unemployment rises. Even the incomes of those people still working fall. This means that they are able to buy fewer goods and services. Sales fall further, and the economy goes into a deeper recession.

Perhaps the worst outcome of the contraction of business activity is *cyclical unemployment.* As business activity declines, workers are laid off. They have no income and are not able to provide for their families. If the contraction is severe, such as in the Great Depression, the problems caused by unemployment can be far-reaching. Without income, people are not able to meet mortgage and other credit payments. In time, some people may lose their homes and other possessions.

During the Great Depression soup kitchens set up by charitable organizations provided free food for many unemployed workers.

The Bettmann Archive

Fiscal Policy. One function of government is to try to solve problems of business cycles—such as inflation, recession, and depression. In the past, our government has used fiscal and monetary policies to achieve economic stability.

Fiscal policy involves government taxation and spending. In times of inflation, demand and spending are often greater than production. In such times, fiscal policy should be designed to cut spending. One way to fight inflation is for government to increase taxes. This will lower the disposable personal income. Each person will have less to spend on goods and services. Fiscal policy to fight inflation should also cut government spending. Business and personal spending tend to increase when there is more government spending. But in times of inflation, spending needs to be reduced.

Fiscal policy to fight a recession is the opposite of that used to fight inflation. Spending and employment need to be increased. To encourage spending, government can cut taxation and increase its own spending. Lower taxes will increase disposable personal income, thus giving people more to spend on goods and services. Greater government spending will increase business activity by using more resources, such as unemployed workers.

Monetary Policy. In Chapter 11, you read that the Federal Reserve System is able to control the supply of money with monetary policy. During times of inflation, spending needs to be cut. The Federal Reserve System cuts spending by reducing the amount of money in circulation. First, the Federal Reserve System can raise the reserve requirement. All depository institutions must hold reserves with the Federal Reserve System equal to some part of their deposits. By raising the requirement, the Federal Reserve System can limit the amount of money available for loans. Second, the Federal Reserve System can raise the interest rate on loans it makes to depository institutions. In turn, these institutions will tend to raise the interest rate on loans they make. People are less likely to borrow money if interest rates are high. Third, the Federal Reserve System can sell government securities it owns. This will also remove money from circulation.

In times of recession, a monetary policy to increase the amount of money in circulation is needed. This calls for the Federal Reserve System to lower the reserve requirement, lower interest rates, and buy government securities.

The effectiveness of fiscal and monetary policies as ways to maintain economic stability has been questioned. Some people question the usefulness of fiscal and monetary policies because they take so long to work. And during the early 1980's, traditional fiscal and monetary policies had a limited effect on *stagflation*—inflation with rising unemployment. Stagflation, inflation, and unemployment will be looked at more closely in Chapter 13.

Section Checkups

1. *What is a country's Gross National Product?*
2. *Why does a decrease in total spending cause a decrease in business activity?*
3. *How can fiscal and monetary policies be used to fight inflation?*

Section 3
The Impact of Government

Since the Great Depression of the 1930's, the federal government has played a greater part in our free enterprise economy. Today, the impact of government is felt in nearly every part of our economic life. But the kind of impact government has had is the subject of much discussion. Some people feel that government has had a negative effect on our economy. They also feel that our economy will work more efficiently if government involvement is lessened. However, other people feel that government has had a beneficial effect. They believe that government is needed to help maintain economic stability, growth, and equality. As you read this section, ask yourself the following questions: *What has been the impact of federal regulation on the economy? Why do some people feel that the role of the government in the economy should be reduced? Why do some people feel that government's role in the economy is necessary?*

Government and the Economy. As our country faces the economic problems of the 1980's, there is growing disagreement as to the part federal government should play in our economy. A number of Americans feel that government has a negative impact on the economy. They believe that government involvement lessens economic freedom. They point out that government regulations may hurt business activity and can stop our free market system from working efficiently. Also, they feel that taxation destroys individual and business incentive, since higher earnings are tied to higher taxes.

Other Americans hold a different view. They feel that government has a positive impact on the economy. This point of view sees some regulations as protection for workers. Other regulations are viewed as protection for consumers from questionable business practices. It is also argued that our government has passed laws that ensure the efficient working of the market system. And these people state that taxation provides money for important social programs.

Opposition to Regulation. Government regulations are not new. Throughout our country's history, all levels of government have passed laws that regulate business activity. Some of these laws require people to hold licenses before they can enter certain businesses. Other laws set standards for business operations or for the quality of finished goods. Still other laws set up agencies that make sure these standards are met. But what has been the impact of regulation on our economy?

Most Americans agree that some government regulation is needed. However, there is disagreement as to how much is needed. A number of economists, business leaders, and consumers are beginning to question government's part in our economy. They feel that regulation has caused a marked increase in production costs. For example,

(Text continues on page 216.)

Innovation and Opportunity
David Arlasky and the Chapman-Lok

When Chapman Industries Corporation of Elk Grove Village, Illinois, asked David Arlasky to design an automobile security system, it did not realize he had some inside information. As well as being a mechanical engineer, Arlasky was also an expert on car theft. While in college, Arlasky had worked for a number of banks, repossessing cars from people who had failed to repay loans. Few of these people were willing to return the cars, so more often than not, Arlasky had to find ways to get into the cars to take them away. Arlasky found the task of entering locked cars fairly easy. He could normally do it in 10 to 15 seconds. Many of the methods he used were similar to those used by car thieves.

When Arlasky began to build the automobile security system, he tried to devise one that would foil all the tricks used by car thieves. The final result was the "Chapman-Lok." When the Chapman-Lok is used, it automatically locks the hood and the ignition system. A special key is needed to unlock the Chapman-Lok. According to Arlasky, with one of these systems a car is virtually theftproof. The only way to steal a car protected with a Chapman-Lok is to tow it away or to cut the hood using a blowtorch.

Chapman Industries Corp.

More than a million cars are stolen each year. And more than half of these are never recovered. Car theft can be a very expensive business for insurance companies. So, many insurance companies offer reduced rates to car owners who have their cars fitted with the Chapman-Lok. Some companies will not offer insurance coverage unless the car has a Chapman-Lok.

To date, more than two million locks have been sold. Yet only one car protected by the Chapman-Lok system has been reported stolen. Even though these statistics are impressive, Arlasky is more pleased with what a car thief told him. "You guys are hurting my business," the car thief said.

The "skills" that David Arlasky developed while working his way through college proved useful in our free enterprise system. The Chapman-Lok has helped David Arlasky to become a millionaire.

This is one cartoonist's view of the effect of government regulation of industry.

many workers have to be hired just to handle the paperwork required by government agencies. Further, safety standards set by some federal agencies are often very costly to implement and may not always improve safety. It is also stated that the quality standards set by some government agencies are often unnecessary. Competition among producers should ensure high quality products at reasonable prices without strict regulations.

Higher production costs caused by government regulation have increased the cost of doing business for some companies. To stay in business, companies have covered these costs by raising prices. In this way, government regulation has affected consumers.

Government regulation may also be the cause of certain hidden costs. For example, because of costly research and testing standards set by the FDA, drug companies may decide not to develop certain new drugs that might be helpful. Even so, many Americans feel that in the field of drug research, such strict regulation is needed.

Support for Regulation. Many people do not view the overall economic impact of government as harmful. These people feel that government regulation has had a positive effect. For example, in their view safety and health regulations have led to safer working conditions and a healthier environment. As a result, fewer working hours have been lost through accidents and illness. Also, the requirements of such agencies as the FDA have given consumers the chance to buy untainted food and safer drugs. Without government acting as a watchdog, businesses, in their push for profits, might not consider such things as health and safety.

Those people who favor government regulation agree that regulations can, and often do, increase costs. However, from their point of view even though consumers may pay for government regulation through higher prices, the benefits they receive outweigh the costs.

The Impact of Taxation. A second major point of disagreement arises over taxation. Some people feel that high rates of taxation destroy both business and individual incentive. First, many people become less willing to invest in business because increased earnings lead only to higher taxes. Second, it has been estimated that the average worker has to work from January to May to earn the money he or she has to pay in taxes. If people receive only about 60 to 70 percent of their yearly income after taxes, they are not likely to want to work as hard.

The opposing view is that tax rates are, in fact, not as high as is believed. Although a person may earn an income that could be taxed at a rate of more than 40 percent, the actual rate paid may be far less. For example, when figuring their income tax, many people claim deductions for dependent relatives, interest paid on loans, bad debts, and so on. Because of these deductions, what people actually pay in income tax is much lower than the stated rate. Thus, there is less of a loss of incentive than is claimed.

Those who share this view also note that taxation is an important part of fiscal policy. By changing the levels of taxation and government spending, the federal government can control the level of business activity. Thus, taxation can be used to stabilize our economy. Taxation can also be used to redistribute income and wealth. In this

United States Department of Agriculture inspectors grade meat to ensure that the quality is consistent.

Murray Lemmon/USDA

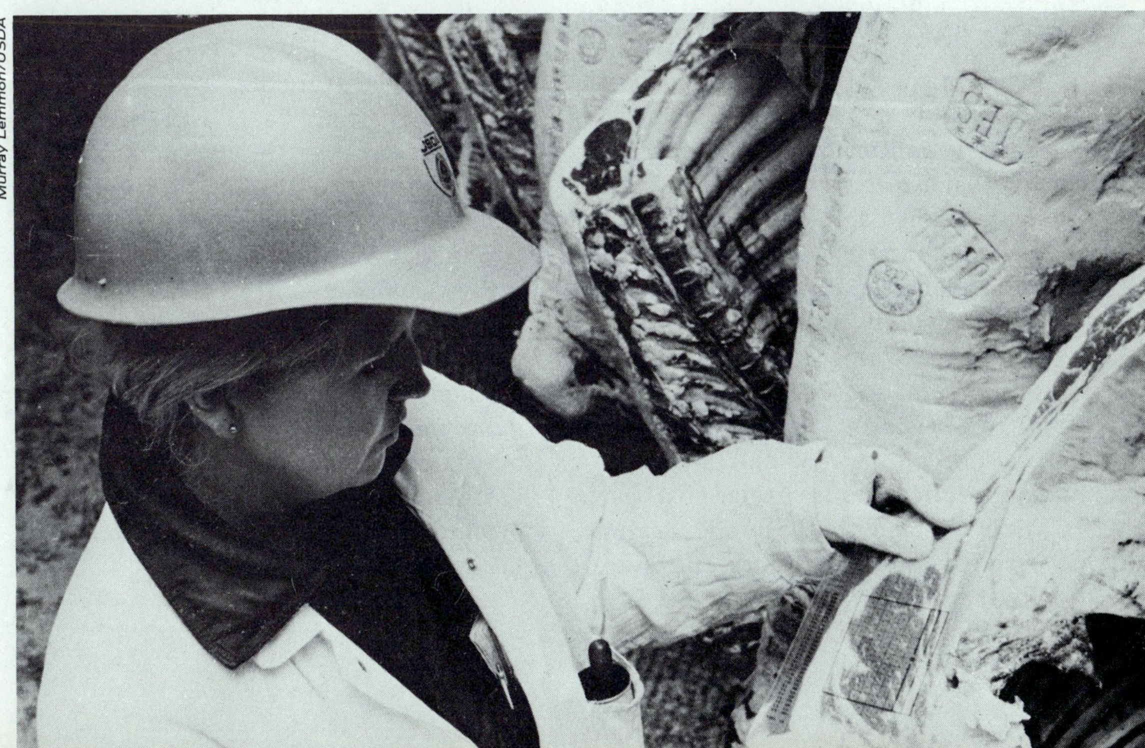

way, there is a more equal spread of economic power. Finally, the revenue gained from taxation pays for the many important programs that government offers.

Public Sector or Private Sector? Today, a number of people are questioning whether government should provide certain goods and services. They feel that some of these goods and services should not be provided at all. Many others could be better provided by private business. By and large, these people feel that politicians and government bureaucrats often do not do what is best for our country.

Probably every American would agree that the purpose of government is to do what is best for the country. But many Americans feel that this is not always the case, particularly at the federal level. In their view, politicians are often moved by the demands of special-interest groups. Industrial and labor groups, and such different organizations as the National Rifle Association and the Consumers' Union, try to influence politicians. Because of this influence, bills that are economically unsound may be passed. These bills may benefit certain special-interest groups at the expense of the common good. During election years, politicians often support programs that are attractive to voters rather than those that are economically sound. For example, few politicians are willing to vote for higher taxes in an election year, even though higher taxes may be in order.

Another point raised is that government is less efficient, since there is no incentive for it to be efficient. However, in the private sector, competition and the drive for greater profits lead to greater efficiency.

These criticisms of the public sector do, in part, have some substance. However, it is very hard to judge exactly which activities would be better handled by private business. Few people doubt that such things as national defense should be a function of government. Or that the production of agricultural goods is better handled by private business. But it is hard to say if other things, such as health care, could be better handled by the private sector or by government.

More or Less Government? A number of Americans feel strongly that the role of government should be reduced. In their view, if government's role is increased, economic freedom will be lessened. However, other people have stated that increased government involvement might increase economic freedom. For example, government rarely produces the public goods it provides. Highways, bridges, and dams, for the most part are built by private contractors. By giving government contracts to private business, the number of people taking part in economic decision making is increased. And by providing public goods, government is giving people the chance to enjoy goods that otherwise would not be available.

In the past few years, there have been calls for economy in government. Many people have said that this could be achieved by reducing government spending. In this way, government would be using fewer of our country's scarce resources. But other people have noted that reducing government spending may not lead to economy in government. Cutting certain government programs just to save money may not lead to greater economy. Both the *costs* and the *benefits* of a program should be closely studied before decisions to cut that program are made.

There appears to be a general feeling in our country that government may be getting too big. Clearly, cutting back on present government programs will be a difficult task. And it is not likely that government will be asked to do less in the future. Rather, it will be asked to be more efficient in what it already does. In that case, government will have to end any duplication of services that are offered by its agencies. And regulations that do not benefit consumers but tend to hinder business activity will have to be dropped. If these changes are made, it is possible that there will be less waste of our scarce resources and that the market system may work more efficiently.

Section Checkups

1. *Why do some people feel that government regulation has had a negative impact on our economy?*
2. *How might taxation affect business and individual incentive?*
3. *How might government involvement in the economy aid economic freedom?*

Chapter Summary

All levels of government play some role in our economy. Today, government, especially the federal branch, performs a number of important economic functions. It makes efforts to maintain our market economy. It provides important public goods and services. And federal government takes steps to ensure our country's economic stability. To pay for these functions, our government collects taxes.

Even though our country's economy has been growing, there have been business cycles, or periods of ups and downs in business activity. These business cycles differ greatly. However, they all have four phases—expansion, peak, contraction, and trough. Business cycles can have severe effects on the economy. To control these effects, our government uses monetary and fiscal policies.

Most Americans agree that our government has a part to play in the economy. But there is little agreement as to how large a part this should be. A number of people feel that government actions have a positive impact on the economy. Therefore, government's role should be enlarged. Other people feel that our economy will work efficiently only if government's role is limited. However, most people feel that it is unlikely that government's role will be reduced.

Reviewing the Chapter

Identifying Terms

Explain or identify the following:

Public goods	Business cycle
National debt	Depression
Balanced budget	Recession
Progressive tax	Inflation
Regressive tax	Stagflation

Analyzing Information

1. What special characteristics does the national debt have?

2. How does government try to limit inequalities in income and wealth?

3. How might psychological factors cause business cycles?

4. What fiscal and monetary policies might be used to control a recession?

5. How might taxation have a positive effect on the economy?

6. Why might politicians support unsound economic programs in election years?

Analyzing Visual Material

1. Study the table on page 206. According to the table, how much of the national debt is owed to banks and the Federal Reserve System? Which single group owns the largest part of the national debt? About what percentage of the national debt is owed to individuals? Is the national debt mostly American owned or mostly foreign owned?

2. Carefully study the cartoon on page 216. What point, do you think, is the cartoonist trying to make? Is this a favorable or an unfavorable view of the role government plays in our economy? Which government agencies might require businesses to submit paperwork? In your opinion, does government play too great a part in our economy? Give reasons for your answer.

Research and Projects

1. Research your state's system of taxation. What kinds of taxes does your state collect? How much money does your state raise from these taxes? What programs and services are provided with this money? Using this information, write a report on your state's system of taxation. Be prepared to present your report to the rest of the class.

2. The class should divide into groups of five. In these groups, discuss whether or not the federal government should provide welfare and unemployment programs. Make notes of the various arguments for and against such programs. Select a speaker to present your findings to the rest of the class.

3. Draw a cartoon showing the views of people who feel that government plays too great a part in our economy. The illustration on page 216 can be used as a guide.

Unit 3
Reviewing the Unit

Understanding the Unit

1. What are the four types of business organizations?

2. How do the operations of stock exchanges and investment banks differ?

3. How do the forces of supply and demand influence wage levels?

4. Which issues are usually covered in collective bargaining agreements?

5. What are the functions of money?

6. How does the Federal Reserve System increase the amount of money in circulation?

7. What can the federal government do to maintain the stability of our economy?

8. Why do some Americans feel that government involvement in the economy should be reduced?

Questions for Discussion

1. In your opinion, are government regulations imposed on business organizations too restrictive or not restrictive enough? Give reasons for your answer.

2. In your opinion, should all groups of workers be given the right to strike? Are there any groups of workers who should not be allowed to strike? Give reasons for your answers.

3. Do you think credit cards should be included as part of the money supply? Give reasons for your answer. What are the advantages and disadvantages of using credit cards?

Recommended Reading

Economic Report of the President. Washington, D.C.: U. S. Government Printing Office, current year. A yearly review of the country's economic situation and proposals for future economic policies.

Hughes, Jonathon R.T. *The Governmental Habit.* New York: Basic Books, 1977. A historical review of government involvement in the American economy.

Miernyk, William H. *The Economics of Labor and Collective Bargaining,* 2nd ed. Lexington, Mass.: D. C. Heath, 1973. A study of the role of labor and collective bargaining in the economy.

Myers, Margaret G. *A Financial History of the United States.* New York: Columbia University Press, 1970. A thorough historical study of money and banking in the United States.

Paridis, Adrian A. *How Money Works.* New York: Hawthorn Books, 1972. A short, easy-to-read account of the workings of the Federal Reserve System.

Preston, Paul, and Thomas W. Zimmerer. *Business: An Introduction to American Enterprise.* Englewood Cliffs, N.J.: Prentice-Hall, 1976. A review of the role of business in the American economy.

Economics at Work

Making economic choices: Expanding the business

After two years of solid, hard work, your frozen-yogurt bar is finally beginning to make a sizable profit, a little in excess of $20,000. Even though it has been a struggle, you have enjoyed the freedom of being your own boss. All the business decisions were your own, even though you did ask people for advice. You now have to make a decision concerning how to use your profits. With your accountant you have made a thorough study of the field, and you have found there is a market for your product. But you both feel that economic conditions are somewhat uncertain at this time. Even so, you have discussed the following four possible courses to follow in using your profits:

1. Make few changes to the business, but pay yourself a much larger salary.

2. Keep the business operating at the same level, but hire a manager to handle affairs. You will have to pay the manager a salary in excess of $15,000 a year.

3. Invest your profits in the business by buying more capital goods. Yogurt dispensers, coffee machines, and so on can be bought for about $18,000. This expansion will require hiring two more workers, so your labor costs will rise.

4. Accept an offer from a friend to form a partnership. With the money capital you both have available, you can expand the business and cover the extra costs of new staff. Managerial duties can be shared between you and your partner. However, with a partner there are two salaries to be paid. Also, you will have to consult your partner before any business decisions can be made.

Using this information, choose which course you wish to follow. Then write a report stating the course you have chosen. Explain the reasons for your decision. Also in your report, answer the following questions: How are the problems you face in making your decision similar to those faced by other owners of sole proprietorships? Do directors of large corporations face such problems?

Be prepared to present your report to the class and to discuss and defend your course of action.

Illinois State Toll Highway Authority

Unit 4 Challenges Facing Our Free Enterprise System

Chapter 13 Challenges on the Domestic Scene

SECTIONS 1 Economic Growth
2 Economic Stability
3 Economic Security

Marathon Oil Company

As we move into the 1980's, many countries, including the United States, are facing important economic challenges. Generally speaking, these challenges can be divided into three groups: economic growth, economic stability, and economic security. To a large extent, the way we meet these challenges will be determined by our future energy supplies. Finding new sources of fossil fuels and developing alternative energy sources will greatly affect our ability to achieve economic growth, economic stability, and economic security.

Section 1
Economic Growth

Economic growth is important to all countries. For growth to take place, a country must increase its supply of the factors of production. Also, there must be an increase in the total spending in the country's economy. In the past few years, questions have been raised about the growth of the American economy. As you read this section, ask yourself the following questions: *What methods are used to measure economic growth? What requirements must be met for economic growth to take place? What are the limits and possibilities of economic growth in the United States?*

What Is Economic Growth? In general terms, economic growth is marked by an increase in a country's output. Some economists view growth in terms of a country's total output. In other words, growth is marked by greater production of goods and services. However, other economists feel that growth is marked by an increase in a country's *per capita*—per person—output. This second definition looks at the productivity of each person in the country.

The second view is, for the most part, more useful. It recognizes that even though a country's total output may increase, there may not be economic growth. For example, if a country's population is growing at a faster rate than its output, the economy would, in fact, be in a decline.

Measuring the Economy. To find out how well an economy is doing in terms of growth, we must have a way to measure this growth. One method of measurement used by governments is the Gross National Product (GNP). As you read in Chapter 12, a country's GNP is the market value of all the final goods and services produced in that country in a given year. Only final goods and services are included in the GNP in order to avoid double counting. That is, the value of the tires, the steel, and the upholstery used to make a car is not counted. Only the value of the final good, the car, is counted in the GNP.

However, some problems arise when estimating a country's GNP. A number of economists feel that there are some things not counted in the GNP that should be included. For example, a homemaker's services to the family are not counted. Yet, if the homemaker took a part-time job, the salary earned from the job would be included in the GNP. The value of people's leisure time is also not counted. These economists also point out that GNP does not accurately reflect changes in the quality of goods and services that may have taken place over the years. Also, GNP does not show the kinds of goods and services being produced. For example, GNP does not distinguish between millions of dollars' worth of bombs and millions of dollars' worth of consumer goods.

Adjusting the GNP. Adjustments of GNP figures to give a more accurate picture of a country's wealth can be made fairly easily. For example, a country with a GNP of 100 million dollars will be very wealthy if its population is very small. However, if the country has a large population, it will be very poor. A country's GNP can be adjusted for population by dividing the GNP by the number of people living in that country. The result is the country's *per capita GNP*. Per capita GNP figures make it easier to compare the wealth of various countries.

Comparisons between yearly GNP figures can also be made. But figures should be adjusted for any inflation or deflation that may have occurred. For example, if the
1 current dollar GNP figures of the United States for the years 1960 and 1981 were compared, it would appear that output had risen by more than five times. (See table on page 227.) However, due to inflation, the dollar used to measure GNP in 1981 buys less than the dollar used to measure GNP in 1960. GNP figures can be adjusted for any price changes by using GNP price levels in 1972 as a base. This is called *constant dollar GNP* or *real GNP*. It measures only the change in the real output in any economy. Real GNP figures show that between 1960 and 1981 output in the United States little more than doubled.

Estimating a country's GNP is not an easy task. Even so, it is a good measure of changes in the yearly level of economic activity. If real GNP figures fall for two consecutive quarters—six months—economists say that the economy is in a recession. However, if real GNP figures rise steadily for a number of years, it can be seen that the economy is growing. By studying GNP figures, economists can estimate how rapidly this growth is taking place.

The Importance of Economic Growth. In the United States, most people have grown up with the idea that life will be better for them than it was for their parents. And many Americans believe that things will be even better in the future. For these beliefs to be fulfilled, our economy must continue to grow.

Economic growth is important for a number of reasons. First, with continued economic growth our standard of living will go on rising. With greater production there will be more products to consume. These products could make everyday life more comfortable. Also, economic growth could lead to more leisure time. Increased efficiency and productivity should mean that workers will be able to spend less time at work without losing income.

Second, economic growth could help to solve such problems as poverty. As the economy grows, more people should be employed and earning an income. More goods and services will be produced, which could be used to help the needy. And, with a growing economy, government would be able to offer more needed services. With more people earning higher incomes, and companies earning more profits, there would be greater tax revenues to pay for these services.

Finally, economic growth in the United States could help other countries. A healthy economy in the United States often can provide the funds for greater aid to developing countries. Aid in the form of money, capital goods, and technical knowledge should help the economies of these developing countries to grow. Healthy

1. Between 1960 and 1983, current dollar GNP figures increased by more than six times. Real GNP figures, however, only doubled.

*U.S. GNP, 1960–1981 (in billions of current and constant dollars)**

Year	GNP Current Dollars	Percent Change Over Previous Year	GNP Constant (1972) Dollars	Percent Change Over Previous Year
1960	507	+ 4	737	....
1961	525	+ 4	757	+3
1962	565	+ 8	800	+6
1963	597	+ 6	833	+4
1964	638	+ 7	876	+5
1965	691	+ 8	929	+6
1966	756	+ 9	985	+6
1967	800	+ 6	1,011	+3
1968	873	+ 9	1,058	+5
1969	944	+ 8	1,087	+3
1970	993	+ 5	1,086	....
1971	1,077	+ 9	1,122	+3
1972	1,186	+10	1,186	+6
1973	1,326	+12	1,255	+6
1974	1,434	+ 8	1,248	−1
1975	1,549	+ 8	1,234	−1
1976	1,718	+11	1,300	+5
1977	1,918	+12	1,372	+5
1978	2,156	+12	1,437	+3
1979	2,414	+12	1,483	+3
1980	2,626	+ 9	1,481	....
1981	2,922	+11	1,510	+2

Sources: Economic Report of the President *and* U.S. Bureau of Economic Analysis.

As the table above shows, our country's GNP has grown. It is important to note that when measured in current dollars, the GNP shows a greater growth than when it is measured in constant dollars—adjusted for inflation.

* In 1983, current dollar GNP stood at $3,310 billion and constant dollar GNP was $1,535 billion.

economies in the Third World countries, in turn, could help the United States. These countries could provide new markets for American goods and services. And we could respond by buying certain goods and services from Third World countries. This would free some of our resources for other, more important, purposes.

Supply Factors of Economic Growth. If our economy is to grow, we must have more and improved factors of production. First, more natural resources of higher quality are needed. Second, we need to invest more in capital goods. And third, the American labor force must grow in both size and quality.

In certain cases, it may not be possible to increase our supply of the factors of production. Recently, we have suffered increasing scarcity of certain natural resources. But scarcities can be overcome, and the United States can enjoy further economic growth. This can be achieved by using the resources we have more efficiently. One way greater efficiency can be gained is through new technology.

Greater availability of resources and greater technical knowledge will have an impact on the economy. An increase in the total output of goods and services will be possible. But this is not the whole picture of economic growth. Other important elements need to be considered.

Other Factors Affecting Growth. With an increase in the quantity and quality of the factors of production, it is possible for the economy to grow. But two other elements must be present. First, there must be an increase in *aggregate demand*—total spending in the economy. In other words, if economic growth is to take place, there must be greater demand for goods and services. Second, the increased supply of resources must be used to ensure the fullest production from them.

For example, the application of new technology makes economic growth possible. However, the greater production that might result from the new technology would be wasted if there was no corresponding increase in demand. Also, the new methods would have to be used in those businesses that would give the greatest returns. Using new technology in a business that would not make a sizable difference in output would not aid overall growth.

Limits and Possibilities of Growth. In recent years, questions have arisen about the growth of the American economy. A number of Americans have voiced doubts that rapid economic growth is desirable. They state that rapid industrialization has almost used up our scarce natural resources. In return, they argue, industry has polluted the land, the air, the rivers, and the oceans. They also state that economic growth has helped little in solving such problems as poverty. These people do agree that economic growth has given us a high standard of living, but only in a material sense. They accept that we do have many more goods and services to consume. Even so, they feel that the quality of life is getting worse. Such things as boring jobs, the hectic pace of life, and pollution cause us to enjoy ourselves less.

While some Americans question whether further economic growth is needed, others question whether it is possible. These people state that the resources of the earth are limited. They argue that if industry continues to use these resources at its present rate, the resources will soon be exhausted. Also, the earth is able to absorb only so much of the waste products of industry. Like a sponge soaking up water, the earth will soon reach its saturation level. In their opinion, these things make further economic growth impossible. If the United States is to survive into the twenty-first century, growth will have to be limited.

Even though many Americans have doubts, some Americans still believe that

Jungwanchi/Gamma—Liaison

In recent years, alternative energy sources have been sought. The windmill in the picture above generates enough electricity for a whole house.

further economic growth is possible and needed. They state that the technology we have has not been fully applied. For example, only 3 percent of the earth's surface is farmed, and much of that is farmed inefficiently. As we develop new technology, new stores of natural resources can be used. For example, in the last few years new developments in the oil industry have made drilling in the Arctic areas possible. However, resources such as oil and other fossil fuels are limited, so both government and private business are seeking alternatives. Experimentation is under way in such areas as solar energy, geothermal energy, wind power, and wave power. Finally, throughout time human beings have proved to be very adaptable in handling problems. There is no reason why the problem of economic growth should defeat them.

Section Checkups

1. *What is the difference between current dollar GNP and constant dollar GNP?*
2. *How does economic growth in the United States help other countries?*
3. *Why do some Americans doubt that economic growth is desirable?*

Section 2
Economic Stability

Economic stability is a major goal of most countries. There are a number of problems to overcome if economic stability is to be achieved. Inflation and unemployment must be controlled. In the past few years, many industrialized countries have faced a new problem. This is a high rate of inflation with high unemployment at the same time. As you read this section, ask yourself the following questions: *What are the two types of inflation? Why is full employment important to the economy? What are the characteristics of stagflation?*

Inflation. If economic stability is to be achieved and maintained, a number of problems have to be overcome. One problem is inflation. Inflation is a widespread rise in prices that lessens the buying power of each dollar. In general terms, there are two kinds of inflation—*demand-pull* and *cost-push.*

Demand-pull inflation happens when people try to buy more goods than can be produced. This gap between the amount demanded and the amount produced can happen if the economy's resources are already fully used. Or it can happen if the increase in production is slower than the increase in demand. When demand is greater than supply, the level of prices is pulled up. If demand continues to be greater than supply, inflation will result.

Cost-push inflation happens when the costs of production go up. To increase production, businesses may be willing to pay higher wages to workers and higher prices for the raw materials needed. But to make a profit, the businesses must raise the prices of their products. Increased prices will lead to demands for higher wages and higher prices for raw materials. In turn, this will be followed by the businesses raising their prices further. If this pattern continues, inflation will result.

Measuring Inflation. In the United States, one measure of the rate of inflation is the Consumer Price Index (CPI). The CPI measures the changes in prices of a "basket," or group, of goods and services a typical American consumer might buy. Included in the CPI basket are the costs of such things as food, transportation, medical services, and housing.

The CPI is expressed in percentage terms to make yearly comparisons easier. With 1967 as the base year, the cost of buying the basket of goods and services in 1967 equals 100 percent. The cost of the basket in other years can then be given as some percentage of the 1967 cost. For example, the cost of the basket in 1981 was [1] 266.2 percent of the 1967 cost. (See table on page 231.) In other words, in 1981 it cost $2.66 to buy the same amount of goods and services that cost $1.00 in 1967. Therefore, a worker who made $100.00 a week in 1967 would have to make $266.20 a week to be as well-off in 1981. It must be remembered

1. The cost of the basket in 1983 was 298.4 percent of the 1967 cost. In other words, in 1983 it cost $2.98 to buy the same amount of goods that cost $1.00 in 1967.

Consumer Price Index, 1960–1981 *

Year	Consumer Price Index 1967 = 100	Percent Change Over Previous Year
1960	88.7	
1961	89.6	+ 1.0
1962	90.6	+ 1.1
1963	91.7	+ 1.2
1964	92.9	+ 1.3
1965	94.5	+ 1.7
1966	97.2	+ 2.9
1967	100.0	+ 2.9
1968	104.2	+ 4.2
1969	109.8	+ 5.4
1970	116.3	+ 5.9
1971	121.3	+ 4.3
1972	125.3	+ 3.3
1973	133.1	+ 6.2
1974	147.7	+10.9
1975	161.2	+ 9.1
1976	170.5	+ 5.8
1977	181.5	+ 6.4
1978	195.4	+ 7.7
1979	217.4	+11.3
1980	244.4	+12.4
1981	266.2	+ 8.9

Source: U.S. Department of Commerce.

The Consumer Price Index (CPI) is used to indicate the rate of inflation. Between 1960 and 1981, there have been 3 years when the rate of inflation has exceeded 10 percent.

that the CPI does not accurately measure the effect of rising prices for every individual consumer or household. However, it is a fairly good measure of changes in the overall price level in the American economy.

* The CPI for 1983 stood at 298.4, a 12 percent increase over 1981.

Recession. Economic stability can also be threatened by downswings in the business cycle. During this contraction phase of a business cycle, business activity declines. For the most part, this decline is caused by a fall in aggregate demand.

One result of a fall in aggregate demand is that businesses cut production. A cut in production usually means less work for workers. As they are working less, workers' incomes will fall. With less income, people spend less. This leads to a further fall in aggregate demand. Businesses respond to this by cutting production further and by laying off more and more workers. If this pattern continues, the economy will be in a recession. Any further decrease in business activity would lead to an economic depression.

Unemployment. A good indicator of the extent of a recession is the level of unemployment. Economists recognize three major kinds of unemployment. *Frictional unemployment* is the normal unemployment that results when workers change jobs or wait to take new jobs. As you recall, freedom of choice allows workers to move from job to job to find the kind of work they can do best at the highest level of pay. However, it may not be easy for workers to change jobs. Some unemployment of this kind is bound to happen. But frictional unemployment is viewed as normal. It is not looked upon as a threat to economic stability.

Structural unemployment exists when there are jobs open, but those workers looking for jobs do not have the skills needed for the jobs. Structural unemployment often happens during times of rapid technological change. In these times, many workers lose their jobs as they are replaced by machinery. It takes time to retrain these workers so that they will have the skills needed for the available jobs. In some cases, these workers may be unemployed for a long time.

During a recession or depression, the most common form of unemployment is *cyclical unemployment*. This form of unemployment happens when there is a slowdown in a country's business activity. If a recession is severe, unemployment is likely to increase in many businesses, in most occupations, and in most parts of the country. Even those workers who are able to keep their jobs are likely to work fewer hours and make less money. Most economists feel that cyclical unemployment is a major threat to economic stability in the United States today.

Measuring Unemployment. Unemployment figures usually follow GNP figures. Under normal conditions, when our GNP is high, not many workers are unemployed. However, during times of recession when GNP is falling, many people are out of work.

Unemployment rates are expressed in percentage terms. Finding our unemployment rate is fairly simple. As you read in Chapter 10, our country's labor force is made up of people aged 16 years or older who have civilian jobs or who are looking for work. Our unemployment rate shows what percentage of our labor force is out of work. Those who are reported as unemployed are those people who want to work and who are seeking work, but who cannot find jobs. Therefore, our unemployment rate can be found by dividing the number of unemployed by the number of workers in the labor force. The result is multiplied by 100 to give a percentage. For example,
in December 1981 with 9.4 million people 1
out of work and a labor force of about 106 million, the United States had an unemployment rate of about 8.9 percent.

During times of recession, more and more unemployed workers join the lines at unemployment compensation offices.

Camerique

1. For the month of December 1983, the unemployment rate was 8.1 percent.

(Text continues on page 234.)

Being a Wise Consumer
Writing a résumé

Some of the most important economic decisions you make will concern the kind of work you enter. When making decisions about a job, you need to be very well prepared. You need to know the qualifications required for the job. You also need to know something about the working conditions involved and the kind of income you could make. Finally, you need to have a method of presenting your qualifications and experience to your prospective employer. One way to do this is through a *résumé*—an information sheet about yourself. There are many different ways to write a résumé. Most employers feel that a résumé should be brief, clear, and concise. Other suggested guidelines below will help you write your résumé.

1. Your résumé should begin with some personal information. Such things as your name, address, telephone number, date of birth, height, weight, and general state of health could be included.
2. Some information on your educational background should follow. The names and addresses of your schools and the length of time you attended them should be listed. The major subjects you studied and any awards you may have won should also be included. It is not necessary to give any information on elementary schools.
3. A list of your work experience should be entered next. The names and addresses of former employers, the length of time you worked for them, and the jobs you did should be included. Be sure to mention any special duties, such as supervising other workers, you may have performed.
4. Some mention of your hobbies, your interests, and organizations to which you belong should be made.
5. Your résumé should end with the names and addresses of three or four people who are willing to provide references for you. Be sure you have their permission to use their names before including them.

Make a number of attempts to write your résumé. When you are satisfied with what you have written, put it to one side. After a day or two, look at your résumé again and see if there are any ways to improve it. Your final effort should run no longer than two pages and should be clearly organized and neatly typed on plain, white paper. For further information on how to write a résumé, see your school careers counselor or write to **U.S. Department of Labor, Office of Information, Publications, and Reports, Washington, DC 20210.**

The Goal of Full Employment. Unemployment imposes certain costs on an economy. First, unemployed workers are not producing goods and services that would be available for everyone to consume. Second, if there are many people out of work, it is fairly certain that other resources are not being fully employed. This will mean that factories are not producing at their full capacity. Finally, as unemployment grows, government spending on programs to aid those who are out of work must be increased.

Those people who are out of work also face many problems. They must still live and pay their bills, even though they receive little income while they are not working. Many workers find it difficult or costly to learn new trades or to move to find new jobs. And if business conditions are bad for some time, many workers find it hard to get any kind of work. This continuing unemployment often has a bad psychological effect on some workers. In some cases, they may give up and just stop looking for work.

In the interests of economic stability, a high level of employment is desirable. The full employment of all resources, including labor, is a major goal of the American economy. Many people think that full employment happens only when everyone who wants a job can find one without much trouble. But to economists, full employment does not mean that everyone has a job. Some frictional unemployment always exists. But there is some disagreement as to what percentage of frictional unemployment should be considered normal. Today, economists feel that we have full employment if 4 percent or less of our work force is unemployed.

Stagflation. Over the years, our economy has faced inflation, recession, and unemployment. In the past few years, however, a new problem has arisen. This problem combines the rising prices of an inflationary period with the falling production and rising unemployment of a recession. Economists call this situation *stagflation*. Since the early 1970's, stagflation has beset the economies of most modern industrial countries.

In the mid-1960's, business activity in our country increased as we provided the equipment needed for the war in Vietnam. This started an inflationary period that was prolonged by the rising cost of oil during the 1970's. Inflation has been at a high level ever since. At times during this period of rapid inflation, we also had a recession. For example, in 1974 and 1975 our real GNP fell. Also, in 1975, the unemployment rate was as high as 8.5 percent. And in 1982, we still had a high inflation rate [1] with rising unemployment. Many economists feel that if our country is once again to have economic stability, new policies must be introduced. Such policies must be designed to stimulate the economy during times of recession without causing further inflation.

Section Checkups

1. *What method is used to measure the rate of inflation?*
2. *What three costs does unemployment impose on the economy?*
3. *How does stagflation differ from inflation?*

1. The rate of inflation for 1983 was 3.2 percent. The unemployment rate for the year stood at 9.5 percent but was falling.

Section 3
Economic Security

If the United States is to have a healthy economy, then its citizens must enjoy economic security. Since the passing of the Social Security Act in 1935, economic security has been a concern of the federal government. The Social Security Act and a number of amendments have given many Americans a needed income.

The federal government has also set up programs that offer better educational and job-training opportunities to the needy. And the federal government has introduced programs to help the farm industry. As you read this section, ask yourself the following questions: *Which groups of people benefit from social security insurance? What are the two major categories of public aid? How has the government tried to help farmers?*

Economic Security. Economic growth and stability are challenges for our economy as a whole. But there are challenges that affect individuals more directly. One such challenge is that of economic security. To be secure, every person should be able to enjoy a minimum standard of living. That is, people should have enough of the basic essentials of life—food, shelter, health care, and so on.

Today, all levels of government offer programs that try to bring about a certain amount of economic security. Some programs, such as social security, allow for direct payments to the elderly, the disabled, and the poor. Education and training programs help to prepare people to enter the job market and make a living for themselves: Urban redevelopment programs may offer better work opportunities for people who live in depressed areas. Finally, government sometimes tries to help certain basic industries, such as farming.

Nancy Kaye/De Wys, Inc.

Over the years, technical innovations have enabled disabled people to enjoy active and productive lives. In the picture to the left, a blind student is shown studying in a law-school library.

Social Security. During the years of the Great Depression, economic security was an important concern of the federal government. The suffering caused by the Great Depression was a major reason for the passing of the Social Security Act of 1935. This act set up a system of social insurance—social security—that could help people through times of economic hardship. Taxes were imposed on workers and their employers to pay for this system.

Over the years, the Social Security Act has been amended to expand the benefits offered. Today, such programs as Old-Age, Survivors, and Disability Insurance; Medicare; Medicaid; Unemployment Compensation; and Public Assistance are all part of social security.

Old-Age, Survivors, and Disability Insurance. A very important part of the social-security system is insurance against hardship due to old age, death, and disability. Upon retirement, workers who have paid into the system receive a monthly pension. The amount of the pension, for the most part, is determined by how much the individual worker paid into the system and the size of the worker's family. If a worker who has paid into the system dies, then family members usually are eligible for a monthly pension. The size of the family and the income of the worker determine the amount of the pension. Similar payments are available for people who are disabled and cannot work.

Medicare and Medicaid. Health care, another aspect of economic security, is also covered by our social-security system. In 1965, the Social Security Act was amended to include health-care provisions. Senior citizens and some disabled people under the age of 65 are covered by *Medicare.* This is a health-insurance program that covers both hospital costs and doctors' bills.

Medicare does not provide 100 percent coverage. For stays in a hospital, the patient has to pay about $260 for the first 60 1
days. The rest of the costs may then be met by Medicare. However, if the stay in the hospital or in a nursing home is longer than 60 days, certain other deductibles must be met by the patient. These amount to about

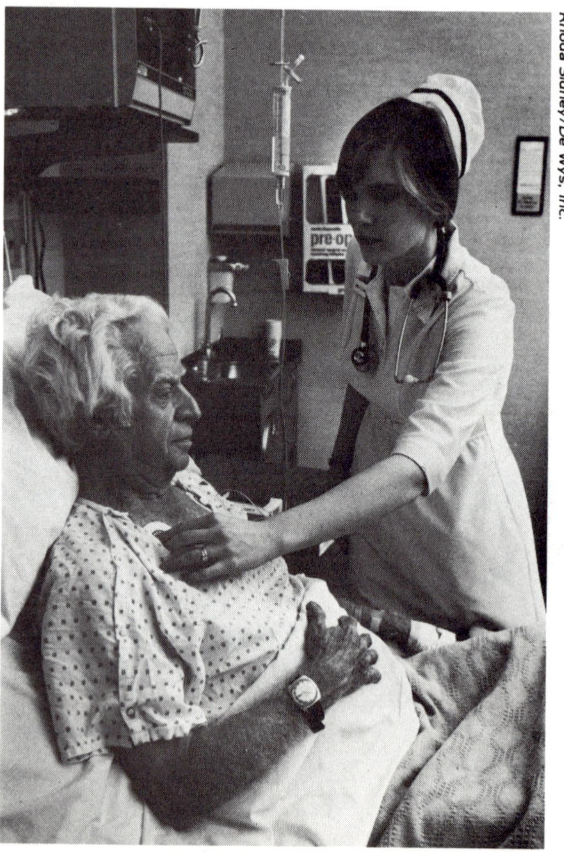

Rhoda Sidney/De Wys, Inc.

The cost of medical treatment can often be a problem for senior citizens. However, the Medicare health-insurance program helps many senior citizens to pay hospital costs and doctors' bills.

1. The patient now has to pay $356 for each stay in a hospital.

1 $25 a day. On doctors' bills, the first $60 is
2 paid by the patient. Medicare then pays 80
percent of all other charges.

Medicare is a federal program and is funded by contributions from workers, taken from their paycheck as part of social-security payments. The federal government also makes contributions to the program.

The poor are also provided with health-care insurance. This program is known as *Medicaid* and is run by the various states. If a state's program satisfies federal guidelines, it can receive federal funds. The remaining costs of the program must be met by the state.

Unemployment Compensation. For the unemployed, economic security is a serious problem. People who are out of work still have bills to pay, even though they have no income. However, there are government programs to help the unemployed.

In the United States, each state has an unemployment insurance program. To pay for these programs, states draw upon the Unemployment Trust Fund of the United States. Money for this trust fund comes from federal and state taxes on employers' payrolls. Some states also require workers to pay unemployment insurance taxes.

About 80 percent of all the workers in the United States are covered by unemployment insurance. When unemployed, workers have to wait a period of time before they can receive benefits. The benefits, and the length of time they are paid, are different from state to state. The amount of benefits paid can run from $25 to $150 a week. Some states pay extra benefits to unemployed workers who have families to support. By and large, unemployed workers can receive benefits for 26 weeks.

Public Assistance. As well as offering senior-citizen pensions and unemployment compensation, the Social Security Act also offers public aid to the needy. Public aid, as with unemployment compensation, is a joint federal and state government responsibility. Public-aid programs are run by the states. Those states whose programs meet federal guidelines receive federal funds to help pay for the programs.

Generally, there are two major categories of public aid. *Supplemental Security Income* (SSI) offers a set minimum income to three groups of people—persons 65 years of age and older, the blind, and the disabled. Such things as social-security benefits and private pensions are counted as part of the minimum income. So, few people receive the full amount of SSI.

Aid to Families With Dependent Children (AFDC) is a program that offers aid to needy children and their parents or guardians. This program is state run, but about half the funds for the program are provided by the federal government. Families may receive aid if the head of the household is dead, is unemployed, is too sick to work, or has deserted home.

Other Programs. Some state governments have programs that allow for direct payments to those in need. One program is workers' compensation, which covers the loss of economic security because of injury or death at work. There is no federal program, but each state has some kind of workers' compensation law.

Most of these state laws allow compensation for loss of pay and for medical expenses if a worker is injured on the job. Some states offer retraining programs for workers who, through their injuries, are not able to continue in their old jobs.

1. Deductibles for hospital stays longer than 60 days now amount to $89 a day.
2. The first $75 on doctors' bills must be paid by the patient. Medicare then pays 80 percent of all other approved charges.

(Text continues on page 239.)

Using Social Studies Skills

Critical reading

Social-security programs have long been a subject of discussion. Below are two excerpts from the debate in Congress on the Social Welfare Reform Amendments of 1979. Read the excerpts carefully; then answer the questions that follow.

Representative Wyche Fowler, Jr.
(D. Georgia)

There are approximately 14,700,000 Americans receiving aid to families with dependent children [AFDC] or supplemental security income. Of this total, fully one-half are children under the age of 18. Two million are elderly poor persons. Two and one-quarter million are blind or disabled. This leaves 3.5 million recipients who are adults in families with needy children. In over 80 per cent of the families receiving AFDC the father is absent. Around 15 per cent of the mothers are working full or part time and another 10 per cent are actively seeking work or are in job training....

...Th[is] bill will not guarantee an income to all, but only to needy children and their families, the elderly poor, the blind, and the disabled.

Representative Charles E. Grassley
(R. Iowa)

...[R]ather than providing incentives for Americans to engage in productive labor, [this bill] will instead penalize those citizens who try to provide for the needs of themselves and their families. The workers are the ones who will shoulder the higher taxes required to finance these so-called reforms....

[This bill] is not welfare reform so much as it is one more step down the road to widespread income redistribution—one more attempt to reward those who do not provide for themselves—one more attempt to penalize those who do work to take care of themselves and their families.

1. According to Representative Fowler, how many elderly poor people receive welfare?
2. Who does Representative Grassley think will pay the cost of welfare reform?
3. According to Representative Fowler, who will be guaranteed an income by the welfare reform bill?
4. What does Representative Grassley feel will be the outcome of the welfare reform bill?
5. How do Representatives Fowler and Grassley differ in their view of people who receive welfare benefits?
6. What kinds of welfare programs do you think should be provided by government? Give reasons for your answer.

The amount of benefits paid differs from state to state. However, compensation for loss of pay is about two thirds of a worker's regular wage. For the most part, workers' compensation programs are funded by state taxes imposed on employers. In a few states, workers are also required to pay taxes toward the programs.

Some programs do not provide for direct payments to individuals. Most of these programs are in education and training. All levels of government spend large amounts of money on education. A major goal of this spending is to offer greater educational opportunity to all Americans.

In the area of training, the federal government's Job Program offers job training to young people from needy families. The Comprehensive Employment and Training Act (CETA) of 1973 allows for federal funds to be given to state and local governments to set up training programs. To receive these funds, these programs must either offer job training to the unemployed or open up public-service jobs to the unemployed.

Agricultural Programs. Agriculture plays a very important part in the American economy. Yet for many years it has been beset with problems. A stable farming industry is considered to be essential for economic security in the United States.

A major problem in American agriculture is that of farm income. Most farm products in the United States are produced by a few large farms. Yet these farms employ less than 10 percent of American farm workers. The vast majority of American farmers work on small farms and account for a very small part of total farm output. As a result, the incomes of these farmers tend to be relatively low.

To combat the problem of low farm-incomes, government has introduced a number of programs to try to help farmers. The United States Department of Agriculture (USDA) advises farmers on how to grow crops more efficiently. The USDA does research in those areas of benefit to farmers, such as crop diseases and fertilizers. Another program run by the USDA, known as the soil bank, offers payment to farmers who leave some of their land fallow rather than plant it with crops. Government also has systems of farm price supports. One such system—*parity price supports*—tries to maintain the relationship between prices for farm goods and prices for other goods. Under this system, farmers are guaranteed a certain price for some farm goods regardless of what price they might receive on the open market.

Programs as Economic Stabilizers. The effectiveness of government programs has long been a subject of heated discussion. Some Americans feel that such programs as social security offer a minimum income for people who otherwise would have none. Economic security is more attainable for those people who receive such benefits.

However, there are other Americans who feel that social security and other government programs hurt our economy. They feel that if the government is willing to give people a living wage in the form of welfare benefits, then these people are not likely to look for work. In this way, large amounts of productive resources—in the form of labor—are lost to the economy.

The performance of government programs concerning farm matters is also a cause of disagreement. Some Americans state that price supports have helped to stabilize the industry. This has meant increases in farm income. On the other hand, other Americans feel that few government programs have helped the small farmer, the one who does need help. They also state that while price supports have increased farm income, the prices paid by consumers for farm products have also risen.

Government programs will always be a subject of discussion. Even so, many people feel that programs offering economic security are needed if we are to have a healthy economy. These people state that such programs as social security allow more Americans to play an active part in our economy.

Section Checkups

1. *What is economic security?*
2. *How do Medicare and Medicaid differ?*
3. *Which federal government programs make provisions for job training?*

Chapter Summary

A major challenge for the United States in the last years of the twentieth century is continued economic growth. Generally, economic growth is marked by an increase in output and can be measured by looking at our country's GNP. In recent years, a number of Americans have questioned whether further growth is possible. However, most Americans feel that growth is both possible and desirable.

Another challenge facing the United States is how to maintain economic stability. In the past, inflation or high unemployment has threatened the stability of our economy. However, in recent years the United States and most other modern industrialized countries have been plagued by *stagflation*—rapid inflation with high unemployment. If we are to have a stable economy, ways must be found to stimulate growth without causing inflation.

Finally, the United States must face the challenge of economic security. Generally, many Americans feel that we all should be able to enjoy a certain minimum standard of living. To this end, all levels of government provide programs that try to establish a certain amount of security for the aged, the disabled, and the needy. The success of these programs has long been a subject of disagreement. Even so, economic security, economic growth, and economic stability are believed to be essential if we are to have a healthy economy.

Reviewing the Chapter

Identifying Terms

Explain or identify the following:

Economic growth	CPI
GNP	Full employment
Aggregate demand	Stagflation
Economic stability	Economic security
Inflation	Medicare

Analyzing Information

1. How can economic growth be measured?

2. What factors have affected economic growth in the United States?

3. What are the three major kinds of unemployment?

4. Why is the goal of full employment so important to the American economy?

5. In what ways has government tried to provide economic security?

6. How has government tried to ensure economic security for farmers?

Analyzing Visual Material

1. Carefully study the table on page 227, which contains information on the GNP of the United States for the years 1960 to 1981. What was the percentage change in the current dollar GNP between the years 1972 and 1973? By how many billions of current dollars did the GNP increase between the years 1978 and 1981? Between which years of the 1970's was there a 6 percent increase in constant dollar GNP? The current dollar GNP for 1981 was about 5 times bigger than it was in 1960. How much larger was the 1981 constant dollar GNP than that of 1960?

2. Study the picture on page 235. How is this blind student able to make full use of library services? What problems do disabled people face in obtaining employment? In your opinion, what should government do to help disabled people find suitable employment?

Research and Projects

1. By writing to the federal Bureau of Labor Statistics, you can obtain monthly information on the Consumer Price Index (CPI). The bureau reports CPI figures for the whole country and for 28 metropolitan areas. Find which metropolitan area is nearest you. Then construct 2 graphs showing how the national CPI and your metropolitan area CPI have changed over the last year. When finished, the graphs can be displayed on the bulletin board.

2. Research the system of workers' compensation offered by your state. Write a report showing the kinds of benefits provided, the way the system is financed, and the number of workers covered by the system. Be prepared to present your report to the rest of the class.

Harold M. Lambert

Chapter 14 Challenges on the International Scene

SECTIONS
1 Importance of International Trade
2 American Trade Policy
3 The Balance of Payments

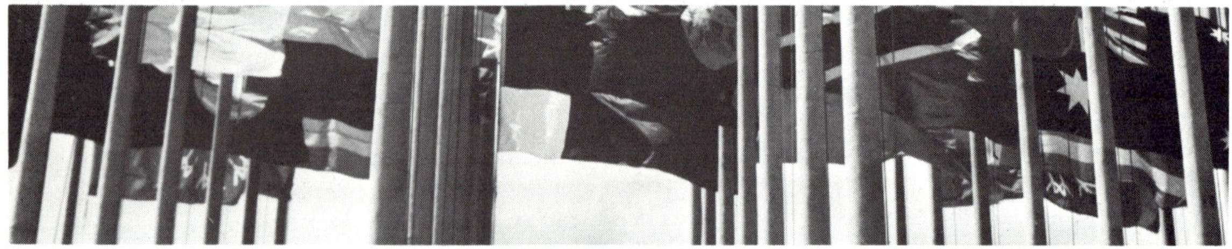

Our American economy is part of the world economy. Thousands of economic transactions link the United States to the economic systems of the other nations of the world. Today, our country is the world's leading trading nation. We import and export most types of natural resources, manufactured items, and agricultural products. The American standard of living is very much affected by our nation's economic relations with other countries. In this same way, the standards of living of citizens of other nations are also tied to their nation's role in the world economy. There is an interdependency among nations in the world economy.

Section 1
Importance of International Trade

Take a few minutes to list the many imported products that you use every day. Perhaps your clothes, eyeglass frames, shoes, or audio and electronic equipment were made in a foreign country. Think about the products that were needed for your transportation to school. The gasoline, the rubber, and possibly the vehicle you used may have originated in another country. These imports are the result of international trade. This section examines the reasons for international trade. As you read this section, ask yourself the following questions: *How does international trade benefit consumers? What are some products that the United States imports? Why do some individuals and some groups oppose free trade?*

Why Nations Trade. International trade allows countries to produce the goods and services that they can make efficiently. Since there is trade among countries, a country can specialize in the production of a limited range of products to use its resources efficiently and then trade with other countries to obtain the goods and services that it does not produce. Without trade, each country would be left to produce everything that its population would need and want. Thus, its people would have to do without some products because no one country could produce all of the goods that are available throughout the world. Without specialization, overall output would drop, and fewer goods and services would be available.

As you know, the countries of the world differ greatly in their productive resources. Climate, labor, waterways, minerals, technologies, and all other resources are unequally distributed among different countries. As a result, countries usually specialize in products based upon their productive resources. Australia, for example, has large tracts of land suitable for growing wheat and for raising sheep for wool production. Therefore, Australia exports large quantities of wheat and wool. Japan, on the other hand, does not have large amounts of land. The Japanese specialize in manufacturing industries that utilize the country's skilled labor force and developed technology. Japan must import wool, wheat, and other raw materials.

Money and International Trade. For international trade to be carried out, people must be able to exchange the money of different countries. Each country has its own money. The *monetary unit* of the United States is the dollar. In Germany it is the *deutsche mark*. In France the monetary unit is the *franc*. These different monetary units, as well as those from other countries, have different values.

People involved in international trade usually must exchange their country's money for the money of another country. Consider the example of a business in Mexico that wants to buy machines from a business in Texas. The Mexican company will have to pay for the machines with American dollars. It will be necessary for the Mexican business to use *pesos* to buy American dollars.

Transactions of money from different countries are called *foreign exchange.* The price of one country's money in comparison to the price of another country's money is called an *exchange rate.* For the Mexican company to obtain enough American dollars to pay its bill, it would need to learn the exchange rate between pesos and dollars. [1] In 1980, one peso was worth about 4 cents in American money. Therefore, one American dollar cost about 25 pesos.

However, exchange rates do not remain constant. In some cases, exchange rates are changed by government action. Or, an exchange rate may be changed because of a sharp increase or decrease in the demand for a country's money. However, most countries try to keep exchange rates relatively stable. They do this partly because international traders and investors are more willing to do business with a country that has a stable exchange rate.

The United States and Trade. The United States is the world's leading trading nation. It imports and exports more products than any other single country. Because the American economy is based on free enterprise, most of the United States international trade is conducted by private businesses. However, the federal government does take some part in international trade as a buyer, as a seller, and as an overall regulator of trade involving products that enter and leave the country.

As you know, the United States is still relatively rich in natural resources. But, despite this abundance, the United States must import a number of essential materials. For example, between 40 and 50 percent of all the oil consumed in the United States is imported. Today, the amount of money spent on foreign oil far exceeds the money spent on any other single import.

The graph on page 245 lists a number of raw materials that are necessary in industry. The graph indicates what portion of each material used by American industries recently was imported from foreign nations. As the graph shows, the United States is completely dependent on foreign trade to obtain diamonds and rubber.

The United States also imports certain foods and manufactured goods. Currently, Americans buy large quantities of coffee, tea, bananas, shoes, and cameras from other countries. In some cases, it would be difficult or expensive for Americans to produce these goods themselves. It should be noted that in some cases, Americans could produce certain goods as cheaply or even more cheaply than other countries. To do so, however, Americans would have to take productive resources away from the production of other goods. And in many cases, this would mean taking resources away from the production of some goods that we make best. Therefore, because our resources are limited, we continue to import some goods, and we specialize in producing those things that we make best.

American Exports. Through specialization, the United States produces many goods for export. Americans specialize in the types of production that utilize our rich

1. As of February 1984, a peso was worth 0.006 cent in American money, and an American dollar was worth about 170 pesos.

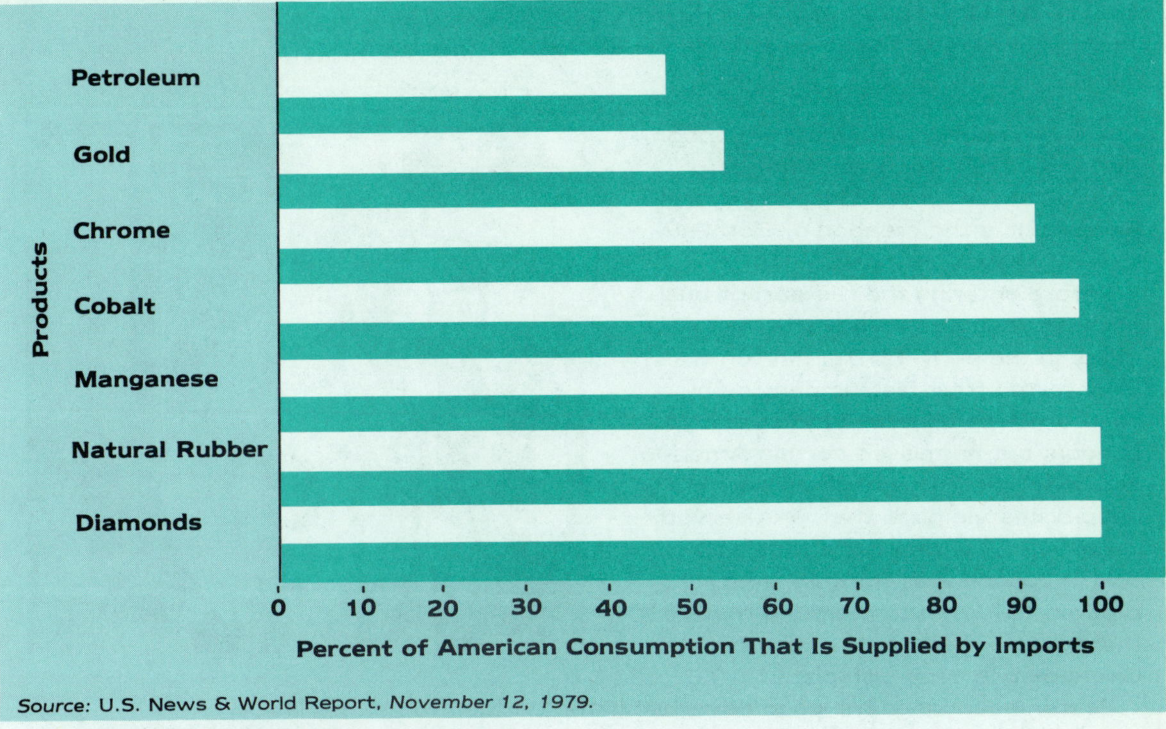

Although the United States is rich in many natural resources, our nation depends on imports for other natural resources.

farmland, our highly skilled work force, and our advanced technology. Millions of American workers are directly involved in producing goods that are sold on the worldwide market.

Today, the United States is one of the world's top food exporters. Many nations depend on grain grown by American farmers. About 25 percent of the wheat, cotton, tobacco, soybeans, and lard produced in this country each year is exported. Industrial products, such as machine tools, tractors, aircraft, and office equipment, are also exported in large quantities. Other nations buy these products from the United States for the same reasons that the United States buys other goods from foreign countries.

Debates Over Free Trade. Throughout America's history, there have been many disagreements over the amount of foreign trade that our country should undertake. These debates continue today. For the most part, these disagreements center on the question of imports. Some people believe that international trade should be carried out without government interference. Others believe that the gov-

(Text continues on page 247.)

Innovation and Opportunity
Chicago pizza in London

A very popular restaurant in London, England, is owned by an American. The restaurant is the Chicago Pizza Pie Factory. It is the creation of Bob Payton, a former Chicagoan.

Courtesy of Bob Payton

Before entering the restaurant business, Payton was an advertising executive. In the early 1970's, Payton was transferred from his company's Chicago office to London. Payton enjoyed London, but he missed certain American specialties. One of them was the deep-dish-style pizza that was served in Chicago. The only pizza that was sold in London was the thin, snack type. In 1977, Payton decided that there was a market in London for Chicago-style deep-dish pizza.

Payton abandoned his job in advertising and decided to risk his life savings on the venture. Carefully, he put together a plan for a restaurant that would bring a bit of Chicago to London. He proposed his plan to investors, raised the needed capital, and located a site.

Gathering the right ingredients and equipment to make his special pizza in London presented challenges to Payton. Unable to find the right blend of cooking oil in London, Payton obtained the recipe used by the oil supplier in Chicago and learned to prepare his own blend. Payton found that wedding-cake pans would work well for cooking and serving the pizzas. Payton also found that cheese imported from Denmark most closely resembled the cheese used by Chicago pizza makers. Payton imported Chicago street and park signs and other Chicago memorabilia to decorate the restaurant. To complete the Chicago-like atmosphere, Payton arranged for tapes of a Chicago radio station to be sent to the restaurant each week for background music, news, and weather reports.

The restaurant has been a tremendous success. Payton has moved his business to larger quarters in London and has opened a second restaurant in Bath. It is common to see lines of customers waiting to enter the restaurants. Some of the customers are Americans traveling in England who, like Payton years ago, miss the pizza that they enjoy at home.

Eric Smith/Liaison

These workers, shown picketing a foreign-car dealer, want the federal government to impose restrictions on the importation of foreign cars.

ernment should restrict or totally ban some imports.

Supporters of *free trade*—international trade without restrictions—believe that Americans, as well as people in all countries, benefit from the free exchange of goods among countries. They argue that industries should compete on the worldwide market. Through this free competition, efficient producers would profit, and inefficient businesses would be forced out of business. Supporters of free trade say that this system would result in the most efficient use of resources. They also say that it would keep consumer prices at the lowest possible level. Furthermore, they claim that free trade offers consumers the widest possible choice of goods. For example, international trade makes it possible for Americans to purchase cheap cotton clothes from India and a wide range of electronic goods from Japan. Supporters of free trade say that American consumers should be able to buy goods produced in other countries.

Arguments Against Free Trade. Opponents of free trade call for our government to impose restrictions on imports They contend that free trade does not always serve the best interests of our country. Opponents of free trade say that restrictions are needed to protect industries at home. There are several reasons given to explain this need for protection.

Many opponents of free trade believe that our country should be as self-sufficient as possible. They claim that America should not have to depend on foreign sources for raw materials and goods. They point out that goods or resources from foreign sources could be cut off during times of war. Those Americans who call for self-sufficiency point to the example of the fuel shortages that faced our country in 1973. During that year, the Arab countries placed an *embargo*—stoppage—on oil sold to the United States.

The oil embargo was set up for political reasons. It resulted in many problems, such as higher fuel prices and gasoline shortages. These problems led many Americans to call for an energy plan that would make our country more self-sufficient.

Further Reasons for Restrictions. Other Americans who call for import restrictions point to the need to protect the jobs and wages of American workers. They claim that workers in some countries are not paid as well as Americans. Low wages allow foreign producers to sell their goods at cheaper prices than can American businesses. In some other cases, foreign-made goods are cheaper because they are produced by industries that have been in operation longer than American competitors.

At times, American businesses have accused foreign producers of competing unfairly by *dumping* their products on the American market. Dumping occurs when a seller prices goods lower than the cost of production. Dumping makes imported goods cheaper than American-made goods. As a result, American consumers would probably buy cheaper, foreign-made goods. American businesses then would lose sales, and they might be forced to pay lower wages or go out of business. It is argued that either outcome would be harmful for the economy. Our government uses several measures to prevent dumping.

The arguments for and against free trade have their merits. The side that one takes often depends upon the benefits received. Free trade can result in more goods and lower prices. For these reasons, most economists strongly support policies that promote freer trade. But free trade can also cause problems for some American businesses. These businesses, and their employees, often ask for protective tariffs and quotas. Balancing the needs and wants of various groups in our economy is difficult. Our government faces these problems as it adjusts our trade policies.

Section Checkups

1. *Why does the United States import some products that could be produced more cheaply in our country?*
2. *Why do some Americans want our country to be self-sufficient?*
3. *How are cheap imports seen as a threat to American business and workers?*

Section 2
American Trade Policy

Our government's trade policy reflects the varied interests and beliefs held by American citizens. In this section you will learn about our country's efforts to limit some trade and to promote other trade. As you read this section, ask yourself the fol-

The duty charged on the items listed here depends on the value of the merchandise and the country of origin. Imports from certain countries enter the United States with lower duty rates than imports from other nations.

Duty rates

Item	Rate A*	Rate B**
Toys	17.5%	70.0%
Tape Recorders	5.5%-7.5%	35.0%
Record Albums	5.0%	30.0%
Transistor Radios	10.4%	35.0%
Silk Clothes	16.0%	65.0%
Embroidered Clothes	21.0%-42.5%	45.0%-90.0%
Leather Shoes	2.5%-20.0%	10.0%-30.0%
Wood Chairs	8.5%	40.0%

*Rates for most-favored nations.

**Rates for communist nations, except Romania, Yugoslavia, Poland, and Hungary.

Source: Department of the Treasury.

lowing questions: *How do tariffs work to restrict imports? Why are certain imports prohibited from entering the United States? Why does the United States promote international trade?*

Import Restrictions. In the United States, the Congress and the President share responsibility for regulating our country's foreign trade. The government limits imports to protect domestic industries and for other reasons. *Tariffs* and *quotas* are two major methods used to restrict imports.

Tariffs are taxes on imports. Tariffs—also called *duties*—are the most common way of limiting imports. Tariffs increase the prices that consumers must pay for imports. The resulting high prices on imported goods encourage consumers to buy *domestic goods*—goods made in our country. Tariffs therefore reduce the price advantage that imported goods might otherwise have.

Different imported goods are taxed at different duty rates. In some cases, goods from one country enter the United States at different duty rates than similar goods from another country. This occurs because our government wants either to discourage or to encourage trade with certain countries for political reasons. The table on this page lists current duty rates for various items.

Quotas restrict imports by placing a limit on the amount of a certain good that may enter the country. Quotas are generally set for a specified period of time, such as a year. The United States has import quotas on many kinds of dairy products, textiles, and steel. There are also quotas set on the importation of peanuts, sugar, and other foods. Once a quota is filled, no more items of the specified type of good can enter the United States until the next quota period.

Other Restrictions. The government also places other restrictions on imports.

U.S. Customs

The foreign-made goods that travelers bring into the United States are subject to duties and to other import restrictions. This Customs Inspector checks the merchandise brought into the United States at the Baltimore-Washington International Airport.

For example, certain goods are completely banned from entering the United States. Some of these items are prohibited because they could pose a direct threat to the welfare of Americans. For this reason, dangerous drugs, some fireworks, and certain weapons cannot be imported into the United States.

Some other items are banned because their production involves threats to the world ecology. Many ivory products and animal furs, for example, are not imported because they require the killing of endangered species of animals. Items produced from certain kinds of whales and birds are also prohibited for the same reason.

Our government also restricts imports by requiring importers to obtain permits. In some cases, the qualifications set up for these permits make it difficult for some traders to sell goods in the United States. In some other cases, our government limits the number of import permits that are issued. The American government also limits imports by establishing certain safety and health standards. Because of these rules, many food products cannot be sent into the United States. Many fresh fruits and dairy products are prohibited from entering the United States. Also, automobiles imported into our country must meet American safety and air-pollution-control standards.

As you can see, there are many different reasons that have led our government to restrict imports. These trade restrictions, however, can also lead to economic problems. High American tariffs, for example, can cause other countries to retaliate against American industries. They might place high tariffs on American-made goods. This would harm the American economy since many American producers depend on exporting their products. Furthermore, foreign countries could retaliate against American tariffs by limiting the amount of resources that the United States could buy. This could cause many problems since Americans rely on foreign sources for many resources. To work for good trade relations, our government has entered a number of different international agreements.

Promoting Trade. The American government has taken a lead in promoting international trade. Much progress toward ending trade barriers has been achieved through international conferences sponsored by the United States. These meetings have helped to bring about an international trade organization.

The members of this organization developed what is known as the *General Agreement on Tariffs and Trade* (GATT). This agreement involves about 85 countries. These countries have agreed to work together to remove barriers to international trade. Representatives from these countries meet to negotiate tariff cuts and to work out rules for trade. The GATT and other international agreements have expanded American participation in international trade. Private businesses also have taken many steps to develop favorable trade relations between the United States and other countries. As a result, American businesses now face fewer obstacles in buying resources or selling goods on the worldwide market.

At the same time, our government has taken steps to solve problems that might be caused by increased trade. For example, the federal government provides financial aid and technical assistance to businesses and workers who are harmed by an increase in imports. The government also extends aid to communities that meet financial hardship because certain trade barriers are reduced or removed.

Balance of Trade. Our government is also concerned with America's *balance of trade*. The term *balance of trade* refers to the net difference between the value of a country's imports and the value of its exports. A country's balance is described as *favorable* if the value of exports is greater than the value of imports.

With a favorable balance of trade, a country would sell more of its products in other countries than it buys from other countries. The opposite situation is referred to as an *unfavorable* balance of trade. An unfavorable balance of trade occurs when a country uses more money for its imports than it receives for its exports. During the late 1970's and early 1980's, the United States had an unfavorable balance of trade.

Earlier in history, a country's balance of trade was considered to be a major indicator of the country's economic health. It was used to show a country's rank among the countries of the world. Each government wanted to maintain a favorable balance of trade. Today, however, a country's balance of trade is not considered as important. This change occurred because countries now undertake many financial transactions beyond the trade of goods and services. Therefore, to examine the American role in international economics, it is necessary to look at the other financial transactions that take place between the United States and the rest of the world.

Section Checkups

1. *What are tariffs?*
2. *How could trade barriers imposed by other countries harm the American economy?*
3. *Why has American government and business worked to promote favorable trade relations with other countries?*

Section 3
The Balance of Payments

The United States is one of the world's leading economic powers. Americans also are involved in a wide range of international transactions. This section explains some of these transactions. As you read this section, ask yourself the following questions: *What is international investment? Why does the United States offer foreign aid? In what ways could the United States attempt to end the balance-of-payments deficit?*

International Investment. Investing in other countries forms another close tie between the American economy and the world economy. *International investment* is a term used to describe the transactions in which money from one country is invested in another country. International investments can be undertaken by government, businesses, or individuals. All international investments involve the movement of some form of capital from one country to another.

By 1980, for example, Americans had
1 over 435 billion dollars invested in foreign nations. Some of this money was taken to foreign countries by American businesses that are *multinationals*—businesses that operate in more than one country. Another part of this foreign investment was made by Americans who bought stocks and bonds of foreign businesses. Dollars deposited in foreign banks or lent to foreign governments are also a form of foreign investment.

Foreign investments are closely related to trade. Consider the example of an American manufacturing company that opens a

This Mobil station in Tokyo is an example of an American corporation operating in a foreign country.

Eric Kroll/Taurus Photos

1. As of 1983, Americans had more than $725 billion invested in foreign countries.

factory in another country. The factory will probably be supplied with machinery and other equipment that is made in the United States. In this way, foreign investments result in increased exports from the United States.

Individuals and businesses from other countries also make investments in the United States. Canadian businesses, for example, had over 6 billion dollars invested in the United States by 1980. Many individuals and businesses from Europe, the Middle East, and Japan also have invested money in the United States.

Foreign Aid. American money is provided to other countries in the form of foreign aid. Foreign aid describes the assistance given by one nation to another. The United States extends more money in foreign aid than any other country. Since 1946 the United States has spent 239.8 billion dollars in foreign aid. The graph on this page shows which nations received the largest shares of that money.

Between 1946 and 1981, the United States extended $239,808,000,000 in foreign aid. The nations receiving the largest shares of this aid are listed on this graph.

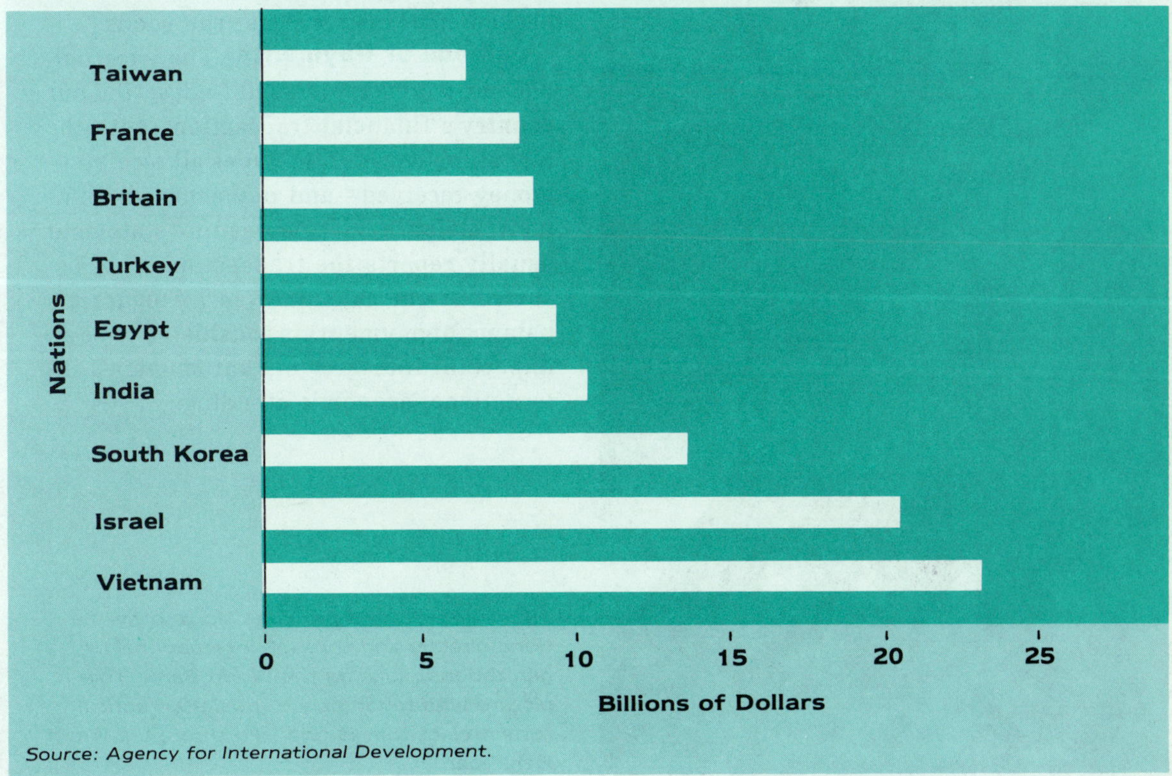

* Israel is now the chief recipient of American foreign aid.

Foreign aid can be divided into two categories. The first category—economic aid—is undertaken by both the American government and by private individuals and organizations. Economic aid is generally aimed at helping less developed countries build their economies. Economic aid also helps other countries deal with pressing problems such as famine, disease, or disaster. There are many forms of economic aid. Loans, grants, food, books, and technical assistance are among the kinds of aid sent by Americans to other countries. The Red Cross and CARE are two examples of private organizations that provide aid to people in all parts of the world.

The second category of foreign aid is military assistance. The American government gives military assistance to other countries to help them build their defenses against internal and external threats. This aid is designed to help other countries maintain their strength and stability. American military assistance has, at times, been used to help other countries to stop the spread of communism.

Foreign aid is also important to our country's international trade. For example, about one third of all American exports are sold to developing countries. In many cases, these nations can afford to purchase American goods and services because they receive aid from the United States. Foreign aid helps these countries become markets for American goods.

Balance of Payments. The term *balance of payments* is used to describe our country's financial transactions with the rest of the world. It includes all *receipts*—money received—and *payments*. A country's balance of payments statement usually reports the transactions that occurred in one calendar year. A country's balance of payments is considered to be an important indicator of that country's international economic standing.

Yosef Hadar/World Bank Photo

The United States provides aid to other nations directly and through international organizations, such as the World Bank. This picture was taken at a Yugoslavian agricultural project that is financed through a World Bank loan.

(Text continues on page 256.)

Using Social Studies Skills
Interpreting circle graphs

Over the past twenty years, both the amount and the nature of American imports have changed greatly. The circle graphs below present information on American imports during 1965 and 1979. Study the graphs carefully; then answer the questions that follow.

American imports

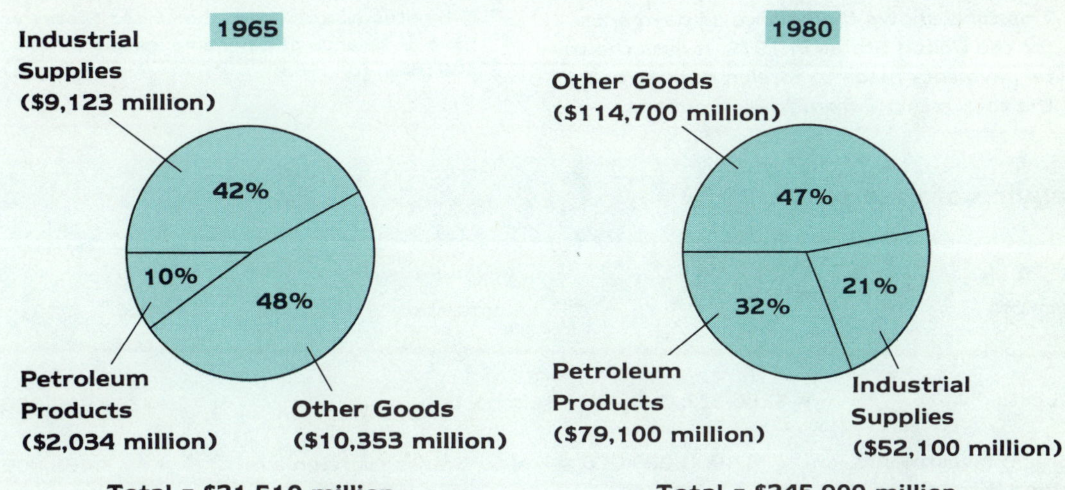

Source: Economic Report of the President.

1. By what dollar amount did the value of American imports increase between 1965 and 1980?
2. By what dollar amount did the import of industrial supplies increase between 1965 and 1980?
3. Which category of imports increased by the largest percent between 1965 and 1980?
4. What percentage of the total imports to the United States were petroleum products in 1965? In 1980?
5. How much more money did Americans pay for petroleum imports in 1980 than in 1965?

The table on this page presents a summary of the United States balance of payments for 1979. The receipts column includes all transactions that involved the receipt of money from other countries. The most important receipt item is the money received for goods exported from the United States. Receipts also include the money that Americans earned through their business investments in foreign countries. Money is also received by the United States because people from other countries buy American services and make investments in American businesses.

Our country's balance of payments also includes those transactions in which Americans paid money to the people, businesses, or governments of other countries. The largest payment item in 1979 was for goods imported by Americans. Payments in 1979 also included American foreign aid, business investments, and money

This table shows the balance of payments for the United States in 1979. It lists the total payments made to foreign nations and the total receipts from foreign nations.

* Estimates suggest that the United States will have a balance-of-payments deficit of about $20 billion for 1983.

Balance of payments, 1979 *

Receipts		Payments	
Exports	$286,312,000,000	Imports	-$280,980,000,000
Foreign Investments in the United States	33,902,000,000	U.S. Grants (foreign aid excluding military)	- 3,488,000,000
Total	320,214,000,000	American Investments Abroad	- 63,423,000,000
		Transfers (pensions, etc.)	- 2,160,000,000
		Total	- 350,051,000,000
Total Receipts	+$320,214,000,000		
Total Payments	- 350,051,000,000		
Balance	- 29,837,000,000		

Source: Survey of Current Business.

Marc L. Salzman

These Americans are shopping in Marrakesh, a city in Morocco. Dollars spent by Americans in foreign nations are included as payments in our balance of payments.

spent to support the American military forces abroad. Money spent by American tourists when they travel in foreign countries is also listed in the payment category.

Our balance of payments indicates the difference between total payments and total receipts. If receipts are greater than payments, our country has a *surplus* in its balance of payments. A *deficit* occurs when our country's payments are greater than our receipts. The table shows that the United States had a deficit in 1979. That is, in 1979 more money was paid out of the United States than was taken in.

Problems of Deficits. The United States has had a continuing overall deficit in its balance of payments since 1950. This means that an increasing amount of American dollars has flowed out of the United States and that more dollars are now being held by the people of other countries. This persistent deficit is a problem for Americans because it affects the value of the dollar.

The value of the dollar on the worldwide market has been affected by this deficit. In
recent years, the value of the American 1
dollar has declined in comparison with the currencies of some other countries as a result of this deficit. The factors of supply and demand shape the value of the dollar. The dollar has declined in value on the international market because the supply of dollars has exceeded the demand. This *devaluation*—lowering of value—makes it more difficult for Americans to import the goods that they need. If this deficit continues, the American dollar may be devaluated even further. Inflation and unemployment are related to the problems of deficits and devaluation.

There are some steps that our government can take to try to reduce the deficit. One of the most obvious ways is to reduce the amount of money that Americans spend on imports. This seems difficult, however, when we consider the amount of money that is presently spent on imported oil. In order to cut the money that is spent on imports, the United States will have to reduce its dependence on foreign oil.

1. Due to high interest rates and a relatively low rate of inflation in the United States, the American dollar was strong against most foreign currencies during the early 1980's.

Another way to reduce the payments deficit is to increase American exports. To do this, American producers will have to become more competitive on the worldwide market so that people in other countries will want to buy more American goods and services. This increase in exports will cause more dollars to flow back into the United States.

There are other methods that our government could use in an attempt to reduce or to eliminate our balance of payments deficit. For example, the United States could reduce its foreign aid. Or, the United States could cut back its military forces stationed in other countries. These steps, however, might interfere with other national goals, such as national security. Obviously, there are no easy solutions to our present deficit problem. However, many economists agree that if the United States dollar is to maintain its position relative to other currencies, the deficit problem must be corrected.

Section Checkups

1. *What is a multinational business?*
2. *What are the two categories of foreign aid?*
3. *Why might a change in the amount of goods exported by Americans result in a change in the balance of payments?*

Chapter Summary

Today, the United States leads the world in trading. Americans import and export a wide range of products. International trade is essential to many areas of our economy. For example, America depends upon foreign sources for much of the oil we use today.

Throughout America's history, there has been a continuing debate over the question of free trade. Some Americans believe that the government should restrict imports with tariffs and quotas. Others think that international trade should not be restricted. At present, our government uses a number of trade restrictions for economic and political reasons.

Americans also play an important part in the world economy through international investments and foreign aid. In all international transactions, it is important that the amount of money that flows out of our country is in close balance with the amount that is coming in. Our country's economic stability and welfare depends on our ability to reduce or to eliminate any long-term deficit in our balance of payments.

Reviewing the Chapter

Identifying Terms

Explain or identify the following:

Import	Embargo
Export	Tariff
Monetary unit	Quota
Foreign exchange	Balance of trade
Free trade	Foreign aid
Dumping	Balance of payments

Analyzing Information

1. What is the advantage of a country's specialization in production?

2. What factors shape the particular specialization of production in a country?

3. Why would a person who is involved in international trade need to know about exchange rates?

4. Why does the United States import goods that it could produce?

5. What is dumping?

6. How might a tariff affect the price that a consumer must pay for an imported product?

7. What is the purpose of the General Agreement on Tariffs and Trade?

8. Why does the American government provide foreign aid?

Analyzing Visual Material

1. Examine the table of duty rates that is shown on page 249. What is the difference between the rates applied to imports from most-favored nations and the rates imposed on imports from some communist countries?

2. Study the graph on page 253. Which nation received the highest amount of American aid? What was the approximate amount of aid that was sent to all nine nations shown in the graph?

Research and Projects

1. Make a list of the products that you use in one day. Indicate which products were imported or were produced from imported materials. Do research to try to learn the origin of several of the imported products. Then, prepare a chart that combines your information with that of the other members of your class. Display this chart on a bulletin board.

2. Prepare and hold a panel discussion on the current debates on import restrictions. Use current magazines, newspapers, or interviews with business owners or workers to learn different viewpoints that should be discussed by the panel.

3. To learn more about foreign investments, prepare a report on the overseas activities of one American business. Oil companies, automobile makers, and business-machine companies are among those that might be examined. Direct communication with the business, either through an interview or a letter, might aid you in your research.

H. Armstrong Roberts

Chapter 15 Other Economic Systems: A Comparison

SECTIONS
1 The Japanese Economic System
2 The British Economic System
3 The Soviet Economic System

A comparison of economic systems shows that all nations have developed economic systems designed to satisfy the needs and wants of their people. But these economic systems usually differ in some respect. For example, nations with free enterprise systems rely largely on supply and demand to determine how resources will be used and what goods and services will be produced. In socialist nations, the government makes some decisions concerning the production of major goods and services. In contrast, in communist nations, all economic decisions are made by the government.

Section 1
The Japanese Economic System

Before World War II, Japan was rapidly becoming an industrial power. Since the end of the war, Japan has developed into a leading industrial nation. Today, Japan's Gross National Product ranks second among the industrialized free world. To a large degree, Japan's free enterprise system has led to the country's rapid economic development. As you read this section, ask yourself the following questions: *What factors helped rebuild Japan's economy after World War II? How does the Japanese government encourage industrial production? What are some of the economic problems facing Japan today?*

Government and the Economy. At the end of World War II, the Japanese economy was at a standstill. In the years that followed the war, economic recovery became the chief goal of the new Japanese government. The efforts and the determination of the Japanese people were combined with economic assistance from the United States to rebuild the Japanese economy. This massive undertaking was successful. In less than ten years, Japan's industrial output reached prewar levels.

The economy of Japan is, for the most part, a free enterprise system. However, there is some government ownership in the economy. The government does own and run the country's telephone and telegraph lines, most railroads, and some airlines. But overall, the Japanese government takes no direct control over most other major parts of the economy.

Even without direct controls, the Japanese government does influence industry. Ministers of the Japanese government often meet with banking and business leaders. Together these officials talk about such things as investments, imports, exports, and inflation. As a result, most major decisions are based upon the cooperative efforts and mutual understanding of government and business leaders.

Oftentimes, the Japanese government encourages certain kinds of businesses. In the 1970's, for example, the Japanese government promoted the production of television sets and computers. To encourage this production, the government-owned Japanese Development Bank offered low-cost loans to companies in these fields. Often subsidies are given to businesses that the government seeks to help.

Japanese Industry. Favorable conditions such as a highly skilled work force and technological development have given rise to rapid industrial growth. Today, Japan is a leading producer of steel, iron, cars, radios, and televisions. Currently, Japan is second in the world in output of cars and third in output of steel.

Photri

These workers are assembling high-precision watches, employing the advanced technology that has helped to make Japan a leader in world industry. Careful attention to detail helps to produce quality merchandise.

Industry in Japan has reached a high level of growth. But the country does not have many natural resources. Japan does not have large supplies of such things as coal, iron, copper, and oil. Japan must depend on foreign suppliers for these needs. For example, Japan imports about 99 percent of its oil.

Much of the Japanese economy is based upon importing raw materials and exporting finished products. Using the high level of technology and the skilled labor force available in Japan, industries are able to manufacture high-quality goods at reasonable prices. Many of the items made by Japanese businesses are designed to compete in the international market. The income from the sale of these exported goods helps to balance the cost of Japan's imports.

Japan's rapid industrial growth has been helped by a high level of capital investment. In the 1960's, for example, the country reinvested about 35 percent of its national income into industry. This resulted in the replacement of old machinery. In turn, the new machinery helped add to the rate of productivity.

Labor in Japan. Another reason that accounts for the high rate of industrial growth is the close employee-employer relationships that characterize many of Japan's industries. For example, Japanese businesses hire workers on a lifetime employment system. That is, employees often stay with one company until they retire. One advantage of this system is that employees have a strong sense of loyalty to their company. Also, businesses are likely to invest time and money in long-range training programs for their employees.

Stable labor-management relations have added to the industrial growth of Japan. Labor unions have existed in Japan on a large scale since 1945. Even though these unions have the right to strike, they seldom do. Informal labor-management councils have been set up in Japanese industries. These groups discuss working conditions, ways of improving productivity, and other important matters. Through these meetings, labor and management representatives have been able to settle differences that might otherwise have caused a strike.

(Text continues on page 264.)

Looking at Careers
The international financial analyst

John D. Firestone & Associates, Inc.

What do international financial analysts do? International financial analysts collect and analyze economic and statistical data. It is the responsibility of international financial analysts to help develop and establish favorable trade policies with other countries. They study topics such as taxes, tariffs, trade barriers, and international exchange rates. International financial analysts may work for the federal government or for multinational corporations.

What qualifications do international financial analysts need? A bachelor's degree in economics or finance is the minimum requirement for beginnng financial analysts. College courses in social sciences and advanced mathematics are also essential. Fluency in a foreign language is considered a plus. An advanced degree is helpful in attaining higher-level positions. Personal qualities that are needed by financial analysts are accuracy, patience, and objectiveness. Although there are no licensing requirements for financial analysts, most analysts belong to professional organizations.

What about pay and working conditions? Financial analysts just out of college will earn an above-average salary, but additional education and experience will expand an individual's earning power. For example, in the early 1980's the average income of financial analysts with a doctorate degree who were working for the government was about 30,000 dollars a year. Financial analysts generally have pleasant working conditions. Much work is conducted from the office, and some travel may be required.

How does a knowledge of economics help? International financial analysts usually combine a knowledge of economic principles with an understanding of international trade relations. In addition, financial analysts utilize economics to make important decisions that may greatly affect international trade. For more information on careers in financial analysis, write to **National Association of Business Economists, 28349 Chagrin Blvd., Suite 201, Cleveland, Ohio 44122.**

In most cases, the wages paid to Japanese workers are decided through collective bargaining. In many industries it is common for workers to receive pay raises based on seniority alone. Many experts believe this practice has helped increase worker productivity. This is because, over a period of time, workers become better at their job. However, this policy is slowly being changed. Many businesses now use a pay system similar to the one in the United States.

Japanese Agriculture. Japan is very mountainous. Only 15 percent of the land is suitable for farming. Farms are often small. They average about 2.7 acres [1.1 hectares] in size. Only 14 percent of the Japanese people work in agriculture production.

All usable land is cultivated in order to meet the food needs of the large Japanese population. Modern farm equipment and scientific methods are used to increase crop yield. Even with its large population and small farming area, Japan supplies 80 percent of its own food needs.

The Japanese government does not closely regulate agriculture. However, the government does try to encourage self-sufficiency. By keeping the price of rice high, for example, the government has brought about an increase in Japan's rice crop and in the income of farmers.

Social Welfare. Since the early 1960's, social-welfare programs have been a main undertaking of the Japanese government. Today, Japan's welfare programs offer many different services. These include income security, health care, retirement benefits, and services for the aged and the disabled. However, these programs have not reached the same level as in Western Europe or the United States.

Health care is provided by the Japanese Health Insurance plan. Under the provisions of this plan, payments are made in cases of sickness, injury, and maternity. About 70 percent of health care and hospital costs are paid for by the state.

Japan's welfare programs are primarily financed through general taxes. About 20 percent of the average worker's income is paid as income tax to the government. Currently, social-welfare costs make up the largest part of the Japanese government's budget.

Japanese farmers use terrace farming, a method that allows even the steep sides of hills to be cultivated.

Artstreet

Comparison of recent American and Japanese consumer prices

Item	United States	Japan
Beef (1 lb)	$ 1.70	$ 12.10
Coffee (1 cup)	.40	1.15
Sugar (1 lb)	.24	.57
Butter (1 lb)	1.79	3.62
Women's Skirt	41.30	33.43
Men's Socks	1.79	2.52
Gym Shoes	15.49	5.50
Toaster	14.50	25.65
Electric Range	379.00	540.40
Movie Admission	3.50	7.00

Source: Various Sources.

Both the United States and Japan have free enterprise economic systems. However, consumer prices differ between the two countries. As this chart indicates, the prices of many items are higher in Japan than they are in the United States. On an average, Japanese workers spend almost 30 percent of their income on food.

The Japanese Consumer. Since Japan's economy is based on free enterprise, the forces of supply and demand determine the kinds of goods made. Generally, the Japanese consumer is able to choose from many different goods.

Overall, many items—such as clothes, appliances, and food—are often high priced. For a price list of selected goods, see the chart on this page. Almost 30 percent of the average worker's income of about $10,000 a year is spent on food. Nearly 10 percent of the average Japanese worker's income is spent on housing.

Because of the small amount of usable land and the large population, land prices tend to be very high. Though land is high priced, many Japanese still prefer single-family dwellings. About 60 percent of the homes in Japan are owner occupied. However, in the crowded capital city of Tokyo, most of the population live in apartments. These dwellings usually consist of three rooms. Two of these rooms serve as both living and sleeping quarters. The other room is a kitchen-dining area. In the past few years, the Japanese people have demanded better living conditions. New dwellings of increasingly better quality are being built. But housing remains scarce.

Economic Problems. The rising rate of inflation is one of Japan's most serious

Japan is a manufacturing nation. Much of the Japanese economy is based on exporting finished products, like these motorcycles, to foreign nations. Maintaining a favorable balance of trade is an important concern of Japanese industries.

Photri

economic problems. Average consumer prices have risen by about 8 percent recently. But the cost of gas and electricity has increased by almost 50 percent. The increasing cost of imported oil is one of the chief causes of Japan's inflation.

In recent years capital investments have decreased. This trend has caused a slowdown of economic growth. Changing this situation may not be easy. Most likely, Japan will have to encourage foreign countries to invest in Japanese businesses.

To be able to get the raw materials it needs, Japan will have to continue good trade relations with other countries. As a manufacturing country, Japan must also sell finished goods to other countries. This may cause other countries to try to limit the import of Japanese goods to protect their own businesses. At times some Americans have called for government regulations to keep down the number of Japanese cars on the American market.

Japanese society is troubled by inadequate social services. Although social services are improving, the availability and quality of these services have not kept pace with the rapid growth of the economy. For example, hospitals in Japan are often overcrowded and sometimes in need of repair. Thus, Japan is far behind most Western countries in terms of social welfare.

Today, Japan is a leading industrial power. In past years, Japanese businesses have grown at a rapid rate. But some experts question if this high rate of growth will go on in the future. How Japan continues its prosperity and economic growth and meets the wants of its people remains to be seen.

Section Checkups

1. *What type of economic system exists in Japan?*
2. *How do employer-employee relationships influence productivity?*
3. *Why is it essential for Japan to continue to find new foreign markets?*

Section 2
The British Economic System

In a socialist economic system, the government plays a large part in economic decision making. But private ownership is not eliminated. Oftentimes, the government owns certain major industries in such fields as transportation, communication, and heavy industry. A mixed economic system—part government ownership and part private ownership—exists in Great Britain, where the government owns certain basic industries. As you read this section, ask yourself the following questions: *What was the purpose of the National Insurance Act? Why does the British government own certain industries? What trouble does Britain's economy face?*

Socialism in Great Britain. Socialism in Great Britain began in 1945. After World War II, the British economy was in shambles. Many people believed that the government should plan the country's economic recovery. And they said the government should also control the means of production. A Labour, or socialist, government was voted into office in 1945. Its leader, Clement Attlee, became the country's prime minister.

The socialist government of Great Britain came to power through democratic means. Similarly, the socialists' plans were started through democratic processes—through laws passed by the legislature. Thus it is said that socialism has come to Britain through evolution, not through revolution.

Nationalization of Industry. A major characteristic of socialism in Great Britain is the government's ownership of key industries. Government-owned industries are called nationalized industries. Over the years these industries were bought from private owners by the government. As a result, many large industries—such as the coal mines, the steel industry, railroads, and an airline—are owned and run by the government. It is the aim of the government to run these businesses for the public good.

From the socialists' point of view, government ownership and operation of key industries has certain advantages. This is because they believe that private entrepreneurs often have different business goals than the government. For example, private individuals running a factory expect to earn a profit. If the owners fail to earn this profit, they may shut down the factory. On the other hand, socialists believe the government does not run a factory only for profit.

Before a socialist government would think about closing a factory, other parts of the economy would be considered. The closing of the factory may greatly add to unemployment and increase the payment of unemployment compensation. Furthermore, the government has more resources to use for investment than do private owners. A socialist government could use public monies to improve the factory and make it profitable. Keeping such a factory open may serve the public's interests.

Many of the key industries have been nationalized. But much private ownership still exists. The textile industry, retailing, and agriculture are among the fields that, in general, are privately owned and managed. In this way, Great Britain has a mixed economy. Private ownership exists along with government ownership and some central planning.

Politics and the Economy. Today in Great Britain, there are two major political parties, the Labour party and the Conservative party. These two political parties hold different beliefs on the role of the government in industry. In general, the Conservative party favors more free enterprise than does the Labour party.

Perhaps the difference between these political parties can best be seen through the example of the steel industry. Between 1945 and 1951, the Labour government had nationalized the steel industry. In 1953, when the Conservative party was in power, the steel industry was sold back to private owners. However, in 1967 the government, under control of the Labour party, once again nationalized the steel industry. Thus, in Britain, the political party in office directly influences the government's role in the economy. Such dramatic changes in governmental policies seldom occur in the United States.

Social Welfare in Britain. One primary concern of the Labour government has been social welfare. The enactment of legislation extending social services is fundamental to the socialists' belief that the individual's welfare is the responsibility of the state. In Great Britain social-welfare programs were started on a large scale shortly after World War II.

G. R. Roberts

Nationalization of key industries is an essential part of a socialist economic system. This is a view of the Port Talbot Iron and Steel Works, part of the nationalized steel industry in Great Britain.

One of the first laws called for by the Labour party was the National Insurance Act. It was passed in 1946. This law provided for many different kinds of government aid. Financial aid was given to citizens in cases of unemployment, sickness, maternity, and retirement. Also, death benefits were paid to families to help pay funeral costs.

Today, under the National Insurance Act and other laws almost the whole population of Britain is protected from economic hardship in some way. Workers, for example, are compensated for loss of pay while they are sick or disabled. If needed, these benefits are paid until the worker reaches retirement age. Upon retiring, the worker is paid a pension by the government.

Another important program started by the Labour party was the National Health Service. Under this plan most health care and hospital care is given free of charge. Prescriptions are either free or very low priced. Through a system of socialized medicine Britain's population is assured of medical care.

The British Consumer. The British government owns and runs certain industries. It does not control the entire British economy. In many parts of the economy, the forces of supply and demand largely determine what goods are made and the prices for these goods. The British are able to select from a variety of consumer goods. Generally, food prices are often a little higher than in the United States. But prices for clothes and appliances are often lower. A subcompact British car, for example, costs about $4,900, while an American subcompact car may cost about $6,000.

As you have read, most health care and dental services, as well as other services, are provided for the British consumer. In most cases, the British consumer does not pay when these services are used. The cost of these services, for the most part, is covered through general taxes and paid for by the government.

Both Great Britain and the United States have a progressive tax structure—that is, individuals in higher income brackets are taxed at a higher rate. But taxes in Great Britain are generally higher. About 30 percent of the average British worker's income is collected as income tax, compared to about 20 percent for the average single American. The rate of taxation in Britain increases markedly as income increases. For example, personal income beyond $52,500 is taxed at about 80 percent. This [1] means that with an income of $62,500, an individual might keep only $2,000 of the last $10,000.

A large part of an individual's income goes to cover the costs of housing. Roughly 50 percent of the houses in Britain are owner occupied. The rest of the dwellings are rented from private owners or from the government. Single-family dwellings are usually two-story buildings with the living rooms and kitchen downstairs and the bedrooms and bathroom upstairs.

With the British urban population near 77 percent of the total population, housing shortages exist in many cities. Also, many dwellings were built before 1919, and some are in rather poor condition. An average of about 300,000 new dwellings are being built each year to meet housing needs. But adequate housing is still relatively scarce.

Economic Problems. The economy of Great Britain has been troubled with problems for which there are no easy answers. One problem is the inflation that has

1. Personal income above $52,500 is now taxed at about 60 percent. A person with an income of $62,500 would keep about $4,000 of the last $10,000.

accompanied the rising standard of living since World War II. During the 1970's, inflation grew at about 10 percent a year. In the early 1980's it rose to about 19 percent.

Many economists believe that the demands of some labor unions for higher pay have added to the high rate of inflation. Inflation problems have been made worse by labor-management troubles. Often, British unions strike to achieve their goals. Some strikes in key businesses seriously hurt the British economy.

In the 1979 elections, the Conservative party gained control of the government. Under the leadership of Prime Minister Margaret Thatcher, steps were taken to fight inflation by cutting government spending and controlling the money supply. In 1980, spending for education, housing, and foreign aid was lowered. The outcome of the Conservative government's 1
plans remain to be seen.

A second problem has been the almost continual deficit in the balance of payments. Britain needs to import large quantities of raw materials and food. Britain's exports have not been sufficient to offset the cost of these imports. As a result, more money has flowed out of Britain than has flowed into the country.

In response to this problem, the British government has sought more favorable trade agreements with other countries. On January 1, 1973, for example, Great Britain joined the European Economic Community—the Common Market. Through this new economic relationship with European countries, Britain has hoped to stimulate its own economy. The lower tariffs among Common Market member nations have helped increase British exports. However, the trade agreements of Common Market membership also present some drawbacks to the British economy. The long-term effects of Common Market membership are still not clear.

Since the end of World War II, Great Britain has democratically changed its economy to a socialist system, while still retaining much free enterprise. The Labour party has nationalized many of the key

Sven Simon/Katherine Young

Great Britain's Prime Minister Margaret Thatcher came to power in 1979. A member of the Conservative party, she ended controls on wages and prices, revised the tax system, and lowered income taxes by an average of 15 percent.

1. By the end of 1983, inflation in Britain was down to about 4 percent.

industries and introduced many social reforms. But many economic problems—such as inflation, shortages of key markets, and dependence on foreign suppliers—continue to exist. The direction that the mixed economy of Great Britain will take in the near future will greatly depend upon which political leaders the voters elect.

Section Checkups

1. *When did socialism begin in Britain?*
2. *How does the British government finance its social-welfare programs?*
3. *Why did Great Britain join the Common Market?*

Section 3 The Soviet Economic System

Today, the Soviet Union is one of the world's leading industrial nations. It is controlled by a communist dictatorship. Unlike Americans, Soviet citizens have little freedom. They also have little say about how their economy operates.

According to Soviet law, all property—the land, factories, banks, and so on—is owned by the people. But in fact, almost all property and almost all economic activity are controlled by the government.

Since 1917, the Soviet Union has developed from a backward agricultural country to one of the world's leading economic nations. This change did not come without cost. As you read this section, ask yourself the following questions: *What is the role of the* Gosplan? *Why does the Soviet government control industrial production? How are wages and prices controlled in the Soviet Union?*

The Beginnings of Communism. As you have read, the ideas of modern communism can be traced back to the ideas of a German philosopher, Karl Marx. In the *Communist Manifesto* and *Das Kapital,* Marx outlined the way he thought communism would take the place of capitalism.

Marx viewed society as an economic struggle between the rich upper class and the poor working class. In Marx's view, the working class would ultimately seize power from the wealthy and set up a classless society—communism. Karl Marx believed communism would first come about in an industrialized country. It did not. Instead Communists took power in Russia in 1917. At that time Russia was a backward farming country.

After the Russian Revolution of November 1917, the Communists, under the leadership of Lenin, took over the Russian government. Lenin, a follower of Marx's ideas, planned to establish a communist dictatorship. Lenin and the Communists quickly took over the means of production—land, factories, farms, and businesses. Strikes were outlawed. Rapid industrialization became the chief goal.

In the years since the revolution, the Soviet economy has been controlled by the government. The government, in turn, has been under the control of the Communist party. Through a planning commission, known as the *Gosplan,* the Soviet government has made all major economic decisions for the country. The *Gosplan* has answered the three economic questions: What should be produced? How should products be produced? For whom should products be produced?

Soviet Control of the Economy. A command economy exists in the Soviet Union. The forces of supply and demand—as we know them—have little influence in determining production. Instead, the Soviet government runs the economy through the *Gosplan.*

The *Gosplan* is made up of a chairman and an 11-member board. It also includes about 100 scientists, sociologists, and economists. This group of individuals decides such things as how many cars will be made, how much wheat will be grown, and how much steel will be produced. These decisions are based upon what the Soviet government has said it needs.

The *Gosplan* usually makes an economic plan for a five-year period. There are several steps taken in the development of this plan. First, the *Gosplan* analyzes data and evaluates how resources will be used. Second, the *Gosplan* passes on its recommendations to regional ministers, who in turn discuss the plans with farm and plant managers. Third, each manager prepares a report, which is evaluated by the *Gosplan.* Fourth, the *Gosplan* prepares a final plan. This plan is then sent to the leaders of the government for approval. When it is put into effect, the plan spells out what will be produced, how much will be produced, and how it will be sold. The plan is implemented on a year-to-year basis.

The Kremlin, in Moscow, is the center of power of the Soviet government, which makes all economic decisions.

Tass from Sovfoto

Industries in the Soviet Union. In the past, Soviet five-year plans have emphasized the growth of heavy industries. The production of machinery, steel, chemicals, and so on has been stressed. Current planning continues to stress the growth of heavy industries. The production of military equipment is also important in the Soviet Union. Because of the emphasis on capital goods and military products, the production of consumer goods has often fallen short of the demand.

To meet its production quotas, the *Gosplan* uses several means. First, higher income is used to reward workers who surpass quotas. Second, emotional appeals are used to motivate workers. For example, good workers are given "hero medals." The third means is through pressure. Social and economic pressure is used by the Communists to be sure that their plans are carried out. An unproductive worker, for example, may receive a cut in pay. Or the worker may be removed from government housing. If the problem is serious enough, the worker may be fired. Since the Soviet government is the only employer, it can be very hard for a worker to find new housing or another job.

Even though labor unions do exist in the Soviet Union, they do not work to protect the interests of the Soviet worker. Instead, unions in the Soviet Union are used by the Communist party to carry out the current five-year plan and to increase production. These labor unions do not negotiate wages, and the workers do not have the right to go on strike. A worker's wages, as well as the prices the worker must pay, are set by the *Gosplan*. The government, not the forces of supply and demand, determines wages and prices in the Soviet Union.

Soviet Agriculture. One of the goals of the Communists is to be independent of foreign food suppliers. Each five-year plan directs the Soviet Union's agricultural production. Currently, about 2.25 million square miles [5.8 million square kilometers] of land is being farmed. About 50 percent of the population lives on farms.

Two types of farms are found in the Soviet Union—state farms and collective farms. Privately owned farms have been almost completely eliminated.

State farms are government owned. Usually, these farms are huge in size, averaging about 112,000 acres [45 320 hectares]. Normally, 400 to 500 families live on a state farm. Workers on this type of farm receive a regular wage from the government. The entire crop is turned over to the government.

Collective farms are cooperatives composed of many peasant families. These farms vary in size. In most cases, each family on a collective farm keeps a small plot of land for private use. But the rest of the farm, the buildings, and the farm machinery are collectively owned. Through its five-year plans, the government determines what crops are grown on the collective farm. Part of the harvest is kept for use on the collective farm. A fixed amount of the crop is sold to the government at very low prices. Any surplus may be sold or traded. However, after quotas have been filled, there is rarely a surplus.

The agricultural goals set by recent five-year plans have not often been achieved. The communist government has tried to improve production through the use of science and technology. But production has remained low. Weather conditions often have caused crop failures. In addition,

(Text continues on page 275.)

Using Social Studies Skills

Understanding a cartoon

Magazines and newspapers often use political cartoons to illustrate their viewpoint. Political cartoons often *satirize*—ridicule or poke fun at—a prominent person or a government's policies. Cartoons of this type are designed to entertain. But the cartoon's real purpose is to make a point. To make this point, the cartoonist often uses symbols that the reader must understand. Political cartoons are used throughout the world because they can be understood in spite of language differences. The political cartoon at the right is taken from a Soviet magazine, *Krokodil*. The viewpoint expressed by the editors of *Krokodil* is most often strongly anti-Western. However, this cartoon satirizes some of the inefficiencies of Soviet industries. Study the cartoon carefully; then answer the questions that follow.

Sovfoto

Krokodil

1. Whom does the man in the cartoon represent?
2. In what type of business or industry is this cartoon taking place?
3. What is the finished product the worker is expected to make?
4. Why do you think the smaller piece of material has a higher price tag on it?
5. What do you think the cartoonist is saying about waste and inefficiency in the Soviet Union?
6. What do you think the cartoonist is saying about the pricing system in the Soviet Union?

E. Shulepov/Tass from Sovfoto

This picture shows the winter-wheat harvest on a Soviet state farm. The farm's goals and activities are determined by the government.

Soviet farm workers are not highly motivated to produce more. Lacking incentives because they cannot profit from increased production, Soviet farmers produce far less than do farmers in our free enterprise system. As a result, the Soviet Union frequently needs to import grain to feed its people. In the 1970's, the Soviets imported about 6 million tons [5.44 metric tons] of wheat and corn a year from the United States.

The Soviet Consumer. The average consumer in the Soviet Union plays a far smaller role in the Soviet economy than does a consumer in the United States. As you know, in our free enterprise system, the consumer influences what is produced. The American consumer has a wide choice of goods to purchase. However, this is not the case in the Soviet Union. The Soviet consumer's choices are restricted because the government decides what goods should be produced. Although some consumer goods must be produced, Soviet five-year plans stress the production of heavy industries at the expense of consumer goods.

To control what the Soviet consumer is able to buy, the *Gosplan* often sets high prices for consumer goods, such as cars and televisions. Setting prices in such a manner has two effects. One, many consumer items can be afforded only by communist party leaders, government officials, and national heroes. Two, consumer goods are priced to keep consumption low. In this way goods are rationed by price. High prices and low wages shape consumer demand in the Soviet Union.

In the late 1970's, the Soviet workers' wages increased by about 4 percent a year. This extra income has led the Soviet consumers to want more consumer goods. And even though the communist government has attempted to produce more consumer goods, the available goods have not satisfied the Soviet consumers.

Goods that are thought to be necessities by the average American consumer—meat, stylish clothes, and cars—are not readily available to the Soviet consumer. For example, in the Soviet Union a small sedan costs about $10,000—more than twice the average worker's annual salary. The cost of the car must be paid in full when it is ordered. The customer then waits about a year for delivery. For a comparison of prices in the Soviet Union and the United States, see the chart on this page.

Housing is another problem in the Soviet Union. About 30 percent of the urban Soviet population shares part of its living quarters. Many families live in a single room that serves as living room, dining room, and bedroom. Often families share bathroom and kitchen facilities with at least one other family. Although construction of new housing is under way in most Soviet cities, housing shortages are likely to exist in the Soviet Union for many years to come.

There is a significant difference between the buying power of the Soviet consumer and the American consumer. As the chart below shows, consumer and luxury items are priced beyond the reach of the average Soviet consumer. Unlike prices in the United States, prices in the Soviet Union are not determined by the market forces of supply and demand but are determined by the Soviet government.

Comparison of recent American and Soviet consumer prices

Item	United States	Soviet Union*
Car (Compact)	$6,200.00	$10,000.00
Bus Fare	.75	.08
Ballpoint Pen	.29	1.50
Dental Checkup	32.00	Free
Chicken (1 lb)	.65	2.25
Loaf of Bread (1 lb)	.62	.24
Jeans	18.50	45.00
Hardcover Novel	12.95	3.00
Daily Newspaper	.25	.05
Vacation (2 weeks, per person)**	900.00	120.00

*Many goods and services are subsidized by the Soviet government.

**Vacations: U.S. figure is for a major resort city.
Soviet vacations are subsidized by workers' unions.

Source: Various Sources.

Today, most economists agree that the Soviet Union has made great progress. However, its attempts to become completely self-sufficient have not succeeded. Industrial output has fallen short of the goals of the various five-year plans. And agricultural goals have not been met in recent years. As a result, the Soviet Union's dependence on foreign trade has increased. Perhaps more importantly, the desires of the Soviet consumer have not been satisfied.

Section Checkups

1. *When did communism begin in the Soviet Union?*
2. *How does the* Gosplan *motivate workers so that production goals are achieved?*
3. *Why has agricultural production in the Soviet Union often fallen short of the* Gosplan's *goals?*

Chapter Summary

The economy of Japan is, for the most part, a free enterprise system. Even though there is almost no direct government control of the economy, many industries are influenced by the government. Stable labor-management relations, a skilled work force, a high level of technology, and excellent management have helped Japan's economy grow at a rapid rate. As a leading manufacturing country that lacks natural resources, Japan must import most of its raw materials. Japan must also depend upon foreign markets for the sale of much of its output.

A mixed economy exists in Great Britain. The British government owns and operates key industries. Privately owned businesses continue to exist. Social welfare is a chief concern in Britain. A high rate of taxation covers the many social programs available in Great Britain. Because Great Britain is chiefly a manufacturing country, it must depend on foreign suppliers for much of its raw materials. Today, inflation and a lack of foreign markets are two problems facing Great Britain's economy.

The economy of the Soviet Union is controlled by the communist government. The *Gosplan*, an office of the Soviet government, makes almost all economic decisions for the country. Industries are told what to make, and farmers are told what to grow. Wages and prices are set by the *Gosplan*. The choice of consumer goods is limited. However, even with all the control of the economy, the communist government has not met its goal of self-sufficiency.

Reviewing the Chapter

Identifying Terms

Explain or identify the following:

Capital investment	Labour party
Self-sufficiency	Margaret Thatcher
Nationalization	Command economy
Central planning	*Gosplan*
Conservative party	Heavy industries

Analyzing Information

1. In what ways have stable labor-management relations aided the growth of Japanese industry?

2. How does the Japanese government influence industrial production?

3. What advantages do socialists see in the nationalization of key industries?

4. How does the social-welfare program in Great Britain affect British consumers?

5. How does the *Gosplan* determine the economic goals of the Soviet Union?

6. In what ways do the plans of the *Gosplan* affect the Soviet consumer?

Analyzing Visual Material

1. Examine the photograph of the Japanese factory workers on page 262. How do you think the uniforms the workers are wearing are related to the type of work that they are doing? Do you think the workers' uniforms might affect the quality of the finished product? Explain.

2. Look at the table on page 265. Which of the listed consumer items costs less in Japan? Would you say the prices for food items are higher or are lower in Japan than in the United States?

3. Study the table on page 276. Which of the listed consumer items are priced lower in the Soviet Union than in the United States? Why do you think the price of a car in the Soviet Union is high?

Research and Projects

1. Imagine that you are a Japanese entrepreneur starting a new industry. List the benefits, privileges, and advantages you would be willing to give to your employees. Report to your class why you think these things would increase productivity. Discuss how you would evaluate each benefit and its effect on productivity.

2. The government of Great Britain controls several aspects of the British economy. To determine the extent of this influence, collect newspaper and magazine articles on the British economy for one week. Report your findings to the class.

3. To understand the full extent to which the *Gosplan* controls the Soviet economy, research two or three of the individual five-year plans. Note which areas of the economy have been stressed and which have been neglected. Summarize your findings in a report to the class.

Randy Dieter/Corn's Photo Service

Chapter 16 The Future of American Capitalism

SECTIONS 1 Society and Economic Stability
2 Growth and Technology
3 Maintaining Free Enterprise

As we look to the future, new challenges await us. In the past, our free enterprise system has helped us to become a leading economic power. Our economic system can enable us to continue our growth and development in the years to come. If we achieve this economic growth in the future, we will have the opportunity to maintain a high standard of living while at the same time reducing social problems, such as poverty and unemployment. Thus, most observers agree that maintaining our free enterprise system is essential if we are to keep the many economic freedoms we now enjoy.

Section 1
Society and Economic Stability

A large part of the economic success of the United States can be attributed to the free enterprise system. The American free enterprise system has given rise to one of the highest standards of living in the world today. And free enterprise has allowed more freedom than is found in most countries in the world. However, our economic system now faces new challenges. Our future depends upon how we, as a people, meet these challenges. As you read this section, ask yourself the following questions: *How has the government tried to eliminate poverty? In what way may population growth be an economic problem? What employment patterns seem to be developing for the future?*

Free Enterprise and Stability. Freedom is the basic ingredient of our economic system. Our free enterprise system answers the three basic economic questions by allowing people to make their own choices, to compete in a market system, and to own and to use private property. Economists agree that the free enterprise system has served the country well. Americans enjoy one of the highest standards of living in the world. And our nation is one of the strongest and most productive countries in the world. But it is not perfect.

For the United States to keep its position as a leading economic power, a stable economy must be a national goal. A stable economy is, in general terms, an economy with high employment, little or no inflation, price stability, and economic growth. A stable economy does not experience frequent and sharp ups and downs in economic activity.

Today, our free enterprise system faces the challenges of a changing society. Social and economic problems must be solved. These problems include such things as inflation, poverty, unemployment, discrimination, and education. The causes of these problems are many and complex.

Poverty. Poverty is not limited to one area or to one group of people. Poverty-stricken people live in all areas of our country—both urban and rural. Poverty-stricken individuals are people of all ages, races, and ethnic groups. In 1980, for example, the government estimated that
about 29.3 million people in the United 1
States were living in poverty. Clearly, poverty is a major problem. It is a problem for which no easy answers are available.

Officially, a family of 4 with an income
of less than $8,414 is considered to be liv- 2
ing below the poverty level. Currently, about 13 percent of the people in the United States are said to be living in poverty. If this 13 percent rate were to remain constant, by the year 2000 there would be over

1. As of 1983, about 34.4 million Americans were living in poverty.

2. In 1983, the poverty-level income for a family of 4 was $9,862. About 15 percent of all Americans lived in poverty in 1983.

This table shows the number of years it takes for a nation's population to double at certain rates of growth. Many nations today face economic problems because of rapid population growth.

Population doubling time

Population Growth Rate Percent	Number of Years to Double Population
0.5	139
1.0	69
1.5	46
2.0	35
2.5	28
3.0	23
3.5	20
4.0	17

1 36 million poverty-stricken people living in the United States.

The federal government has spent billions of dollars to fight poverty. For exam-
2 ple, in 1981 the government spent over 9 billion dollars on the food-stamp program alone. Yet poverty continues.

In the future it will be necessary for both government and industry to work together to solve the poverty problem. Both government and business must create conditions that allow as many people as possible to earn a living. Some experts suggest that the government pay the poor a minimum income and offer them incentives to earn more than this minimum level. Others plan new public-service programs. However, experts agree that for poverty programs to be successful, these programs must remove the causes of poverty.

Stability and Population Growth. The population of the United States has been growing at a rate of just less than 1 percent per year since the 1970's. By the year 2000, it is estimated that about 280 million people will be living in the United States. This growing population may present an economic problem for our free enterprise system.

For example, in 1980 the civilian work force was made up of over 100 million people. By 2000 this figure may rise to as much as 135 million workers. Obviously, it will be necessary to create many new jobs for all these additional people. However, new technology in existing industries will most likely result in fewer workers producing more goods. Thus new industries and new opportunities must be developed. Our economy must be able to meet this rising need for jobs. If not, many more people may be unable to find jobs. Any rise in unemployment seems certain to add to the number of people living in poverty.

Some economists are concerned that the United States may not be able to support so large a population in the future. These economists are worried that our natural resources may not meet our needs. They also fear that our businesses may not be able to continue to grow and create new jobs to support a growing population. Therefore, a number of economists and other social scientists have suggested that a lower population growth rate could result in less unemployment. Less unemployment, in turn, should be a key to a more stable economy.

1. If a 15 percent rate continued, by the year 2000 there would be more than 40 million Americans living in poverty.

2. In 1983, the federal government spent over $12 billion on the food-stamp program.

(Text continues on page 283.)

Using Social Studies Skills

Interpreting graphs

Demographers are scientists who study populations. Their studies show that the percentage of the American population 65 years of age and older will increase significantly in the future. There are two main reasons for this increase. First, the average life span of Americans will continue to increase slowly. Second, Americans are having fewer children. The graph shows the percentage of Americans 65 years of age and older for the years 1900 to 2025. Study the graph carefully; then answer the questions that follow.

U.S. population, age 65 and older, 1900–2025*

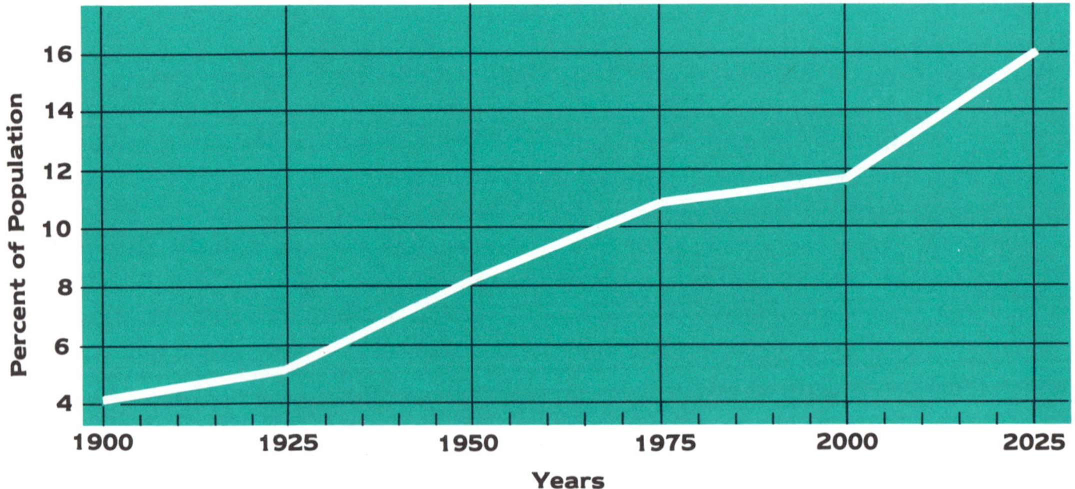

*1980–2025 figures are projected.

Source: U.S. Census Bureau.

1. About what percentage of the American population will be 65 years of age and older in 2025?
2. In what year did Americans 65 years of age and older make up about 8 percent of the population?
3. By what year is the percentage of Americans 65 years of age and older expected to reach 16 percent?
4. In 1900, 4 percent of the population was 65 years of age and older. By what years will there be about 3 times that percent?

Future Employment Patterns. To have a stable economy, we must find ways to prevent high rates of unemployment in the future. Lowering unemployment must be a major goal of government and business. To reach this goal, economists and other experts have tried to determine some of the job needs of tomorrow.

No one is able to predict the future. But five trends appear to be likely. First, computers and machines will continue to replace many unskilled and semiskilled workers. Second, more highly specialized skills will be needed for employment. Third, people will probably work fewer hours. Thus, workers will have more leisure time. Fourth, job discrimination based on race, sex, or age will decrease. And the fifth trend is that workers will change jobs and careers more frequently.

Obviously, these trends are not new. In the past few decades, for example, white-collar jobs have increased more rapidly than have blue-collar jobs. This reflects the trend toward more people working in service-type jobs, such as doctors, social workers, accountants, and engineers. (See circle graphs on this page.) To be qualified for these kinds of jobs, workers need to have special skills.

A continuing trend seems to be the increase of white-collar workers, who now make up over half of the American work force.

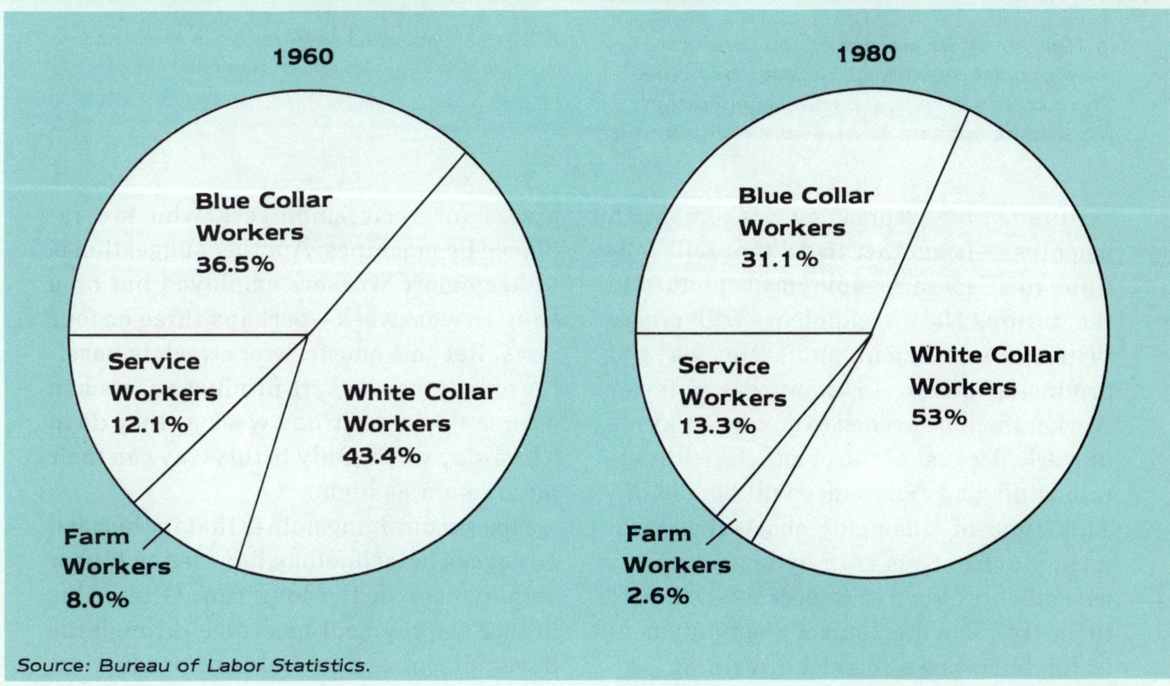

Percent of American female population employed, 1900-1980*

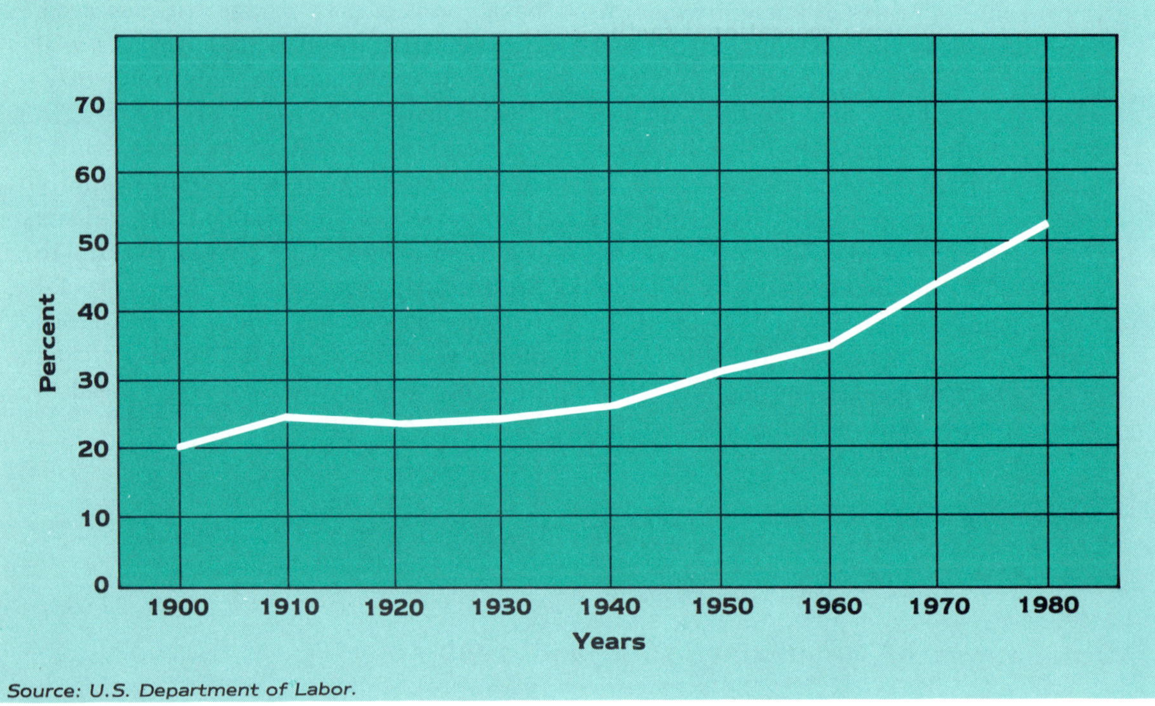

In 1980, over 50 percent of the American female population worked outside the home. The increase in female participation in the work force appears to be a continuing trend.

* By 1983, about 53 percent of the female population worked outside the home.

Automation—replacing workers with machines—is another trend that will continue to affect our employment picture in the future. New technology will create faster, more efficient, and easier ways of producing goods. In many cases fewer workers will be needed to do certain kinds of work. Because of this, workers with certain skills and experience will be laid off. This type of unemployment—structural unemployment—is seen by many experts as a chief problem of tomorrow. One way to partly solve this kind of unemployment is for businesses to set up training programs for their employees who are replaced by machines. Another suggestion is to keep more workers employed but on a shorter workweek—perhaps three or four days. But this shorter workweek is possible only if the workers produce as much in a three-day or four-day week as they do in a five-day week. Only in this way can their pay remain as high.

One encouraging note is that in the past, advances in technology have led to higher employment in the long run. Often, this higher employment has come through the development of new fields of production.

In years to come, for example, as people spend less time at work, they will have more free time. Many people may use their leisure time by using recreational facilities, or by going to concerts, art shows, or amusement parks. One likely outcome of these activities will be the growth of the recreation and entertainment industries. In this way, many new jobs may be created in these fields.

The need to create new jobs remains a challenge for our economy. Our economic system must solve the problem of unemployment. Only through our efforts will our free enterprise system continue to meet the challenges of our changing economy.

Section Checkups

1. *About how many people were living in poverty in 1980?*
2. *What are the five trends facing workers in the future?*
3. *Why are some economists concerned about rapid population growth?*

Section 2 Growth and Technology

Economic growth is an important part of the American free enterprise system. But economic growth is the result of many factors. In the past, one of these factors has been advances in technology. In the years to come, Americans must look to new technology as one answer to the challenges that face our free enterprise system. As you read this section, ask yourself the following questions: *What is the relationship between economic growth and new technology? What are some of the steps that might be taken to meet America's future energy needs? In what ways might solar energy be used in the future?*

Growth in the Future. Most economists agree that economic growth is needed if we want to raise America's standard of living. Growth provides more goods and services, which help satisfy the needs and wants of our growing country.

Economic growth is related to advances in technology. This technological growth often results in a more efficient use of natural resources. By combining or using our resources in new ways, economic output and growth can be increased.

It is not easy to measure the amount of technological advancement taking place in a country. One way is to look at the new

Chevrolet Motor Division, General Motors Corporation

The production of this electric car was made possible by research and new technology. Technological advancements are an important part of economic growth.

goods produced. For example, microwave ovens and home video recorders came about through new technology. But these advances could not have been made without investment.

Technological advancement and investment are closely connected. The amount of money spent on research and development is often a good measure of a country's technological growth. For example, in 1960 American government and business spent about 13 billion dollars on research and development. By the early 1980's, how-
1 ever, this figure had risen to over 51 billion dollars. Even allowing for inflation, there has been sizable growth in spending for research and development.

Today, almost everyone agrees that technological growth will be very important in the future. But there is some concern that not enough is being spent to keep up this growth. There is also a growing pressure on many businesses to take more risks in research and development.

But faced with rising prices, many American businesses are hard pressed to meet the current costs of research and development. Thus some ways to encourage investment in this area have been suggested. One suggestion has been to cut income taxes. In this way people may be able to save more money, and this money could be used for investment. A second suggestion is to allow businesses to reduce their taxes by allowing credit for money spent on research and development. A number of economists feel that these steps, or others, are needed to ensure tomorrow's growth.

1. American government and business spent more than $75 billion on research and development in 1982.

Energy and the Future. In an industrialized society, economic growth also is dependent upon the efficient use of energy. Today, one of the most pressing problems facing our free enterprise system is the continuing need for more energy. Commonly used fuels, such as oil and natural gas, are becoming scarcer. Thus, it is clear that we need to develop other sources of energy.

The amount of energy needed by the United States has increased greatly in the past few decades. In 1970, for example, 483 million barrels of oil were imported by the United States. By 1980 this figure had risen to over 3 billion barrels. Even with 1
the emphasis on energy conservation, most experts agreed that our energy needs would continue to increase in years to come. (See graph on this page.)

Experts predict that our energy needs will continue to increase in the future. Residential/commercial and industrial requirements are expected to increase the most. As this graph shows, our overall energy demands will be twice as great as they were in 1960.

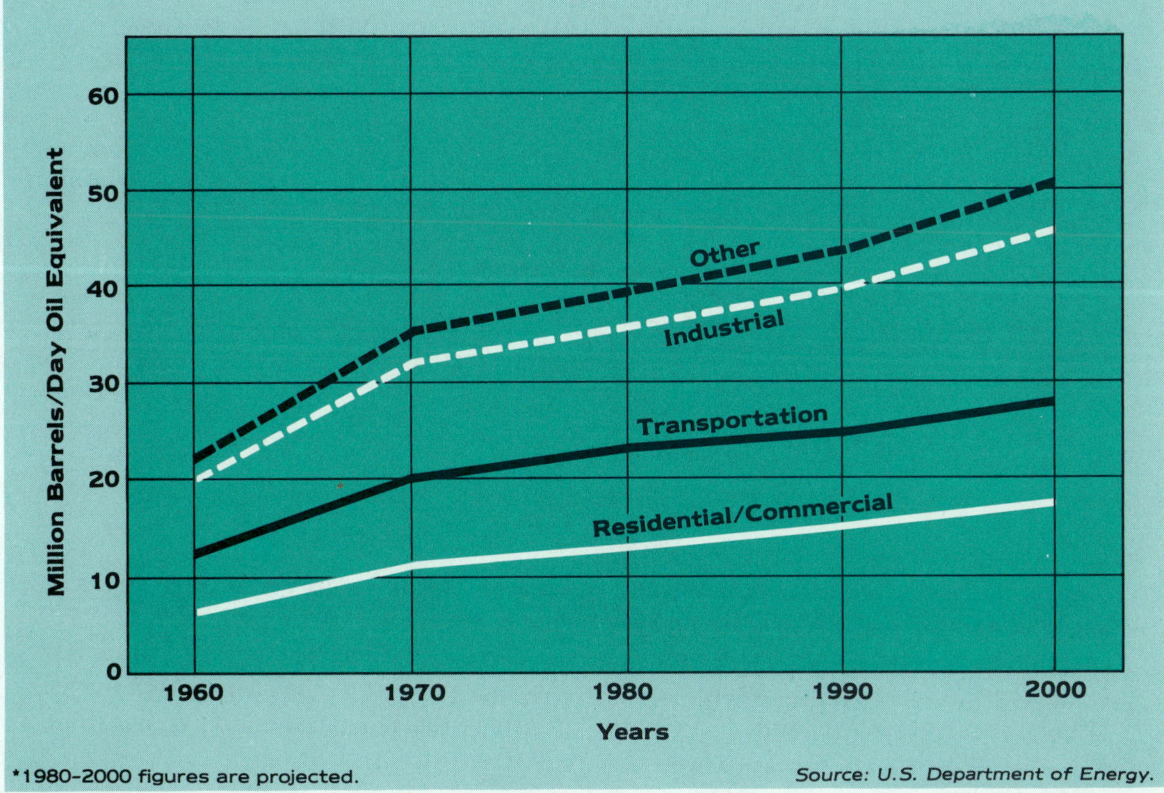

1. The United States imported about 3.5 billion barrels of oil in 1983.

Alternate energy sources—advantages and disadvantages

Energy Source	Advantages	Disadvantages
Coal	Plentiful; technology available for use	Possible pollution from extended use
Fusion	Produces great amounts of energy; unlimited source of energy; low levels of radioactivity	Technology not available until 2000 or later
Geothermal	Plentiful source; technology developed on limited scale	Difficult to reach deep sources; may contain pollutants
Nuclear Breeder Reactor	Makes fuel as it burns fuel; in theory, fuel unlimited	Technology not available until 1990 or later; high levels of radioactive waste
Nuclear Fission	Uranium, used in fission process, in plentiful supply	High levels of radioactive waste; expensive to build nuclear plants
Solar	Unlimited energy source; causes no pollution; technology developed on limited scale	Limited use in cloudy or cold climate; difficult to store and transmit; expensive to convert buildings to solar energy
Wind	Technology developed on limited scale; may provide up to 10 percent of American electricity by 2000	Difficult to store and transmit energy; energy source not constant

Source: Various Sources.

There are several alternate energy sources currently available. Each energy source, however, has advantages and disadvantages. Before any of these energy sources are used on a wide scale, it will be necessary to weigh costs and environmental concerns against expected advantages.

Several ideas have been offered to help meet our energy needs. Some, like making gasoline from sawdust, do not seem to be technologically possible on a large scale. Other ideas, however, appear to hold answers to our future needs. Some of these ideas are shown in the table above.

Currently, nuclear energy provides about 2 percent of the energy used in the 1
United States. Nuclear energy comes from

1. Recent figures show that nuclear energy now provides over 4 percent of the energy used in the United States.

fission—the splitting of atoms of elements like uranium. Some engineers say that by the year 2000, about 25 percent of the energy needs of the United States could be met by nuclear power.

But some scientists and most environmentalists have serious questions about the use of nuclear energy. They point out that nuclear plants cause great amounts of waste heat and tons of radioactive wastes. If left untreated, these wastes may contaminate the earth. As a result, studies are being carried out to find new and safer ways of using nuclear power.

Another source of power, which is already in use throughout the world, is solar energy. New technology has allowed scientists to change sunlight into electrical power. An advantage of solar energy is that it is readily available. Also, it is environmentally safe. The trend toward the use of more solar energy should continue in the years to come.

Technology and the Future. There has been rapid growth in technology in the past 50 years. However, most economists and scientists agree that future advancements will come about even more rapidly. In the free enterprise system, entrepreneurs are able to take risks and innovate. Two likely outcomes of these actions will be greater advances and more economic growth. Another likely outcome will be new products and services for the American consumer.

One rather dramatic plan being talked about is in the field of transportation. Recently, several engineers and scientists developed plans for an underground high-speed train. The technology for this kind of system already exists. By using magnetic waves, the train cars could be floated through underground tunnels at speeds of about 50 miles per minute. Thus, a passenger could go from New York to Los Angeles in less than an hour. Even though the cost of building such a system is thought to be about 250 billion dollars, the American consumer could have a fast, cheap, pollution-free way to travel.

Another innovation could revolutionize the field of dentistry. In the future, people may be able to take a pill that would eliminate cavities. And a vaccine may be available to prevent gum disease. Some dentists believe that this kind of treatment could be available within 15 years.

Technological developments may also bring forth changes in architecture. In years to come, architects will be designing homes and buildings with this new technology in mind. For example, walls may be constructed to allow the sun's rays to heat buildings in the winter, yet keep out the sun's heat during the summer. This kind of wall also would allow fresh air into the house while keeping out dirt and noise.

Today it appears certain that in the future Americans can expect continued technological growth. It also is certain that the future of our free enterprise system depends, in large part, upon the successful use of this technology.

Section Checkups

1. *How are economic growth and technology related?*
2. *What are the benefits of solar energy?*
3. *Why are some scientists concerned about the use of nuclear energy?*

Section 3
Maintaining Free Enterprise

Maintaining free enterprise is essential to the continuation of our basic freedoms. However, the success of our economic system is dependent upon many things. Basically, our success in the future rests upon how America's government, businesses, and consumers react to new conditions. As you read this section, ask yourself the following questions: *In what new ways may industries and communities work together in the future? How may the role of the government in our economy change? Why may consumers' spending habits affect the American economy?*

The Role of Business. Many economists believe that businesses will face new challenges in the years to come. These people feel that it is likely that our society will call upon businesses to take a larger role in solving many of our social and economic problems. Production and profit will remain as the major goals of business. But businesses will also have to become even more aware of society's concerns. One top concern will be the safety of workers. Pollution control and equal job opportunities will also be important.

In the future, industries may be asked to work more closely with community groups. Thus we may see the time when more community leaders become members of a company's board of directors.

Most economists feel that the challenge to innovate will certainly remain for businesses in the future. And these innovations will create many new products for the American consumer. New innovations should bring about higher levels of production. New jobs will also be created.

Many experts believe that consulting with employees on problems will become a standard practice for many companies. Recently, for example, a major car maker set up weekly meetings with its factory workers. The outcome of these talks has been significant. Productivity has gone up, and quality has improved. Employee satisfaction has also increased. These and other improvements will undoubtedly mean that this kind of discussion may be a trend in the future.

In the years to come, most people agree that labor unions will still work for the good of their members. But unions may also take an active interest in company management. Labor unions may be represented on a company's board of directors. In 1980, for example, United Auto Workers President Douglas Fraser was elected to the board of directors of the Chrysler Corporation.

Many observers also feel that in the years to come, management, unions, and workers will work even more closely to-

Camerique

Consultations among business leaders, union representatives, and community leaders may result in increased worker productivity.

gether to improve the quality of life. This, in turn, should help all people in our society.

The Role of Government. Lately, there has been a growing concern over government regulation of our economy. Some economists favor this regulation. They believe that government regulation helps in many ways. They feel it protects consumers, helps to create jobs, works to prevent pollution, and helps American industries. These economists warn that reducing government regulation could harm our economic system.

Other economists, however, strongly believe that there is far too much government control of business. These economists feel that government regulation is raising costs and hurting business. Many economists believe that there must be less government regulation of our economy in the future. These economists have put forth several ideas. First, the government's overall role in the economy must be limited. Less regulation of business should encourage people to take risks and invest. Second, government spending should be cut. More of the country's capital will be available for expanding private businesses and creating more jobs if the government reduces taxes and cuts spending. Third, government regulations that cost money but do not add to production, such as antipollution devices, should be cut back.

It is impossible to see exactly what part our government will play in years to come. Clearly, some government regulations, such as fair-employment laws and antimonopoly laws, help maintain the free enterprise system. But the call for less government involvement in the economy is growing. But at the same time the government is being asked to limit imports to protect American business. And as the 1980 election campaign showed, Americans continue to look to the government to stop inflation and fight recession.

The Role of the Consumer. American consumers have always been resourceful. Using the freedoms that are part of our free enterprise economic system, consumers have worked hard to meet their needs and wants. In the future, consumers must spend their money wisely.

(Text continues on page 293.)

Being a Wise Consumer
Car costs and gas mileage

Conserving fuel is a popular and wise thing to do. As gasoline becomes scarcer and prices increase, conserving gasoline will become increasingly important. One way to cut gasoline costs is to own and drive a car that gets many miles per gallon of gas. But how much should a person be willing to spend on a car to save on gas?

Many people are spending thousands of dollars for small, fuel-efficient cars. But some of these people are not always aware of how much money they can expect to save on gas. In many cases car dealers raise the price of fuel-efficient cars because of the increase in demand. And some dealers add handling and delivery fees to the cost of the car. These fees, plus other options, may cost $2,000 or more. Therefore, a car buyer should determine how many years of driving would be required to get this amount of money back.

By looking at the table, you can see that based on 10,000 miles of driving a year and gasoline at $1.50 per gallon, the fuel bill for a car that averaged 20 miles per gallon would be $750 per year. If the car averaged 30 miles per gallon, the fuel bill would be $500. By buying the car with the better mileage, the motorist would save $250 over 1 year's time. If gas prices remained constant, over 5 year's time the motorist could save $1,250.

It is important to consider the price of the car and projected fuel costs when shopping for a car. The car buyer defeats the purpose of trying to save on gasoline costs if the car costs more than the buyer can ever expect to save on gas.

---

*Yearly cost of gasoline**

Miles per Gallon	Expense at $1.50 per Gallon	Expense at $1.75 per Gallon	Expense at $2.00 per Gallon
10	$1,500	$1,750	$2,000
15	1,000	1,166	1,333
20	750	875	1,000
25	600	700	800
30	500	583	666
35	428	500	570
40	375	438	500

*Based on 10,000 miles of driving

Futurists—those who try to predict future trends—feel that in the 1980's consumers must know the overall effects of their spending. Recent events, for example, have shown that too much credit buying tends to increase the chances of inflation. And when spending increases, saving declines. Banks and other savings institutions do not have enough money to make business loans. This condition can seriously affect economic growth. One answer may be to give Americans more information on how our economy works.

If current trends continue, there will be more economic education in our schools. Many economists believe that consumer-education classes will be very important. Education is the key to keeping our free enterprise system working. Only with well-educated consumers will we be able to continue to understand and to solve our economic problems in the future.

Section Checkups

1. *What will most likely continue to be the main goals of businesses?*
2. *What are the three ways that some economists suggest that government regulation be limited?*
3. *Why are consumer-education programs important for the future of the free enterprise system?*

Chapter Summary

Our free enterprise system has led to the high quality of life that most Americans enjoy today. But problems still exist. Therefore, in the future, ways must be found to help solve such problems as poverty, unemployment, and discrimination. Two important steps needed to meet these problems are greater economic growth and a more stable economy.

Economic growth and stability are important goals for America. Innovations and new technologies are made possible by economic growth. If growth is achieved, Americans can look forward to future innovations in such fields as energy, transportation, health care, and architecture.

In years to come, it seems likely that business managers and workers will work even more closely together to improve working conditions and to increase productivity. And many economists believe that government regulation of our economy will have to decrease. As these changes occur, the consumer will still play one of the most important roles in our free enterprise system.

Reviewing the Chapter

Identifying Terms

Explain or identify the following:

Stable economy	Technology
Poverty	Fission
Poverty level	Futurist
Automation	Consumer education

Analyzing Information

1. Why must economic stability be a national goal?

2. What are two of the problems facing our economic system?

3. Why do some economists favor limited population growth?

4. How does a rapidly increasing population present an employment problem?

5. What can be done to encourage business investment?

6. What are some of the technological improvements Americans can look forward to in the future?

7. What advantages do some economists see in reducing government regulation of our economy?

8. How may improved communication between employees and employers help businesses in the future?

Analyzing Visual Material

1. Compare the circle graphs on page 283. What was the change in the percent of blue-collar workers between 1960 and 1980? What was the change in the percent of white-collar workers for the same period? Which group of workers decreased the most between 1960 and 1980?

2. Examine the graph on page 284. In 1900 about what percent of the female population was employed? What percent of the female population was employed in 1960? How did the percent of the employed female population change between 1900 and 1980?

Research and Projects

1. Several plans to fight poverty have been tried in the past. Study several of these American poverty programs and decide which have been the most successful. In a report to the class, explain the type of plan you would recommend to eliminate poverty in America.

2. Americans can expect many advances in technology. Collect newspaper and magazine articles about new inventions and innovations. Use these articles to prepare a booklet and present a report to the class.

3. The future of our economy greatly depends upon meeting our energy needs. Choose one energy source and write a brief report on its advantages and disadvantages. Explain your findings to the class.

4. Interview a business owner to find out what plans the company has for the future. Present your findings to the class.

Unit 4
Reviewing the Unit

Understanding the Unit

1. In what ways do the American people benefit from economic growth?

2. How does our federal government attempt to bring about economic security for Americans?

3. How does the American economy depend on international trade?

4. How do import restrictions affect American consumers?

5. What is meant by the devaluation of the dollar?

6. Why would import restrictions set by the United States and other nations present problems for the Japanese economy?

7. How does the Soviet method of determining wages and prices differ from the way that wages and prices are determined in the United States?

8. What energy sources might be used to meet our country's future energy needs?

Questions for Discussion

1. Do you think the federal government should undertake programs such as social security and unemployment insurance? Explain your position on this matter.

2. Do you favor or oppose free trade? Discuss the reasons behind your opinion.

3. In your opinion, what, if any, changes should be made in the federal government's role in business?

4. What steps do you think an American citizen should take to be prepared to meet the economic challenges of the future?

Recommended Reading

Aliber, Robert Z. *The International Money Game*. New York: Basic Books, Inc., 1973. An easy-to-understand description of international foreign exchange.

Duignan, Peter, and Alvin Rabushka, eds. *The United States in the 1980's*. Stanford, Calif.: Stanford University, 1980. A collection of essays that explore the major issues of the 1980's.

Ebenstein, William, and Edwin Fogelman. *Today's Isms*. Englewood Cliffs, N.J.: Prentice-Hall, Inc., 1980. An in-depth study of communism, fascism, capitalism, and socialism.

Ike, Nobutaka. *Japan: The New Superstate*. San Francisco: W. H. Freeman and Company, 1974. Illustrated study of Japan with a chapter on the future.

Mishan, E.J. *The Economic Growth Debate*. London: George Allen & Unwin Ltd., 1977. An assessment of economic growth and the overall needs of society.

Phillips, Owen. *The Last Chance Energy Book*. Baltimore: The Johns Hopkins University Press, 1979. An explanation of current energy supplies and future energy options for the United States.

Economics at Work

Making economic choices: Trade and foreign exchange

Imagine that you are the owner of a clothing store. You are planning your spring line of clothing. You must decide where to buy 400 men's shirts and 400 women's blouses. You have checked with a number of different suppliers and have found that garment companies in New York, Toronto, and Mexico City are offering the type of cotton clothing that you want to sell in your store. The shirts and blouses produced by these different suppliers are of similar design and similar quality and would sell for about the same price in your store.

Listed below are the wholesale prices charged by each company. The prices include all packaging and shipping costs, but these prices do not include the 20% tariff that must be paid on imported cotton garments. Also listed below are the exchange rates for American dollars, Canadian dollars, and Mexican pesos. Use this information to determine where you would get the best price for the garments that you want to buy. You need not buy the shirts and the blouses from the same supplier.

Supplier	Price per Blouse	Price per Shirt
New York	$7.00	$6.00
Mexico City	125 pesos	137 pesos
Toronto	$6.89 (Canadian dollars)	$6.61 (Canadian dollars)

Exchange Rates

Mexican Peso = $0.04 (U.S.) Canadian Dollar = $0.87 (U.S.)

In order to determine the best buy from these alternatives, you will need to convert the foreign prices into American dollars. For example, you must figure how many American dollars it would take to buy a blouse priced at 125 Mexican pesos. The exchange rate shows that one Mexican peso is equal to $0.04 in American currency. It is also necessary to convert the Canadian prices into American dollars. Remember, a 20% tariff will be collected on all imported cotton garments. You must figure this charge as part of the price of any garments imported from Canada or Mexico.

Glossary of Terms

This glossary contains definitions of words and terms that are used in this book and are important to the study of economics. The number at the end of each definition indicates the chapter in which the word or term is first used.

A

Advertising. The process of making known the goods and services that are available and, through various methods, persuading the customer to purchase them. **(6)**

Agency shop. A work place in which workers are not required to join a union but must pay a fee to the union to cover the cost of services provided by the union. **(10)**

Aggregate demand. A term that refers to the total spending in the economy. **(13)**

Aid to Families With Dependent Children (AFDC). A form of public aid that offers assistance to needy children and their parents or guardians. **(13)**

Allocation. A term that refers to the process of the distribution, or sharing, of resources. **(1)**

Arbitrator. One who settles disputes between two parties, especially labor-management disputes. **(10)**

Automation. The use of machines instead of human labor. **(1)**

B

Balanced budget. A determination of future income and expenses for a specific period of time in which expenses are equal to income. **(12)**

Balance of payments. A term used to describe a nation's financial transactions with the rest of the world. A balance-of-payments statement shows the total payments made to foreign countries and the total receipts from foreign countries for a specified period of time. **(14)**

Balance of trade. A term used to refer to the net difference between the value of a country's imports and exports. **(14)**

Barter. A system in which goods and services are exchanged for other goods and services without using money. **(11)**

Blacklist. A list of workers not to be given employment because of their union activities; now illegal. **(10)**

Bond. A written promise to pay back borrowed money plus a set rate of interest at some specified date in the future. **(9)**

Boycott. A term used to indicate the refusal to buy goods or services in protest. **(10)**

Broker. A person who acts as an agent between two or more persons involved in a business transaction. For example, a real-estate broker represents buyers or sellers in the sale or rental of property. **(7)**

Brokerage firm. An organization that acts as an agent for investors in the buying or selling of securities. **(9)**

Budgeting. The preparation of a plan of expected future income and expenses. **(8)**

Business cycle. A term describing the recurring ups and downs of economic activity. **(12)**

C

Capital. All the tools, machinery, equipment, inventories, storage, and distribution facilities used in the production of goods and services; one of the factors of production. **(1)**

Capital goods. Goods such as tools, machines, and factories used to produce other goods. **(1)**

Capital investment. Money used to purchase real capital to be used in the production of goods and services. **(15)**

Capitalism. An economic system based on private ownership of property and the freedom of individuals to engage in economic activity as they see fit. A capitalist economic system uses the profit motive to stimulate production and competition to insure efficiency, and consumer sovereignty is expressed through market purchases of goods and services to determine what is produced. **(2)**

Central planning. A term describing the activities of a central authority in determining what, how, and for whom goods or services will be produced. **(15)**

CETA. The Comprehensive Employment and Training Act, passed in 1973, in which federal funds are provided to state and local governments to set up employment-training programs for young people from needy families. **(13)**

Charge account. A form of consumer credit extended by a retail store or bank in which the consumer purchases items without paying cash and agrees to pay for the purchases at some later date. Often a finance charge is added to the outstanding balance. **(8)**

Clayton Antitrust Act. An act of Congress aimed at preventing monopolies that lessen competition. **(9)**

Closed shop. A work place in which only workers belonging to the union could be hired; now illegal. **(10)**

Collective bargaining. The negotiation of contracts by employers and unions. **(10)**

Command economy. An economic system in which all major economic decisions are made by a central authority. **(15)**

Common Market. An organization of Western European nations set up to remove tariff barriers within their borders and establish other common economic policies; also known as the European Economic Community (EEC). **(15)**

Common ownership. Ownership by all the people. **(2)**

Common stock. Shares of corporate ownership that allow the owner to vote for the board of directors and to receive a share in the profits. **(9)**

Communism. An economic system in which all economic goods are owned by society as a whole. Private property is eliminated. **(2)**

Communist Manifesto. A pamphlet written by Karl Marx and Friedrich Engels in 1848 that outlined and explained the basic philosophy of communism. **(2)**

Competition. Rivalry among sellers of similar goods or services to attract consumers. **(3)**

Complementary goods. Goods that are consumed together. Automobiles and tires are complementary goods. **(5)**

Condominium. A form of housing in which the purchaser owns a unit in a multiunit dwelling and a share of the common areas, such as hallways and lobbies. **(8)**

Conglomerate. The result of the merger of companies in different industries. **(9)**

Conservative party. One of the chief political parties in Great Britain. The Conservative party favors more private enterprise and less government ownership. **(15)**

Consumer. The purchaser or user of final goods and services. **(1)**

Consumer cooperative. An association of consumers who join together to try to purchase products in large quantities and at low prices. **(9)**

Consumer education. Instruction that teaches consumers to make the best possible economic decisions. **(16)**

Consumer Price Index (CPI). A measure of the change in prices of a group of goods and services necessary to maintain a typical standard of living, compiled by the Department of Labor. **(13)**

Consumer sovereignty. The concept that consumers determine what is produced through their purchases. **(8)**

Controlled economy. An economic system that for the most part, is regulated by the government. The government may or may not own the means of production. **(1)**

Cooperative. A business whose owners are its customers, operated to provide its owners with some kind of advantage other than profit. **(9)**

Corporate charter. A document that makes a corporation a legal entity. **(9)**

Corporation. A business organization authorized by law to act as a legal person, though it may be owned by one or more individuals. **(9)**

Cost-of-living adjustment. Wage or pension increases given to maintain purchasing power. **(7)**

Craft unionism. The organization of a labor union based on one skilled trade or of two or more closely related skilled trades. **(10)**

Credit limit. The maximum amount that a consumer can charge to a charge account. **(8)**

Currency. A term that refers to paper money and coins. **(11)**

Cyclical unemployment. Unemployment caused by decreased economic activity. **(13)**

D

Demand. The amount of a product consumers are willing and able to buy at all possible prices at a particular time. **(2)**

Demand deposit. A checking account in a commercial bank. For example, funds held by consumers, businesses, and government agencies in their checking accounts are demand deposits. **(11)**

Demand schedule. A schedule that shows how many units of a product will be demanded by consumers at different prices, other things being equal. **(5)**

Demographer. A person who undertakes the study of populations—their size, movement, and vital statistics. **(16)**

Depression. A relatively long period of exceptionally slow business activity. Typical traits of such a period are somewhat lower prices, low profit levels, much lower production levels, and high rates of unemployment. **(12)**

Devaluation. The lowering of value of one nation's currency in terms of the currencies of other nations. **(14)**

Discount rate. The interest rate charged by the Federal Reserve System to a member bank when making a loan. **(11)**

Discrimination. Unequal treatment of individuals by others, especially in matters such as employment opportunities, educational facilities, and so on. **(7)**

Dividend. A share of profits paid to stockholders. **(9)**

Dumping. The selling of imported goods at prices lower than the cost of production. **(14)**

Duty. *See* Tariff.

E

Economic goods. Scarce material items that people are willing to pay for in order to satisfy their needs and wants. **(1)**

Economic growth. An increase in productive capacity and in material living standards over time. **(13)**

Economic profit. A term that refers to business income that exceeds costs; the money left to the entrepreneur after all costs of production, including a normal profit, have been paid. **(6)**

Economics. The study of individuals' and societies' efforts to satisfy unending wants through the use of limited resources. **(1)**

Economic security. Protection against loss of income. **(13)**

Economic stability. *See* Stable economy.

Economic system. The way that people have developed for the production and consumption of goods and services in a particular country or area. **(1)**

Economizing. The practice of making economic choices; using resources efficiently. **(1)**

Efficiency. A term that refers to making the best possible use of available resources; using as few scarce resources as possible to produce as many final desired outputs as possible. **(4)**

Elastic demand. A situation in which the quantity demanded varies greatly as the price of the particular goods or services increases or decreases. **(5)**

Embargo. An order of a government forbidding trade or commerce. **(14)**

Entrepreneurship. The organization and coordination of land, labor, and capital for the purpose of innovation and risk-taking in a production process; one of the factors of production. **(1)**

Equilibrium price. *See* Market price.

Exchange rate. The price of one nation's money in terms of another's. **(14)**

Export. Goods shipped to other countries. **(14)**

F

Factors of production. Elements that combine to produce economic goods and services: land, labor, capital, and entrepreneurship. **(1)**

Fascism. A political-economic system in which private ownership of the means of production exists, but the government largely determines what products will be produced. **(2)**

FDIC. The Federal Deposit Insurance Corporation, created by the United States government in 1933 to protect depositors' money in banks. **(11)**

Federal Reserve System. The central banking system of the United States, set up by the Federal Reserve Act of 1913. It is responsible for controlling the nation's money supply and maintaining the value of the nation's currency. **(11)**

Finance charge. The fee added to the unpaid balance of a charge account. **(8)**

Fiscal policy. The use of government taxation and spending programs to influence economic stability. **(12)**

Fission. The splitting of atoms, resulting in the release of large amounts of energy. **(16)**

Fixed income. An income set at a certain amount and not adjusted with changes in the cost of living. **(7)**

Foreign aid. Assistance given to one nation by another. **(14)**

Foreign competition. Rivalry among sellers of domestic products and sellers of foreign-made products. **(6)**

Foreign exchange. A term that refers to the transactions of money between different countries. **(14)**

Freedom of choice. The term used to describe economic freedoms, including the right to organize and participate in any lawful business, to select a job freely, and to make consumer decisions. **(3)**

Free economy. *See* Market economy.

Free enterprise. The freedom of individuals and private businesses to organize and operate for the purpose of profit in a competitive market system with minimal government regulation. **(2)**

Free goods. Items that people need, are plentiful in supply, and can be had without conscious effort. Fresh air and sunshine are examples of free goods. **(1)**

Free trade. A term that refers to international trade without restrictions. **(14)**

Frictional unemployment. Normal unemployment that occurs when workers change jobs or wait to take new jobs. **(13)**

FSLIC. The Federal Savings and Loan Insurance Corporation, which insures depositors' money in savings and loan associations. **(11)**

Full employment. In economic terms, when four percent or less of the labor force is unemployed. **(13)**

Futurist. A person who tries to determine future trends. **(16)**

G

General Agreement on Tariffs and Trade (GATT). An agreement involving about 85 nations to work to remove trade restrictions. **(14)**

Gosplan. The agency of the Soviet government that makes all major economic decisions for the country. **(15)**

Grievance procedures. Provisions of a contract that set up step-by-step ways of solving labor-management disputes during the lifetime of the contract. **(10)**

Gross National Product (GNP). A term that describes the market value of all final goods and services produced by an economy in one year. **(12)**

H

Heavy industries. Industries that produce machines, chemicals, steel, and other capital goods, but not consumer goods. **(15)**

Household. A social unit that provides productive resources. **(7)**

I

Import. Goods received from other countries. **(14)**

Income. Payments received for goods or services. **(7)**

Income redistribution. Any system that adjusts the allocation of incomes among households in a manner different from that which is determined under the market system. **(12)**

Incorporate. To form a legal corporation. **(9)**

Indivisible goods. Goods that must be produced and consumed in such large amounts that private business could not produce them profitably. **(12)**

Industrial unionism. The organization of a labor union made up of the workers of an entire industry. **(10)**

Inelastic demand. A situation in which the quantity demanded changes little as the price of a particular good or service increases or decreases. **(5)**

Inferior goods. Goods for which demand decreases as the income of consumers increases. **(5)**

Inflation. A widespread rise in the prices of goods, services, and resources. **(12)**

Innovation. The introduction of new products or new methods of production. **(6)**

Installment loan. A type of loan in which payments are made on a regular, often monthly, basis. **(8)**

Interest. The price of capital. **(5)**

Investment. The purchase of goods or services in the hope that their value will appreciate over time. Expenditure of funds for capital goods. **(4)**

Investment banker. A banking specialist who purchases new issues of stock from a corporation and then sells the stock to the public at a profit. **(9)**

L

Labor. Human physical and mental activity used to produce goods and services; one of the factors of production. **(1)**

Labor force. All persons aged 16 or over who are gainfully employed or are seeking employment. **(10)**

Labour party. One of the chief political parties in Great Britain. The Labour party is a prosocialist party. It favors government ownership of key industries. **(15)**

Laissez-faire. An economic policy based upon no intervention by the government in economic affairs. **(2)**

Land. A general term meaning all the things in nature that can be used to produce goods and services—natural resources; one of the factors of production. **(1)**

Law of diminishing returns. A principle of economics that describes a condition that exists when adding more of one factor of production, such as labor, to fixed amounts of other factors of production yields a lesser increase than the previous addition yielded. **(4)**

Lease. A legal contract for the possession of property for a specified time and for a specified rent. **(8)**

Limited liability. An advantage of a corporation in which the owners of a corporation can lose only what they have put into the business if the business should fail. **(9)**

Limited partnership. A situation in which individuals may invest in a partnership without risking all their personal possessions. **(9)**

Liquid. A term applied to certain assets that are easily converted to cash. **(8)**

M

Market. Any place where buyers and sellers meet to make exchanges and where goods and services that are similar tend to have similar prices. **(5)**

Market economy. An economic system in which the forces of supply and demand direct economic decision making. **(1)**

Market price. The price at which the amount that producers want to sell is equal to the amount that consumers want to buy; also called equilibrium price. **(5)**

Market system. The basis of the American economy, through which free economic choices are put into effect. *See also* Market economy. **(3)**

Mass production. The production of goods in large quantities, usually by means of machinery and frequently by reliance upon interchangeable parts and division of labor. **(1)**

Medicaid. A program providing medical assistance to low-income persons, funded largely by state and local government, usually supplemented by federal grants. **(13)**

Medicare. A federal program of health-care insurance, usually for persons 65 years of age and over, providing both hospital and medical coverage. **(13)**

Mercantilism. A controlled economic system in which the government regulates imports, exports, manufacturing, shipping, and so on, to bring greater wealth, stability, and power to the country. **(2)**

Merger. One company combining with or buying another. **(9)**

Mixed economy. An economic system in which there exist elements of government regulation or ownership and elements of the market system. **(3)**

Monetary policy. The actions of the Federal Reserve System that affect our money supply and the availability of credit. **(11)**

Monetary unit. The basic unit of currency of a nation. **(14)**

Money. Anything that is acceptable as a medium of exchange. **(11)**

Money wages. The dollar amount of a worker's paycheck. **(10)**

Monopoly. A single seller of a good or a service. In general terms, a seller of a good or a service who has considerable control over prices and output is said to have some degree of monopoly power. **(3)**

Multinational. A company with holdings in many countries. **(9)**

N

National bank. A commercial bank chartered by the federal government and belonging to the Federal Reserve System. **(11)**

National debt. The amount of money the federal government owes. **(12)**

National income. A term that refers to the total income earned in a nation through the production of goods and services during the year. **(7)**

Nationalization. The process whereby private industry is purchased and operated by the government. **(15)**

Nationalized. The state of an industry owned by the government. In most socialist countries, basic industries are nationalized. **(2)**

Natural resources. The wealth provided by nature that can be used in the production of goods or services or that provides satisfaction in its natural state. Examples of natural resources are soil fertility, woodlands, climate, mineral deposits, and so on. In economic terms, identical to the concept of land. *See also* Land. **(3)**

Near-money. Government bonds and savings accounts that are held by individuals and that are easily converted to cash. Near-money is not considered part of the money supply because it normally is not used as a medium of exchange. **(11)**

Needs. Items necessary for survival, such as food, clothing, and shelter. **(1)**

Nonprice competition. The competition among sellers involving methods other than pricing, such as improving products, advertising, and offering additional services. **(6)**

Normal good. A good for which demand increases as the real income of consumers rises. **(5)**

Normal profit. The minimum required return to keep an entrepreneur in a certain business. **(6)**

No-strike clause. The provision of a contract by which workers agree not to strike during the lifetime of the contract. **(10)**

NOW account (negotiable order of withdrawal account). An interest-paying savings account from which money can be withdrawn by check. **(11)**

O

Oligopoly. A market situation in which there are only a few sellers of a good or service. **(9)**

Open shop. A situation in which workers who do not belong to the union may be hired and are not required to join the union. **(10)**

P

Parity price supports. A system that sets farm prices in an attempt to maintain the relationship between prices for farm goods and the prices for other goods. **(13)**

Partnership. An association of two or more persons to own and operate a business organization. **(9)**

Partnership contract. A written agreement between co-owners of a business organization. **(9)**

Patent. The exclusive right granted by a government to make or sell an invention for a period of years. **(3)**

Patronage dividend. The earnings or savings received by a member of a cooperative based on the amount of business the member has done with the cooperative. **(9)**

Pension. Payments at regular intervals to retired workers. **(13)**

Per capita GNP. A nation's Gross National Product divided by its population. **(13)**

Personal income. The annual income received by persons from all sources. **(7)**

Poverty. The condition in which one lacks the comforts of life and has inadequate amounts of the necessities. **(16)**

Poverty level. An official minimum income needed for the bare necessities of life. A family's income that falls below this minimum is evidence that the family lives in the condition of poverty. **(16)**

Preferred stock. Shares of corporate ownership that allow owners to receive dividends first, before common-stock holders, but that do not allow owners to vote for the board of directors. **(9)**

Price-fixing. A situation in which competing businesses join together to decide prices for their goods or services; now illegal. **(3)**

Private property. A term that refers to the ownership of productive resources and personal property and the right to use them without interference from others. **(3)**

Producer cooperative. An association of producers who join together to try to sell their products at a higher price. **(9)**

Production. The process of creating goods and services to satisfy human wants. **(1)**

Productive resources. *See* Factors of production.

Productivity. The measure of goods and services made with a set amount of resources for a given period of time. **(4)**

Profit. The price of entrepreneurship. Also, income remaining after all costs of operating a business are paid. *See also* Economic profit. **(3)**

Profit margin. A method of reporting profits in which profits are disclosed as a percentage of a business's net sales. **(6)**

Progressive tax. A tax system that takes a larger proportion of income from high-income people than from low-income people. **(12)**

Proxy. Written authority to vote on behalf of another at a stockholders' meeting. **(9)**

Psychic wage. Nonmoney satisfaction a person receives for doing a certain job or working in a certain part of the country. **(10)**

Public goods. Goods provided by governments that help to satisfy the collective wants of people and that could not be provided adequately by the private sector. **(12)**

Public utility. A privately owned business organization that provides an important service for the public, usually subject to some government regulation. **(3)**

Q

Quota. A government limit on the amount of a good that may be imported within a specified period of time. **(14)**

R

Rate of profit. A method of reporting profits, in which profits are disclosed as a percentage of the amount of money invested in the business; also called stockholders' equity. **(6)**

Real GNP. A nation's Gross National Product adjusted for inflation. **(13)**

Real income. The goods and services one is able to purchase with one's dollar income. **(7)**

Real wages. A term that refers to what the money received as wages will buy. **(10)**

Recession. A situation in which business activity is slowing down or contracting. Typical traits of such periods are decreasing prices, decreasing profits, and increasing unemployment levels. **(12)**

Regressive tax. A tax system that takes a smaller proportion of income from high-income people than from low-income people. **(12)**

Rent. In economic terms, the price of land. Also, the term *rent* may refer to the payment for the use of a capital good, such as a tool or machine. **(5)**

Rental income. Income that comes from allowing real property to be used in production. **(7)**

Repossess. The act of a creditor taking back merchandise purchased on credit for which payments have not been made. **(8)**

Reserve requirement. The percentage of a bank's total deposit that it must keep in its own vaults or in a district Federal Reserve bank. **(11)**

Right-to-work law. A law stating that workers do not have to join unions to keep their jobs. This law makes union-security clauses illegal. **(10)**

Risk. To take the chance of incurring a loss in the hope of making gains. **(6)**

S

Savings. Personal income that is not spent; also the retained income of businesses. **(8)**

Scarcity. The universal condition of individuals wanting more goods and services than they can produce or obtain, given the fact of limited resources. **(1)**

SEC. The Securities and Exchange Commission, set up by the Securities and Exchange Act in 1934. Its purpose is to protect investors in the securities market. **(9)**

Security. A general term for a stock certificate or bond. **(9)**

Self-interest. Concern for one's own personal well-being. **(3)**

Self-sufficiency. The ability of an economic system to provide for itself without being dependent upon foreign trade. **(4)**

Seniority clause. A provision of a contract stating that benefits and promotions will be given according to the length of time workers have been employed by the company. **(10)**

Service cooperative. An association of consumers who join together to offer members special services, such as credit on favorable terms. **(9)**

Shortage. An excess of quantity demanded over quantity supplied at some price. **(5)**

Skilled worker. A person with special training in a particular occupation, craft, or trade. **(4)**

Socialism. An economic system in which the major means of production are owned and operated by the government; small businesses are usually privately owned and operated. **(2)**

Social Security System. Established by the Social Security Act of 1935, this program provides old-age, survivors, disability, medical, and unemployment insurance. This program is financed through taxes imposed on both employers and employees. **(7)**

Social-security tax. A tax imposed on employers, employees, and self-employed persons to finance social-security benefits. **(2)**

Social welfare legislation. Laws passed by a legislature that provide some type of assistance for specific groups within a population. **(15)**

Sole proprietorship. A business owned and controlled by one person. **(9)**

Specialization. The procedure of becoming more expert in some relatively narrowly defined process by engaging in that process to the exclusion of other activities. **(4)**

Speculator. One who takes risks in buying and selling securities in the hope of making a large profit. **(9)**

Spillover benefit. A benefit that comes about because some good or service is produced or consumed but that goes to some party other than the producer or consumer. **(12)**

Spillover cost. A cost that comes about because some good or service is produced or consumed but that falls on some party other than the producer or consumer. **(12)**

Stable economy. In general, an economy with high employment, little inflation, price stability, and economic growth. **(13)**

Stagflation. Inflation with rising unemployment. **(12)**

Standard of living. A term that refers to the amount of goods and services consumed by a nation or the citizens of that nation. **(1)**

Stock exchange. The marketplace where securities are bought and sold. **(9)**

Stockholder. A person who owns shares of stock in a corporation. **(9)**

Strike. A planned work-stoppage by employees in an effort to gain acceptance of their demands. **(10)**

Strikebreaker. A person brought in by an employer to take the place of a striking worker. **(10)**

Structural unemployment. A situation in which jobs exist, but the workers looking for jobs do not have the necessary skills for those jobs. **(13)**

Supplemental Security Income (SSI). A form of public aid that offers a minimum income to persons 65 years of age and over, the blind, and the disabled. **(13)**

Supply. The amount of a product producers are willing and able to sell at all possible prices at a particular time. **(5)**

Supply schedule. A schedule that shows how many units of a product will be supplied by producers at various prices, other things being equal. **(5)**

Surplus. An excess of quantity supplied over the quantity demanded at some price. **(5)**

T

Taft-Hartley Act. The Labor-Management Relations Act of 1947, which outlawed the closed shop and forbade unions from making political contributions. It also organized the National Labor Relations Board and amended the Wagner Act. **(10)**

Tariff. A tax on imported goods. **(14)**

Technology. The application of scientific discovery to production resulting in new products or new processes of manufacture. **(3)**

Time deposit. A savings account not subject to immediate withdrawal. **(11)**

Traditional economy. An economic system in which economic decision making is based upon customs, beliefs, and traditions. **(1)**

U

Underwrite. To agree to purchase a new issue of stock. **(9)**

Unemployment. A situation in which one is unable to find gainful employment when being willing and able to work. **(13)**

Unemployment insurance. A program of the Social Security System that provides workers with funds while temporarily unemployed. The cost of the program is usually funded by employers, and it is administered by the states. **(13)**

Union-security clause. A provision of a contract that sets up a union shop. **(10)**

Union shop. A work place in which the company may hire whom it wants, but workers must join the union after a set period of time, frequently 30 days. **(10)**

Unit pricing. A way to determine the price of a product in comparable units of measure. **(5)**

Unlimited liability. A disadvantage of a sole proprietorship and some partnerships that makes the owner or owners personally responsible for all debts incurred by the business. **(9)**

Unskilled worker. A person who lacks training to perform a particular type of job. **(4)**

Urban area. A town or a city with a population of more than 2,500 persons. **(3)**

V

Vault cash. The currency kept on hand by banks to meet the demands of depositors wishing to make a withdrawal. Vault cash is not considered part of the money supply. **(11)**

W

Wage. In economic terms, the price of labor. **(5)**

Wagner Act. The National Labor Relations Act of 1935; it gave workers the right to organize and set up collective bargaining procedures. **(10)**

Wants. Items that are not necessary for survival but make life more comfortable. Cars, color televisions, and dishwashers are examples of wants. **(1)**

Warranty. A guarantee by a manufacturer or seller to stand behind a product and to replace or repair the product if it should prove defective within a specified period of time. **(9)**

Worker's compensation. A law stating that employers must provide specific benefits for workers injured while at work. **(13)**

Y

Yellow-dog contract. An agreement that an applicant for employment will not join a union if hired; now generally illegal in the United States. **(10)**

Index

The following abbreviations are used in this index: *c.*, chart; *cart.*, cartoon; *diag.*, diagram; *g.*, graph; *ill.*, illustration; *m.*, map; *q.*, quotation; and *t.*, table.

C

D

F

G

H

I

J

K

L

M

N

O

P

S